D0297768

JOHN
PAUL
GEORGE
RINGO
& ME

Acknowledgements

The author would like to thank the following people for their invaluable help with the preparation and production of this book:

- Denise S Gardner for enabling access to the Bill Carlson Collection of photographs
- Sean O'Mahony for permission to use pictures by *The Beatles Book* magazine's official photographer, Leslie Bryce
- Peter Rhodes and Alex Wilde for access to a wonderful collection of Beatles memorabilia
- Mary Cockram (aka Anne Collingham) for her visual and verbal memories of The Official Beatles Fan Club
- Mark Lewisohn for his professional generosity
- And Corinne Barrow for her time-consuming research work

My very special thanks to:

- The enterprising production team at Boutique Editions Ltd, particularly my editor Julian Newby and Andy Ewan, Debbie Lincoln and Richard Woolley
- The enthusiastic publishing team at André Deutsche, particularly Lorna Russell and Lydia Drukarz
- John, Paul, George and Ringo, without whom …

This edition published in Great Britain in 2011 by
André Deutsch
An imprint of the Carlton Publishing Group
20 Mortimer Street
London W1T 3JW

Text copyright © Tony Barrow 2005, 2011
Design copyright © Carlton Books Ltd 2005, 2011

The right of Tony Barrow to be identified as the author of this work has been asserted by him in accordance with the Copyright, Designs and Patents Act 1988

All rights reserved. This book is sold subject to the condition that it may not be reproduced, stored in a retrieval system or transmitted in any form or by any means, electronic, mechanical, photocopying, recording or otherwise without the Publisher's prior written consent.

A catalogue record for this book is available from the British Library.

ISBN: 978-0-233-00327-6

Typeset by E-Type, Liverpool
Printed and bound in Great Britain by CPI Mackays, Chatham ME5 8TD

JOHN
PAUL
GEORGE
RINGO
& ME

TONY BARROW

Edited by Julian Newby

ANDRE
DEUTSCH

Contents

THE FAB FOREWORD

THIS BOOK IS neither a biography of The Beatles nor an homage to their music. The Beatles wrote and recorded some of the most durable songs in the history of the pop and rock music business, and pretty well everyone in the world has access to their greatest work on the group's comprehensive collection of CDs – or on vinyl if you're lucky. But even those who know the music well and play the Fab Four's recordings regularly have little or no first-hand knowledge of what John, Paul, George and Ringo were really like as people during the Sixties, and that's what this book is all about.

Only a handful of professional aides and business associates worked as part of The Beatles' permanent entourage for any length of time, and fewer still remain alive today. I was with The Beatles as their personal press and publicity officer between 1962 when they released their first Parlophone single, 'Love Me Do', until 1968 when the band's insidious break-up was well under way.

Planning each stage of The Beatles' PR strategy, co-ordinating their on-tour press conferences in places as far apart as Tokyo and Toronto, Munich and Minneapolis, arranging their media interviews and photo shoots throughout the Beatlemania years and beyond, I got to know John, Paul, George and Ringo very well. Travelling with them around the world on their biggest and most dangerous concert tours in 1965 and 1966, I was uniquely placed to witness at first hand not only their carefully developed public personalities, but also their private pleasures, tantrums and mood swings. I was there to see the unprecedented highs and horrendous lows of their momentous and remarkably action-packed career, the brightest moments in their extraordinary success story and the darkest times when the less attractive aspects of being the world's top pop megastars brought all of the Fab Four terrifyingly close to death.

Let me set the scene. I remember the Sixties as years of political dissent and cultural revolution, radical new freedom of expression among younger people and massive changes in all sectors of the arts, from film to fashion. Music smashed through racial and religious barriers that had gone unchanged and unchallenged by previous generations. Sexual taboos were explored and in many cases dismantled forever. In 1962 America's president John Kennedy built up the West's protective missile sites in Turkey, and so in reply Russia's president Khrushchev put Soviet weapons of mass destruction into Cuba and pointed them at the US. Helen Gurley Brown's *Sex And The Single Girl* was published and AT&T launched Telstar 1, the planet's first communications satellite. In America the Beach Boys released their debut album, *Surfin' Safari*, Bob Dylan's first album came out, and Marilyn Monroe committed suicide. The Twist was the international dance craze but British fans were still bopping away to bands led by Messrs Acker Bilk, Chris Barber and Kenny Ball at the tail end of the trad jazz boom. In 1962 the *Sunday Times* launched its colour supplement, Cliff Richard made the movie *Summer Holiday*, the first James Bond film, *Dr No*, was premiered in London and The Rolling Stones got together. The latest television shows in the UK included 'Steptoe And Son', 'Dr Finlay's Casebook', 'Z Cars' and 'The Saint'. In soccer, Tottenham Hotspur won the FA Cup for the second year running and in Test-Match cricket Australia retained the Ashes. This was the age of Mateus Rose wine from Portugal and tinned Fray Bentos meat pies from Argentina. Most of us in the UK didn't know a pizza from a piazza.

Just like the rest of us randy, fertile and forthright young men of 1962, The Beatles boasted among friends about their first unso-phisticated sexual conquests, from sticky-fingered gropings in local bus shelters to "going all the way" with ready, willing and able Mersey Beat groupies who kissed and much more, but never did tell. According to some of the girls who knew The Beatles best in Liverpool and later, the boys went into graphic detail about each new female in their love lives, carefully separating the "good lays" from the "ice maidens" and openly awarding points to past partners in the presence of new girlfriends who were left in no doubt as to what they were expected to live up to. Paul used the combination of his cute baby-faced good looks and charming chat-up patter to gain a reputation in Liverpool as the "greatest bird puller" of the four. The others felt they came off second best although by all accounts it was George, the youngest of The Fabs, who was eventually the most prolific when it came to putting notches on his bedpost. Partly because he was the group's founder and apparent leader, girls found John "wickedly exciting" and "irresistibly gorgeous". But John's private handicap was a woeful shyness with women, which came as a surprise to most outsiders who knew only the brasher and cynically cruel sides of his dynamic public persona. Sadly I don't think John found true love until he hooked up with Yoko Ono. So far as casual sex is concerned, Ringo was the least involved, but then as the late-arriving drummer he also had an inferiority complex which he tried hard to conquer. It wasn't only a matter of sex; Ringo was the least involved in most of the group's activities and felt disadvantaged by being the last to join the line-up of the group. Towards the end of The Beatles' short working lifespan when individual tempers began to flare, the group tended to gather at Ringo's house for business meetings because it felt like a neutral zone.

In the following chapters I try to put the reader in the picture on key occasions from The Beatles' historic house party with Elvis Presley at his Bel Air home in the Hollywood Hills, to the very private scene of John's tearful backstage preparation for the most emotional press conference of his life following the "We're more popular than Jesus" furore. No outsiders were present at these or various other equally personal moments, but I can tell you candidly and honestly what happened because I was there and have not had to rely on handed-around third-party reports. You may notice that I have not dwelt on certain sections of the group's story. This is either because I think other authors have dealt with them adequately in biographies and there is nothing fresh or interesting for me to add, or simply because I wasn't there in person and I prefer not to re-tell any details through the (often bleary) eyes of others.

I have not set out to write a complete history of The Beatles here but to give a highly personal account of my time in the Sixties with John, Paul, George and Ringo. For example, I have no first-hand accounts from the film locations for *A Hard Day's Night* and *Help!* for one good reason – I wasn't the "unit publicist" in either case and I didn't have the right union ticket to let me work on film sets. Therefore I stayed at home base and my coverage of location anecdotes is based on what The Beatles told me at the time or soon afterwards. Otherwise I was an on-the-spot eye-witness to most of the private and public events I have written about in this book.

I am deliberately setting out here my own inevitably biased view of what it was like to work with the boys. Where appropriate I have quoted things The Beatles – or one of my colleagues among the group's inner circle – told me. But wherever possible I have avoided re-distributing testimony from outsiders because that's where so many fictional myths and false impressions have been created and spread by other writers in the past. For the same reason I have restricted my story to the Sixties. After The Beatles went their separate ways in the Seventies, so did I, representing scores of top international music stars and other entertainers including Neil Sedaka, Bob Monkhouse, The New Seekers, Tony Bennett, the Bay City Rollers, David Cassidy, Gary Glitter, The Monkees and Helen Shapiro.

In his autobiography, Bob Monkhouse referred to me as his "benign PR man". I hope this meant that he placed me at the opposite end of the human spectrum from shag-and-share story trader Max Clifford and his ilk. With the over-development of so-called cheque-book journalism, the fundamental nature of showbusiness PR has changed dramatically and in my view degenerated woefully since the Sixties and Seventies. I wouldn't want to touch the job now and I haven't been tempted to do so since 1980. For me, the saddest part of leaving the business was disconnecting myself from the good guys: David Soul; David Cassidy; Ray Davies; Cilla Black; Gerry Marsden; Judith Durham; Bob Monkhouse; Helen Shapiro; Nicky Chinn and Mike Chapman, The Jackson Five and a handful of other clients who became my buddies, pals and mates.

Since quitting the PR business in 1980 to return to my first love, freelance journalism, I have written millions of words on The Beatles' story, attempting along the way to put right at least a few of the factual mistakes contained in the work of some unreliable fellow travellers. The definitive history of The Beatles may never be published and I can tell you why. If you picture a massive jigsaw puzzle made up of a million pieces you have some idea of the task facing any future writer who takes on the impossible task of trying to compile a totally comprehensive biography of John, Paul, George and Ringo. For a start, some of the key pieces of the jigsaw are missing, long gone, permanently lost, and by this I mean that essential participants in The Beatles' story have died. In chronological order the list began with Brian Epstein, Mal Evans and John Lennon. By now it includes numerous other central characters such as Linda McCartney, Maureen Starkey, George Harrison, Neil Aspinall, the two unrelated Taylors, Derek and Alistair, and a host of peripheral people headed by The Cavern cellar's resident deejay and best of fellas, Bob Wooler. In other cases, the bits of the jigsaw are there but have warped or been deliberately bent so badly that they won't fit and gaping holes are left in the unfinished puzzle. Here I refer to the shameful number of people who have given false testimony to biographers and journalists over the years. This group includes those who have distorted incidents in order to build up their own contributions to The Beatles' story by wilful exaggeration or blatant invention. Finally there are those blameless souls who, when interviewed by authors, discovered they had genuinely forgotten vital facts, the wrinklies whose fading memories of days gone by have left them incapable of providing reliable testimony. Unfortunately some of them bash on regardless and fill in the gaps with what they consider to be harmless fiction.

I hold up my hand and readily admit that I am now a self-confessed, dues-paid, bus-pass-carrying member of the above-mentioned wrinklies' generation. But, thankfully, I have collected and preserved a wealth of reference material, including diaries, jottings and recordings which I can rely on to jog my memory, together with articles that I wrote back in the Sixties when it was all happening. This is the stuff of which this book is made. Please enjoy it.

TONY BARROW

1 | Not Queer, Not Jewish

JOHN LENNON'S FIRST words to me were: "If you're not queer and you're not Jewish, why are you coming to work with Brian Epstein?" This was not said confidentially or quietly but in loud and strident tones that rang out around the bar of the Devonshire Arms pub and turned heads at adjacent tables. I replied, weakly, that I hadn't yet agreed to join Epstein's management firm, NEMS Enterprises, which was true but totally avoided the issue of answering Lennon's original question. For the record, I was not queer, not Jewish. I was pro-actively heterosexual and passively Church of England.

This was in November 1962. The Beatles had released their first single, 'Love Me Do', on EMI's Parlophone label a month earlier and I was here in this small central London pub, just off Manchester Square, W1 – where EMI Records had their head office – to meet the Liverpool group that Epstein wanted me to come and work with as their PR man. Behind his invitation to meet John, along with Paul, George and the band's recently signed new drummer, Ringo Starr, was the thought that an evening with them in a social setting and plenty of booze would surely give the group an opportunity to decide if they could work with me. I think the fact that all of us came from Liverpool and shared the typical Merseysider's distinctively dry and cynical sense of humour helped to melt the ice. Liverpudlians in exile tend to stick together. Like Masons, it's a survival thing. We also shared a mutual interest in music although, having left Liverpool to live in London several years earlier, I was out of touch with the latest news on the so-called Mersey Beat scene. Our version of first-date small-talk centred on The Beatles telling me what was happening back home at the Cavern, the city's most famous music venue, and about their adventures in Hamburg's clubland where they had spent several seasons, while I talked about life in the London record industry and which acts I had seen recently in concert.

The next day Brian Epstein phoned me: "Well, what do you think?" I told him I hadn't made up my mind but we made a lunch date to discuss things further. My hesitation had nothing to do with how I felt about working with John, Paul, George and Ringo, but was based largely on my own lack of self-confidence. I had a good steady job as a writer at the Decca Record Company and I had no experience of working in press and public relations. I had recently married my Liverpudlian fiancée, Corinne – a Crosby girl who first appealed to me because she looked like Ruby Murray – and neither of us felt that this was the right time to desert the relatively secure sanctuary of my Decca job to branch out in a fresh career direction.

My vague ambition was to break into record production or to join the editorial staff of one of the music papers, but for now I was enjoying my job as Britain's only full-time sleeve-note writer. I worked at Decca's Albert Embankment headquarters either initiating notes for the covers of their locally-produced repertoire of pop LP and EP releases or adapting existing notes on our imported product from the US by adding a "u" to "colorful", that sort of thing. One day I'd be interviewing Anthony Newley or Gracie Fields, the next I'd be writing about a Duke Ellington collection, a new album by Ted Heath or an EP from Billy Fury. For the past eight years, since 1954, I had also been writing a regular record review column called Off The Record for the Saturday magazine section of my home-town newspaper, the *Liverpool Echo*. People who knew me wondered why the by-line on my articles was "Disker" rather than Tony Barrow. The answer was that in 1954 I was a 17-year-old sixth-form schoolboy and while the *Echo* was content to let someone so young act as its pop record critic, it was not prepared to admit this in print and insisted that I should use a pen name to sign my weekly piece. I was allowed to choose my own *nom de plume* and I used a word that had caught my eye on a roadside billboard advertising a week's bill-topping appearance in variety at the Liverpool Empire by the American rockabilly singer Guy Mitchell, an international megastar in his day, who was described as "The World's Top-selling Disker".

It was no coincidence that one of the new singles I reviewed in my first column for the *Echo* was 'Cuff Of My Shirt' by Guy Mitchell.

From as early in my teenage life as I can recall, my two main interests were music and writing. The first single I bought in 1951 – the year before a Top Twenty chart was launched in the UK – on a 78rpm 10-inch single, was 'Black And White Rag', played by a black ragtime and boogie pianist named Winifred Atwell on her honky-tonk "Other Piano". To tide me over until someone gave me a brand-new Dansette job to celebrate the landing of my *Liverpool Echo* deal, I constructed my own primitive record-player using an old wind-up gramophone turntable linked to a lightweight electric pick-up, amplifier and speaker. In those (just) pre-rock'n'roll days I was listening to Al Martino, Jo Stafford, Kay Starr, Frankie Laine, Nat King Cole and Doris Day.

I considered myself lucky to be handed the very grown-up responsibility of writing a newspaper column that brought together my two top interests, while I was still at school. During my formative years at Merchant Taylors' School in the north Liverpool suburb of Crosby I was a rebellious pupil who did well at the few subjects I enjoyed – English and History for example – but I allowed the rest to drift. I found it difficult to respect authority, still do. One master reported that my written work was "suavely persuasive but short on facts", which might be seen by some as a prophetic pointer towards my subsequent 20-year stint as a publicist during the Sixties and Seventies!

One year I won my form's essay-writing award and chose to be presented with the *Kemsley Manual Of Journalism* as my prize on Speech Day. When they told me that my choice cost more than the prize was worth I paid the difference, something that had never happened before. There was an official school magazine called *The Crosbeian*, full of awfully stuffy articles and boring statistics about last season's successes by the school's sports teams. By-passing the school authorities, I launched an unofficial rival publication, *The Flash*, a thoroughly amateurish but much more entertaining read consisting of stapled foolscap pages of typewriting and cartoons, which I ran off on a friend's Gestetner duplicating machine and sold for a few pence. I was the publisher, the editor, a prolific contributor and the magazine's only news-vendor, hawking my latest issue around the school quadrangle at breaks and lunchtimes. *The Flash* came out fortnightly and was full of corny Christmas-cracker-style jokes, up-to-date news about school events, some quite vicious classroom gossip about unnamed members of staff (who lined up to buy their own copies!), a local entertainment guide (which got me free cinema tickets) and a sci-fi serial based on the stuff we saw at the Odeon each Saturday morning in the holidays, all contributed on a voluntary basis by my buddies and classmates.

Then I turned my attention to music. Noting the pitiful standard of the semi-pro strict-tempo dance bands hired by the school for end-of-term hops, I went into (very localised) artists' management and promoted gigs at church halls and small dance studios/ballrooms in the Crosby area starring unknown semi-pro jazz and skiffle outfits such as the Noel Walker Stompers, John Oliver's Jazzmen and the Mike McCombe Skiffle Group. At the time I had no idea that I was playing my tiny part in the initial development of a movement that would become known as Mersey Beat. To be frank, my primary motive was profit, up to an amazing £30 per gig, which I hoped to spend on acquiring and keeping an altogether better class of girlfriend. Not far from me geographically and not far behind me chronologically, a youthful John Lennon was growing up on the other side of Liverpool and recruiting classmates at Quarry Bank High School to form his first band, a skiffle-oriented outfit called The Quarry Men. John admitted that his initial interest in running a group was also to improve his chance of pulling more fanciable judies – the word "judy" was prevalent Liverpudlian slang for "young lady" in the Fifties, replacing the more generally used "bint". (Hence a "judy scuffer" was a female police officer on the Merseyside force.)

Like other local skiffle groups, John's was destined to evolve into a rock'n'roll band to fit his personal preference and to meet an emerging, new public demand for local versions of Little Richard, Chuck Berry, Buddy Holly, and Jerry Lee Lewis. Meanwhile, Mersey Beat for my friends and me meant traditional jazz and our idols were the Merseysippi Jazz Band who played for members of the West Coast Jazz Club at Liverpool's Temple Restaurant in the city's business quarter. Traditionally, those of us who enjoyed jazz were supposed to despise rock'n'pop, the stuff that made up most of the Top Twenty best-selling singles. Having been a record reviewer since 1954, I had developed a wide-ranging and readily adventurous appetite for all types of music. When I assessed a new recording my criteria had nothing to do with musical styles or categories. I was interested in the musical quality of each track I played, plus the recording's chart potential. I have the *Liverpool Echo* to thank for forcing me to adopt such catholic tastes and causing me to enjoy just about any style of well-written, well-sung and well-played music throughout the rest of my life.

After Merchant Taylors' I went on to Durham University where I studied as little as possible. Being a student qualified me for deferment of compulsory national service, but the military caught up with me the moment I left Durham and I became one of the final batch of British national servicemen. By suave persuasion and for no valid reason I gained a compassionate posting to RAF Weeton, outside Blackpool, where I spent much of my two years running the RAF Weeton Broadcasting Service, a closed-circuit set-up that made good use of all the new records I continued to receive for review. The station carried commercials for the Weeton Jive Hive, a live-music jazz venue I launched in the local Women's Institute premises. Luckily, the RAF – or my bit of it at least – operated a half-day closing policy on Wednesdays, so I would rush home to Crosby at lunchtime in my battered pre-war Daimler limo, write my Saturday column and file it at the *Echo* offices before driving back to camp with several of my fellow national servicemen as cost-sharing passengers.

Within more or less the same square mile or two of Liverpool's city centre were the Cavern club, the Iron Door, the Casanova and the Jacaranda. The swelling popularity of trad jazz brought other visiting bands into Liverpool from neighbouring towns and cities. Like the Cavern (and, incidentally the Weeton Jive Hive) many venues were not licensed to sell alcoholic drinks. Then, as now, jazz musicians liked to take an extended mid-evening refreshment break between sets and so had to leave the venue to find somewhere that was licensed to serve booze. Increasingly, the jazz fans demanded some sort of live interval music and skiffle began to fill the gap. Some jazz bands had their own built-in skiffle section, but hiring local outfits was a cheap and attractive option for promoters who paid the youthful musicians next to nothing while happily taking in extra admission money from their friends and families who bought tickets at the door. The ready availability of interval work at Merseyside venues led eager young-sters to learn to play and join groups at their nearest youth club or church hall. Unwittingly, some of these most amateurish of groups were the earliest exponents of Mersey Beat.

I never liked to see all the area's 400 semi-professional groups lumped together as part of Mersey Beat because many different types of music were involved, from skiffle and country to rock'n'roll and rhythm'n'blues. I felt it was an insult to compress the whole spectrum of Merseyside's creative and imaginative music-makers into a single category for the convenience of the media. The *Liverpool Echo* was as guilty as anyone else of over-simplifying its classifications by adver-tising The Beatles' forthcoming gigs under the heading "Jazz". Not until the end of May 1964 did that change to "Jazz and Beat", but by then The Beatles had long left the Cavern and the rest of the Mersey Beat circuit.

It was to the *Liverpool Echo*'s Disker that Brian Epstein wrote when he was on the verge of signing up The Beatles for management in December 1961. He wanted me to write about his group in Off The Record. To his surprise, instead of getting a reply from a staff writer at the *Liverpool Echo* offices, he received my letter from London politely but firmly telling him that the column consisted entirely of record reviews and I wouldn't be able to write about The Beatles until they released something, either an album or a single. I suggested that he should contact a feature writer on the full-time staff of the *Echo*, a flamboyant guy named, coincidentally, George Harrison, who had a daily "people" column called Over The Mersey Wall and was always on the look-out for local stories. This wasn't good enough for Epstein, who arranged to come and see me at Decca in my tiny office hidden away in the backwater that was the Sleeve Department. I was more impressed by the man than the music he brought for me to hear. Visually, he made an immediately favourable impression. He was expensively groomed, with carefully cut, slightly wavy hair and polished and manicured fingernails. His suit was hand-made, he had a costly and well-tailored camel coat worn with a dark blue silk scarf with white polka dots, and shining new black shoes, again almost certainly hand-made. He spoke in a superior Oxbridge voice, a bit like a contemporary BBC announcer, revealing scarcely a hint of a Liverpudlian accent. He wasn't at all my idea of how a typical showbusiness manager, agent or music publisher should look. At that time my experience was limited to colleagues at Decca and the men who worked in the music publishing houses of Tin Pan Alley (Denmark Street, just off London's Charing Cross Road) and hung around the Decca offices plugging their songs and their singing discoveries. Most of these were rough diamonds who tended to chew on worn-out cigars and stank of stale tobacco. Brian Epstein was the first finely cut and beautifully polished diamond I'd ever met in the music business.

Brian asked if he might play me a demo disc, an acetate recorded in the Cavern during a performance by The Beatles. He put it on the turntable and I tried to look interested, but all I could hear was great deal of wild screaming and a backbeat. I didn't even identify the tune that was being played. He excused the sound quality by saying the recording was taken from the soundtrack of a Granada television documentary. The disc showed that a visit to the Cavern could be a very exciting experience but it didn't really display the singing and playing of The Beatles to advantage. My sleeve-note proofreader who was sitting at a desk opposite mine but out of Brian Epstein's line of sight pulled all sorts of faces as she listened. Clearly, this one-woman Juke Box Jury was giving The Beatles the thumbs down. As a sleeve-note writer it was not my place to hire or fire the company's recording talent but I handed Brian his acetate and more or less ushered him out with a bit of the old "don't call us, we'll call you". His parting shot was: "The Beatles are going to be as big as Elvis Presley." Presley was a Decca artist on our RCA label at the time and was currently No 1 in the UK charts with the single 'His Latest Flame'.

In all fairness, I felt that somewhere beneath all the audio mayhem from the Cavern audience there might have been some useful sounds coming from the band if only we could have heard them. Epstein's excuse that the poor technical quality of the recording was down to its origin as a documentary soundtrack proved to be a little white lie because Granada did not do anything at the Cavern with The Beatles until the summer of 1962. Brian had made this recording himself on an amateur machine, simply holding a cheap microphone up above his head somewhere in the audience. No wonder he picked up crowd reactions rather than the group's inadequately amplified music from the Cavern's stage.

Against the advice of my proofreader I called our Marketing

Department. I approached them rather than the producers in A & R (Artistes & Repertoire) because I knew that Brian Epstein was a well-respected Liverpool record retailer. Marketing hadn't heard of Epstein but asked if his record shops bore his name. "No," I said. "His family has a chain of outlets in the city but they trade as NEMS, North End Music Stores." At this point Marketing jumped to attention, telling me that NEMS was one of Decca's best customers in the north-west of England and any band they were connected with must be given the courtesy of an audition.

I must confess that my main interest in the group at this point was to get a story for my *Liverpool Echo* column. I was looking for something that would justify a "Local Group Makes Good" headline. I wasn't the only one putting pressure on Decca to give The Beatles a test session. Brian had been pestering his area salesmen. One of the Decca label's up-and-coming young producers, Mike Smith, had been listening to good reports coming down to him from Merseyside and had taken the trouble to travel north to see the band in action at the Cavern in the second week of December.

Set for New Year's Day, 1962, the Decca audition was a disaster for a number of reasons. The Beatles experienced terrible weather – blizzards then heavy rain – on the 200-mile drive from Liverpool to London. They arrived too late to get a decent evening meal or a good night's sleep before reporting to Decca's West Hampstead studios the following morning. Having travelled in luxury by rail and rested comfortably in his favourite Park Lane hotel, Brian Epstein breezed into the studio to find four cold and disgruntled Beatles who were in snappish mood and too miserable to be particularly enthusiastic about making any music. Because of the late arrival of Mike Smith, the audition was delayed, making both Brian and the boys even more nervy and irritable. The final straw was that Brian had dictated what The Beatles should sing and play for Decca's producers. He vetoed the wildest of their up-tempo ravers with which the group rocked Cavern regulars, insisting that more sophisticated material was required for such an occasion. What The Beatles laid down for Decca on that icy New Year's morning was far from disgraceful but they failed to score high marks for choice of songs, musicianship or presentation.

Despite this, Mike Smith told me there was every chance that Decca would sign The Beatles and I printed this good-news story in my *Liverpool Echo* column on January 27. I wrote: "Latest episode in the success story of Liverpool's Beatles: Commenting upon the outfit's recent recording test, Decca disc producer, Mike Smith, tells me that he thinks The Beatles are great. He has a continuous tape of their audition performances which runs for over 30 minutes, and he is convinced that his label will be able to put The Beatles to good use. I'll keep you posted …"

If I had heard the tapes before writing my copy I would have been less keen to jump the gun. The Beatles were not impressive at the Decca session and those who have heard the West Hampstead recordings over the years have agreed with Decca's chief A & R man, Dick Rowe, who turned the group down. Hearing Mike Smith's various test tapes on his return from a Christmas and New Year break, Rowe told the junior producer that he could sign either The Beatles or Brian Poole and the Tremeloes but he guided him towards the latter. Quite apart from the question of comparative talents, Dick Rowe must have known that The Beatles were brought to his department's attention by Marketing and it would be natural for him to resent having pressure put upon his producers by another department. Rowe's preference for Brian Poole and the Tremeloes made commercial sense for Decca as they were local London-based lads and it would so much more convenient and less costly to bring them in for future sessions, publicity appointments, radio broadcasts and other appearances. Mike Smith told me later: "I wanted The Beatles and Brian Poole and the Tremeloes but Dick insisted that I couldn't have both. He was the guv'nor, I was very much his junior." Could Mike have defied his boss by going ahead and doing a deal with Brian Epstein before Dick Rowe returned to his office? Mike confessed to me that he hadn't the authority to sign any acts in Dick Rowe's absence, but had he been allowed to trust his instincts and sign The Beatles on the strength of their stage show in Liverpool he would have gone ahead and done so. He added: "In the studio they were not good and their personalities didn't come across. Maybe they were in awe of the situation."

According to Epstein, Dick Rowe was quite blunt about turning down the group: "Not to mince words, Mr Epstein, we don't like your boys' sound. Groups of guitarists are on the way out. You have a good record business in Liverpool. Stick to that." Rowe also appears to have displayed a surprising lack of interest in, and knowledge of, the thriving Mersey Beat scene. Rowe was blamed by many of his own business colleagues for the rest of his career for not grabbing the yet-to-be Fab Four when he had the chance. The fact that Decca was to sign The Rolling Stones in the not-too-distant future did not delete this great big Beatles-sized blemish on his CV.

The myth is that all the other major London record companies also auditioned and rejected The Beatles in the first half of 1962 as Epstein trudged around the capital trying to find a buyer for his band. This is only half-true because what the others turned down was the same not-so-hot Decca audition tape. So perhaps Epstein's mistake was not financing a further independent test session for The Beatles, re-recording them on home ground in Liverpool rather than relying on the Decca material as his sole selling tool.

During the first half of 1962 Epstein made frequent visits to London, welcomed back on each occasion at Liverpool's Lime Street train station by four over-optimistic Beatles. On these visits he stayed in touch with me, picking my brains about the journalists on the music papers and the most approachable BBC radio producers. He knew the retail side of the record business backwards but he was lost when it came to the creative movers and shakers on the London scene. When he was about to give up his search for a major record label willing to sign up The Beatles, Epstein met Syd Coleman of Ardmore & Beechwood, an EMI-owned publishing company, with offices above the HMV record shop on Oxford Street. It was a chance encounter – Brian had gone in to find a technician to copy his Decca tapes onto discs because he had decided belatedly that these were easier to carry around and more convenient for people at the record companies to play. On hearing a couple of Lennon & McCartney originals on the Decca recording, to Brian's pleasant surprise, Coleman told him: "I like these. I would be willing to publish them." Coleman then pointed Brian in the direction of George Martin at nearby EMI House, promising to call the Parlophone producer and recommend that he listened to the songs. Brian was over the moon when he phoned me that day from Manchester Square to say he had found an open door at last.

Most record producers in those days were "in house" members of staff, each specialising in specific types of artist or music. George Martin's reputation was built on his off-beat comedy connections and both he and his Parlophone label had a less than impressive track record in terms of discovering successful new rock'n'pop talent. He had joined EMI to make recordings of classical music and light orchestras and, although he professed to be interested in what was happening in the rock'n'pop charts, his production roster was dominated by humorists such as Peter Sellers, Spike Milligan, Bernard Cribbins and the Beyond The Fringe group of satirists. Although his EMI bosses let him take on The Beatles I don't believe they expected him to have much success with the group. For the same reason George's fellow pop producers didn't feel threatened by his Liverpudlian protegés. The truth was that George didn't have a full studio workload and The Beatles were useful time-fillers for him and for the label. The full measure of EMI's indifference would become clear a few months later when the time came to release 'Love Me Do'. The company's committee of producers and pluggers gave The Beatles' first single a shamefully low grading, which meant that it would have minimum promotional time and effort spent on it and would get next to no publicity budget. Most importantly, it would be denied the sort of saturation BBC and Radio Luxembourg airplay that turned many an average record into a best-selling single.

George Martin fixed a recording test for June 6, 1962, in Abbey Road's Number Three studio. The producer claimed later that "it was love at first sight". The Beatles were in great awe of their new producer. They put him in the same high-class, high-respect bracket as Epstein because he spoke in a posh voice, dressed well and was a tall, imposing figure of a man. By July, George had made up his mind and promised Brian he would record four titles with The Beatles. This caused Brian to rush off in the heat of the moment to tell Liverpool's *Mersey Beat* newspaper editor Bill Harry an exaggerated version of the latest state of affairs. Treating Epstein as a reliable source, Bill promptly ran a story headlined GREAT NEWS OF THE BEATLES in which he wrote: "Brian Epstein informs *Mersey Beat* that he has secured a recording contract with the powerful EMI organisation … the many people who voted The Beatles the No 1 rock'n'roll group on Merseyside will now have the opportunity to vote their first disc a hit by buying copies as soon as it is released in July." Brian's premature announcement ignored the fact that George Martin hadn't even discussed a release date at this stage or agreed a date when it might be recorded. Epstein couldn't wait to see some product in the shops but on Martin's part it seems there was little or no urgency

What the Parlophone producer did next was to put each of the boys through individual singing and playing auditions in an effort to find a leader. He hoped that a Tommy Steele or a Cliff Richard might emerge and the rest could form a three-man vocal and/or instrumental backing group. Slowly it dawned on him that it would not be right to change the basic nature of the group and he settled for a leaderless foursome in which the singing would shift around constantly from song to song, mainly spotlighting the superior voices of Lennon or McCartney but occasionally giving the others a look-in too. Why shouldn't he experiment in pop as he had done in comedy? Not aware that this great debate was going on behind their backs, John and Paul dug out a bundle of their half-written songs and started to finish the best of them for their first full-blown recording session in the second week of September. As a rule in 1962 singers were not songwriters, or vice versa. Writing pop hits was the trade of specialist tunesmiths who rarely performed their own work other than on a demo disc made for a music publisher to play to record producers. When The Beatles were recording their first single, George Martin was doing a fair bit of business with the music publisher Dick James, who was pushing several catchy new numbers penned by the north London songwriter Mitch Murray. In the circumstances, to let The Beatles record the Lennon & McCartney composition 'Love Me Do' for the top deck of their debut single was a further act of experimentation, or abnormal generosity, on George Martin's part. The Beatles' initial contract awarded them a royalty rate per single sold of precisely one penny – pre-decimalisation, when there were 240 of those to one pound sterling. In other words, The Beatles would have earned a little less than £4,200 to be divided almost equally between them and Brian (around £840 each) if 'Love Me Do' had sold a million copies – a tiny sum for such an achievement, even allowing for the far greater value of £4,200 back then in 1962.

While I was making up my mind whether to accept his offer of a full-time job with NEMS Enterprises, I had one obvious question for Brian Epstein: Why had he not gone to EMI, the most prestigious and successful group of record labels in the business, at the beginning of his search rather than at the end? He blushed and swore me to secrecy, saying this should not on any account be leaked to the media, but he had been to EMI shortly before he came to see me at Decca back in December 1961. EMI had been his first choice. After waiting some time for their decision and hearing nothing, he had moved on in my direction as his next port of call. Soon after Epstein met me, he received a rejection note from EMI. In a letter, dated December 18, 1961, which I saw later, Ron White, EMI's General Marketing Manager, told Epstein that the company had "sufficient groups of this type under contract at the present time". Writing off his first choice of record company, Epstein felt free to look elsewhere and approach other potential producers. At this point he had arranged to come and see me at Decca.

Brian Epstein never talked in public about The Beatles' first-time-round rejection by EMI in December 1961. Most people have always believed that Epstein's first approach in his search for a recording contract was to Decca. Regardless of the differences of opinion between Dick Rowe or Mike Smith, the poor standard of The Beatles' New Year's Day audition might in itself be seen as ample reason for Decca to turn down the group. That being so, EMI had even more justification for reacting in the same negative way. All Epstein gave EMI to go on were recordings made in Germany for Polydor when The Beatles worked in Hamburg studios with singer Tony Sheridan during the spring of 1961. These were totally unrepresentative of The Beatles' later work – they were hired in Hamburg more or less in the role of session musicians and back-up singers. The German bandleader and record producer Bert Kaempfert was interested primarily in Sheridan as a solo recording artist. He watched a show by The Beatles at the Top Ten Club and decided they would do nicely as Sheridan's backing band at his Polydor recording sessions. Kaempfert didn't even care what the band called themselves and there was confusion over whether the single's record label should credit them as The Beat Boys or The Beatles. It was in this capacity that they recorded Sheridan's arrangement of 'My Bonnie', plus the standards 'Ain't She Sweet' and 'The Saints' and (purely as a goodwill gesture on Kaempfert's part) a George Harrison instrumental called 'Cry For A Shadow', this last title being a rather weak spoof of the material played by Cliff Richard's backing group, The Shadows. The material The Beatles recorded for Polydor was substantially inferior to the test tape produced in West Hampstead with Mike Smith on January 1, 1962, but it did give Brian one additional headache which he kept quiet about as far as possible – before he could sign with EMI or anybody else in 1962 he had to negotiate his way out of the unexpired Polydor recording contract.

I saw one other letter that Brian Epstein received from Ron White. Reading between the lines, I felt I could detect a certain degree of annoyance in what White had to say. Dated June 26, 1962, the new letter began: "I was nonplussed and somewhat embarrassed to see details of a contract going through for The Beatles especially in view of my letter to you of the 18th of December, 1961, when I told you that our Artiste Managers did not feel we could use them." Was he not only embarrassed but perhaps somewhat irritated by the way Epstein had crept back into EMI through another door without his knowledge? My impression was that White might well have taken steps to stop George Martin offering Brian and his Beatles any recording agreement had he known about the deal sooner. White's letter continued politely: "George Martin tells me that he has been suitably impressed with them and has made certain suggestions to you which in his view may improve them still further and it is for this reason that he has offered a contract." In Ron White's place I would have resented the clandestine way in which Brian Epstein returned to EMI and in the circumstances I would not have wished The Beatles well with their first release. When the time came, I might have been sorely tempted to pull rank on those in my marketing department who had the power to decide how much promotional attention the single 'Love Me Do' should be allocated.

As the October release date came nearer, Brian Epstein asked me what else I thought he might do to promote 'Love Me Do'. I told him that as a record reviewer I often received press material, biographical notes and photographs, from independent PR consultants who represented the recording artist in addition to whatever material the appropriate record company's press office was churning out to the media. "Can you do a press kit for me on The Beatles?" Brian asked. Here was a potentially dodgy situation. Could I get away with sitting at a Decca desk to write publicity material for an EMI band? I consoled myself with the thought that Decca had never challenged my existing freelance activities. I had used my Decca office for the last few years to play EMI and other review records and then to write about them for the *Liverpool Echo* so, providing I finished my month's sleeve notes on time, it didn't seem to matter whether or not I was moonlighting for anyone else. Brian agreed to give me a one-off fee of £20, to pay for which, I figured later, The Beatles would need to sell almost 5,000 copies of 'Love Me Do'.

I started to compile biographical details about The Beatles, doing my research via lengthy phone calls to each of the boys in Liverpool, because Epstein thought this would be cheaper than paying for me to visit John, Paul, George and the recently-arrived Ringo in person at their homes. To supplement these blind interviews, I collected the rest of my "lifelines" information on the boys (likes and dislikes, favourite foods, physical statistics and so forth) from Freda Kelly who worked in the NEMS Liverpool office and looked after the band's fan mail. John said his hobbies were writing songs, poems and plays, girls, painting, TV and meeting people. Paul liked girls, songwriting and sleeping. George put driving and listening to records ahead of girls, while Ringo's top preferences were night-driving, sleeping and watching Westerns. Their lists of favourite singers were interesting because none of their choices had current chart hits in September 1962. John went for The Shirelles, The Miracles and Ben E King; Paul put down Ben E King, Little Richard and Chuck Jackson; George said Little Richard and Eartha Kitt; while Ringo chose Brook Benton and Sam "Lightning" Hopkins. Their personal ambitions were "to write a musical" (John), "to have my picture in the *Dandy*" (Paul), "to design a guitar" (George), and "to be happy" (Ringo).

In putting together the press kit I set myself a couple of priorities. The first one was to emphasise the spelling of the group's name. If I didn't make a big point of the "ea" in the middle I could see proof-readers and sub-editors around the country carefully correcting it to "Beetles". John sent me a copy of a zany article he had written for Bill Harry's *Mersey Beat* newspaper two months earlier. Entitled Being A Short Diversion On The Dubious Origins Of Beatles (Translated from the John Lennon) the piece was his way of drawing attention to the group's name and early background while getting a bit of useful publicity in *Mersey Beat* in the run-up to their Parlophone record debut.

John's piece began: "Once upon a time there were three little boys called John, George and Paul by name christened. They decided to get together because they were the getting together type. So all of a sudden they all grew guitars and formed a noise."

Further on came John's fantasy version of why the group chose the call themselves Beatles: "Why Beatles? Ugh, Beatles, how did the name arrive? It came in a vision – a man appeared on a flaming pie and said unto them: 'From this day on you are Beatles with an "a"'. 'Thank you Mister Man, they said, thanking him'."

This was my first insight into the creative, quirky mind of John Lennon, wordsmith. But I decided his piece was far too long (and a little too far out) to be included in the press manual. Instead I wrote something shorter which was in my own watered-down version of Lennonesque language. I headed this segment of the press release: IF YOU CAN'T BEET 'EM …

"Beetles did you say, George? Course I've heard of them. Your Grandfather (may he rest in peace) used to put down some powdery stuff to stop them coming in the house."

"No, Grandma. BEATLES. With 'a' before the 't'."

"Hay? No, I'm sure it was powdery stuff. And who ever heard of beetles supping tea?"

"BEATLES, Grandma. It's a group … there are four of them … and they're on Parlophone."

"We haven't got a phone in the parlour, George. Anyway I don't want to hear any more about them. They give me the creeps. Nasty big black things."

"But they're not black, Grandma. They're white … and they're British!"

Inappropriate or what?! But a mere 40-and-a-few years ago "British" and "white" were considered to be virtually synonymous and nobody saw anything controversial about my last line. I'll never know why I chose to use George, the name of a Beatle, because, with the benefit of hindsight, I can see that this could only have created fresh confusion among journalists. So far as I am aware, my nonsense prose was not used anywhere in print but it served my purpose, which was to impress the name of a new band on the minds of editors, journalists, deejays and producers.

My second aim was to give my material a better chance of being spotted among the piles of other publicity stuff that reviewers received in their mail. My hero among London showbusiness PR people was Leslie Perrin, who later represented The Rolling Stones, Lulu and a host of other international bill-toppers. He presented all his written press material on colour-coded paper, keeping one for tour dates, another for record release information and another for biographical data. I followed the same format, picking bright shades to give each page maximum impact. Finally, to justify my fat fee of twenty quid, I had to make sure that the press kit went out to the right people. I knew that the Decca press office had a comprehensive mailing list and that a recently departed member of staff would have taken a copy with him. Over a clandestine lunch in a BBC staff canteen I linked up my material with his mailing list, clinching a little distribution deal that satisfied us both.

Because I was stalling over Epstein's invitation to join NEMS Enterprises, he did a little headhunting and offered the job to Andrew Loog Oldham, a bright young film and music PR consultant who later became manager of The Rolling Stones. Andrew turned down the NEMS job because he valued his independence and did not want to become part of somebody else's company. This must have baffled Epstein because I had given him precisely the opposite reason – I didn't want to leave a thriving record company to join a small management firm. On a temporary basis, Oldham agreed to do the day-to-day donkey work on The Beatles' PR during the launch period. Basically this involved touting them in person round the West End offices of the music papers, taking the boys to meet as many influential pop music journalists as possible and generally spending time with John, Paul, George and Ringo while I remained dutifully tied to my Decca desk. Frankly I would have found this type of PR work frustrating if not downright demeaning.

When Brian Epstein saw the first so-called "white label" promotional copies of 'Love Me Do', made exclusively for pre-release distribution to the media, he flew into a red-cheeked tantrum, the first of many I was to witness once I went to work at NEMS Enterprises. "They've got Paul's name wrong!" he spluttered. The composer credit read: Lennon – McArtney. Adopting his strongest heads-must-roll voice he rang EMI and they calmly and without apology assured him that labels on copies sent to the shops would be corrected. "Not the point," roared a still-on-the-boil Epstein. "Journalists and producers and deejays have the wrong name on their copies."

EMI were not alone in getting it wrong. Around the same time, Bill Harry's *Mersey Beat* printed the caption "Paul McArtney" in bold type beneath a picture of the Beatle and the same error was repeated in the accompanying story.

From the outset EMI Records were content to let us take control of The Beatles' press and publicity affairs. I do not say this to disparage the PR team at EMI, several of whom were creative and enterprising. Later on, I hired two of them, Bess Coleman and Brian Mulligan, to work with me. Presumably the EMI press office was fully aware of the low marketing priority given to 'Love Me Do' by EMI executives but they stood the cost of printing up photographs of The Beatles and sending out biographical sheets. Otherwise, they had many other new releases to service and were glad to off-load most of the responsibility for setting up interviews and photo shoots for any artistes who had their own independent PR people working for them.

Brian Epstein's way of marking the October 5 release of 'Love Me Do' was to make The Beatles the main supporting attraction to Little Richard, already an icon in the eyes of the boys, in a NEMS Rock Spectacular staged a week later at New Brighton's Tower Ballroom. My way of marking it was to give 'Love Me Do' more space than the week's other releases in the *Liverpool Echo* but I had a good excuse for doing this. After all, The Beatles were a local band, the first of the Mersey Beat brigade to break onto the national recording scene. Under a headline that ran BIG DATE FOR THE BEATLES I called 'Love Me Do' "an infectious, medium-paced ballad with an exceptionally haunting harmonica accompaniment that smacks home the simple tune and gives the whole deck that extra slab of impact and atmosphere so essential to the construction of a Top Twenty smasher." Guilty of overwriting? Moi? Other new releases I reviewed that weekend included Bobby Darin's 'If A Man Answers', The Four Seasons' 'Sherry' and The Crickets' 'Little Hollywood Girl'. Top of the pops that week in Liverpool were 'She's Not You' by Elvis Presley and 'It'll Be Me' by Cliff Richard.

In November I went to watch The Beatles record a guest spot on an EMI-sponsored Radio Luxembourg show called Friday Spectacular recorded in a small makeshift studio set up among the offices at the record company's headquarters in London's Manchester Square. EMI encouraged their new signings to come along to these recordings and mime to their singles in front of a small invited audience of teenagers. At this point, Epstein was willing to do just about anything to get an extra radio play for 'Love Me Do' so he said The Beatles would do the gig. A seemingly trivial incident at the show's recording convinced me that the group was going to be significantly more popular than EMI's Marketing Department had imagined. Without naming the group, presenter Muriel Young started to bring the four boys on stage one by one saying: "John ... Paul ... George ... ". Before she could reach Ringo the audience shrieked its approval and rushed forward to the tiny stage. I read a great deal into this. With 'Love Me Do', a debut single, in the shops for only a month and no stage dates in the capital to back it up, all these London kids had bothered to find out the group's first names. To me this indicated extraordinary interest on the part of the fans and I found this little display of adoration more meaningful than Epstein's comparisons with Presley.

Although 'Love Me Do' was Liverpool's top-selling single for several weeks, most of the city's record shops, including branches of NEMS, were left with dozens if not hundreds of unsold copies on their hands. The expectation among local retailers had been that many thousands of Cavern regulars who had put The Beatles at the top of *Mersey Beat*'s popularity poll would race out to buy the single. Curiously, this didn't happen. Rumours circulated accusing Epstein of buying in thousands of singles to hype The Beatles into the national charts. I believe he bought thousands of singles but I also believe he hoped to sell them rather than let them lie and fester in the storerooms about his shops for years to come. Liverpool fans turned their backs on the single fearing that a big chart hit would take their favourite group away from the Mersey Beat circuit, never to be seen again in the local clubs and ballrooms. They weren't far wrong. The lunchtimes and evenings when doting fans could see and touch and chat up John, Paul, George and Ringo in the Cavern were already numbered. In Britain's Top 50 singles chart dated December 27, 1962, published by the music trade's bible, *Record Retailer And Music Industry*

News, 'Love Me Do' rose from 22nd place to its peak position of No 17, while the two top spots were held by Elvis Presley's 'Return To Sender' and Cliff Richard's 'Next Time'.

★

Shortly after my initial meeting with The Beatles, Brian Epstein clinched his deal with me over lunch at a seafood restaurant in London's West End. He said my job title would be Senior Press and Publicity Officer and I would be running the first London offices of NEMS Enterprises. He must have sensed that salary was more important to me than an impressive job title because, over a magnificent meal of Dover sole washed down with Chablis, he said: "Don't tell me your Decca salary, but whatever they're paying you I'll double it." Newly married and struggling to furnish a new flat, this was an offer I wasn't about to refuse. In any case I was beginning to like both the music and the personalities of The Beatles and they had played me their next very promising single, 'Please, Please Me'. We shook hands over the coffee and Cognac. My anxious parents questioned the wisdom of the move, asking if I really knew what I was doing. "After all, Decca is a highly respected company," they reasoned, "And Epstein is just some record dealer with a band of young lads who are unknown outside Liverpool." If they had known that the man was "queer and Jewish", as John and I both did, they'd have used stronger language. Six years later when my stint as The Beatles' PR man came to a natural end, they would say more or less the same thing all over again: "Do you know what you're doing, son, leaving a highly respectable company like NEMS to set up on your own?"

By January 1963, the year in which Beatlemania would break out nationwide, Brian Epstein had upgraded his prediction for the future of his beloved foursome: "They're going to be bigger than Elvis," he told us.

2 | Brian's Boys

"BOYS, I'VE JUST heard your first number one record. Come up and have a listen." With these words producer George Martin called John, Paul, George and Ringo up to his control room after the 17th take of 'Please, Please Me'. The date was November 26, 1962, the place was Studio Two at EMI's Abbey Road complex in St John's Wood, north London.

At this time, having just agreed to take up Brian Epstein's job offer, my immediate mission was to get to know as much as possible about The Beatles before launching the new and grandly named Press and Publicity Division of NEMS Enterprises. I had until May 1, 1963, the date on which he and I had agreed I should start work. As part of my self-imposed learning curve I watched the group go through the boringly repetitive job of creating their second Parlophone single. Today's advanced recording technology would have let them complete this work in a quarter of the time but back in the early Sixties the tiniest mistakes meant "taking it from the top", going all the way back to the beginning and doing the song all over again. Instinctively, I agreed with George's prediction that 'Please, Please Me' would go to the top of the charts and I hoped we were not being persuaded purely by the power of constant repetition.

After 'Please, Please Me' I attended as few recording sessions as possible throughout my six years with The Beatles unless I had business to do with one or more of the boys. I found it more rewarding to wait and hear the finished work on disc in my office the next day. Therefore, it was no problem for me when, in the not too distant future, The Beatles emphatically excluded visitors from their recording sessions, jealously guarding the sanctuary of the studio as their private and personal workshop. To The Beatles, their studio space was no less sacrosanct than an actor's dressing room in the half-hour before curtain-up. Eventually, as sessions became increasingly complex and tense, wives and other beloved womenfolk would be asked to keep their visits brief or stay away altogether, which is why Cynthia Lennon, Jane Asher, Pattie Boyd and Maureen Cox would wait in one of the currently fashionable West End discos – usually the Speakeasy or the Scotch of St James – for their men to finish work and drive down from St John's Wood to join them at two or three o'clock in the morning. The ban extended to non-essential visits by business aides, although very occasionally they would let me take in a handful of reliable journalists and selected photographers. They trusted me to bring in the right people and in the early days at least they recognised the need for media exposure and accepted that publicity opportunities should sometimes take priority over their wishes for workplace privacy. I think the music publisher Dick James was one of those who put The Beatles off the idea of an open-house policy during recording sessions. Boisterous, jovial, hard-working, genial, shrewd, well-meaning Dick couldn't resist the temptation to keep pressing George Martin's intercom button and shouting words of congratulation or encouragement over the speaker system to the group in the studio below as soon as they had finished each take. Brian Epstein's presence was generally tolerated unless he interfered in the music-making process. Then we would hear a sharp rebuke from John on the studio floor: "You go and count our money, Bri. We'll do the music, you stick to the percentages." The Beatles followed the Liverpudlian habit of abbreviating the names of their friends and colleagues, even down to a single syllable when they could. Epstein became "Eppy", Brian was shortened to "Bri". When The Beatles were talking to him they called him "Bri" and when they were using his name in conversation with the rest of us it was "Eppy". They called Neil Aspinall "Nel", not to be confused with "Hel" or "Hely", their nicknames for the teenage chart-topper Helen Shapiro when they toured together in 1963. I knew I was gaining the boys' acceptance when first Paul and then gradually each of the others began to call me "Tone".

The Beatles, particularly John and Paul, thrived on competition and the threat of losing the A-side of their second single to a Mitch Murray composition made them strive hard to put everything they'd got into the recording of 'Please, Please Me'. They knew that George Martin's vote was split between their own song and Murray's 'How Do You Do It?' The group had recorded first versions of both titles at their 'Love Me Do' session a couple of months earlier and Martin had moaned a bit about the tempo of the Lennon & McCartney number, saying it should not be recorded as a slow sentimental ballad but "belted out as a big-sounding fast number", which is what the group now did. To give it a link with 'Love Me Do' (in those days the pop business liked to hear some similarity and continuity between consecutive singles), the plaintive wailing harmonica was featured again, but a perked-up version this time. After the eighth or ninth take The Beatles hoped they had succeeded in satisfying their record producer. As George Martin huddled with his engineer in the control room to hear back a couple of the earlier takes, Paul shouted from the studio floor: "What shall we do now?" Facetiously, Martin yelled back: "Why don't you do 'Blue Moon'?" To everybody's great amusement The Beatles bounced straight into an impromptu up-tempo version of 'Blue Moon'. Some sanity returned to the session with Martin pointing out dryly that time was limited and if nobody minded too much he'd like to hear another take of 'Please, Please Me'.

The single was issued on January 11, 1963, and became the group's first record to benefit from substantial radio and regional TV plugs. Dick James took credit for kick-starting the television promotion by calling in an outstanding favour from the producer of ITV's nationally networked 'Thank Your Lucky Stars', television's top pop show in those pre-'Top Of The Pops' days. The boys were also dutifully plugging their new single twice nightly on the Helen Shapiro tour throughout the month of February. Tour dates were a mighty useful marketing tool that sold thousands of singles or albums in their wake. Nowadays, with music slots on mainstream television in short supply again, touring is still the best way of boosting record sales. By the third week of February 'Please, Please Me' was neck-and-neck with Frank Ifield's 'The Wayward Wind' with both singles sharing the No 1 chart spot in the NME (*New Musical Express*) chart. Each of the weekly music papers published their own charts. The following week in the NME, The Beatles confirmed their No 1 status, no longer sharing the top spot with Ifield. But in other listings, including those published by *Record Retailer*, which was the chart of preference within the music business, they didn't quite make it to the top. For PR purposes I used to switch my allegiance to whichever chart was showing the best results for our current release. I was happy to claim 'Please, Please Me' as The Beatles' first chart-topper on the strength of the NME showing but if things had been different I would have been just as happy to go with whichever paper's list showed it in the best light. Could this have been the beginning of spin-doctoring?

"We've done it!" gasped a deliriously happy Brian Epstein when he heard that the single was at No 1 in the NME. "There'll be no stopping the boys now!" Epstein enjoyed calling his group "the boys" and "my boys", probably because such familiarity implied a sense of owner-ship on his part, and belonging on theirs. "The boys will be busy that evening I'm afraid." "My boys are booked solidly right up to Christmas now." The habit was infectious and spread through The Beatles' tight little circle of aides and business associates. Soon we were all at it. I would say, "I've got the boys coming in for interviews this afternoon … " or "Sorry, but the boys can't do any more radio recordings until the tour is over … " It was only a matter of time before journalists and eventually biographers were writing about "the boys".

Famously, the group recorded its *Please, Please Me* album in one day on February 11, 1963. A set of three, three-hour sessions were squeezed into that day, starting at 10am and ending (15 minutes late!) at 10.45pm. At a later stage in their recording career, when they had acquired the clout to do so, The Beatles would turn music industry tradition upside down, do away with the creatively restrictive budget-conscious three-hour session policy and take as long as they wanted to make each new album. But in 1963 they were still very much under the control of their management and record company. It would be unheard of today to break into the middle of a series of concerts to make an album in nine hours, but this is what happened when The Beatles interrupted their first nationwide tour in a stage show head-lined by the very talented Helen Shapiro. They ducked out of only one date, a pair of Sunday evening performances in Peterborough, and re-joined the tour in Sheffield 48 hours later.

In view of my previous job at Decca it was taken for granted that I would write the sleeve notes for "the boys'" albums. *Please, Please Me* was virtually a "live" performance in that it was made with no rehearsal and as few re-takes as possible, but I didn't refer to this aspect of the production in my sleeve notes because it was not extraordinary in 1963 for a group to complete an LP in a single day of sessions. It was customary in that era for record companies to rush-release a same-title album in the wake of a hit single.

I wrote in my sleeve notes:

"Producer George Martin has never had any headaches over choice of songs for The Beatles. Their own built-in tunesmith team of John Lennon and Paul McCartney has already tucked away enough self-penned numbers to maintain a steady output of all-original singles from now until 1975! Between them, The Beatles adopt a do-it-yourself approach from the very beginning. They write their own lyrics, design and eventually build their own instrumental backdrops and work out their own vocal arrangements. Their music is wild, pungent, hard-hitting, uninhibited and personal." At Decca and then with The Beatles, my writing style for sleeve notes tended to lie mid-way between sensationalist tabloid journalism and PR.

Knowing as a record reviewer that I liked to find who-plays-and-sings-what details in sleeve notes, I went through the album track by track giving that type of information. On my *Please, Please Me* sleeve notes I missed out the aptly-titled 'P.S. I Love You' and there were so many enquiries from the public about this that I hand-wrote on my office copy "sung by Paul with John and George in support behind him".

What I did not write in my notes was that John's throat was bleeding by the end of the day. Having attempted to soothe his increasingly raw and painful throat throughout the sessions with Zubes (as in "Go Suck A … ") lozenges and endless cups of tea, he moved on to ice-cold milk taken straight from the bottle. During his final track, the marvellous but hugely demanding 'Twist And Shout' (which was already the group's most frequently played anthem back home in the Cavern) he was turning the contents of the bottle pink with blood from his throat each time he took another comforting swig. More than one press critic picked out 'Twist And Shout' as the most significant track on the entire album. Without the boot-camp training The Beatles had been through in Hamburg's clubland during the previous several years I doubt if the *Please, Please Me* album would have turned out to be so exciting.

I must have written several million words for professional purposes as a PR man and freelance journalist over the last 50 years, but much to my surprise it is the few thousand that I wrote for LP and EP covers that have generated the most prolonged public interest. I am amazed by the volume of correspondence I receive about my sleeve notes, particularly those I did for albums and EPs by The Beatles. The most often talked about and most frequently quoted note have been those for *The Beatles' Hits*, a seven-inch EP that came out in September 1963 comprising 'From Me To You', 'Thank You Girl', 'Please, Please Me' and 'Love Me Do'.

Part of the notes ran like this: "The four numbers on this EP have been selected from the Lennon & McCartney Songbook. If that description sounds a trifle pompous perhaps I may suggest you preserve this sleeve for ten years, exhume it from your collection somewhere around the middle of 1973 and write me a very nasty letter if the pop people of the Seventies aren't talking with respect about at least two of these titles as 'early examples of modern Beat standards taken from the Lennon & McCartney Songbook'."

Yes, I did get letters, in the Seventies and well beyond, reminding me of these words, but none of them was at all nasty.

At around the same time in 1963 I also wrote the sleeve notes for *With The Beatles*, in preparation for the group's second LP album, scheduled for release in November. I introduced the collection as "fourteen freshly recorded titles – including many sure-fire stage-show favourites". I said they had "set eight of their own original compositions alongside a batch of 'personal choice' pieces selected from the recorded repertoires of the American R & B artists they admire most". Further on I noted that 'Don't Bother Me' marked the disc debut of George Harrison as a composer, adding: "It is a fairly fast number with a haunting theme tune. Behind George's double-tracked voice the rest of the fabulous foursome create some unusual instrumental effects."

Between the writing and the publication of these notes I was compiling a Beatles' press release and was trying to think up a new phrase to describe the group, if possible one that would catch on. I thought of "the fabulous foursome", which I had coined for the sleeve note I did for *With The Beatles* and decided this was a bit of a mouthful. I shortened it to the Fab Four and in time found that I'd come up with a catchy phrase that would still be around and in common use by the media more than 40 years later.

In 1982 I was thoroughly flattered and pleasantly surprised to get a phone call from Phil Collins. I had represented him in his early pre-Genesis days with Flaming Youth. Now he wanted to talk about one of my sleeve notes for a Beatles EP. He said: "You know the one I mean, they're all jumping up in the air above a brick wall on the front cover photograph." I realised he was talking about the 'Twist And Shout' EP and wondered aloud why this was of any special interest to him. "Tell you what," said Phil, "Genesis is bringing out an EP called '3 X 3'. If I get Gered Mankowitz to do a black and white photo just like your 'Twist And Shout' picture but with us three jumping in the air, will you do a spoof sleeve note in the style you used for The Beatles in the Sixties?" I thought it was a great idea and happily wrote a sleeve note that ended: "Prize this copy of '3 X 3'. Apart from being a fine item for any Genesis connoisseur's collection, these tracks seem to appreciate in audio value at each additional hearing." You see I hadn't lost the knack.

When Elvis Costello re-issued his *Kojak Variety* recordings on CD in 2004 he wrote some additional sleeve notes which mentioned the stuff I wrote for The Beatles some 40 years earlier. He said that his CD could do with notes "that tipped a hat to the likes of Tony Barrow" whose liner notes for The Beatles' albums he "had pored over for many hours, as reading them again and again would reveal more story … " My belated thanks to Elvis, not only for the name check, but also for his massive contribution to pop and R&B in the later decades of the 20th century.

Soon after I handed in my notice at Decca I set about looking for suitable premises to house my new press office. Dick James knew that a friend, the composer and recording keyboard performer Joe "Mr Piano" Henderson, was about to vacate a small suite near the top of Monmouth Street, London, WC2. I felt that the location, on the fringe of Covent Garden and close to Denmark Street, was fine and the accommodation was, er, tolerable. Accustomed to Liverpool property rental prices Epstein was appalled at how little this place was offering us for his money – one and a half somewhat dilapidated rooms above a dubious-looking shop with a curtained-off back room that sold second-hand sex magazines. I remember smiling when I saw that the building was called Service House. The deal was done to take over Monmouth Street and I ripped out the seductive lighting and the ancient casting couch but retained Mr Piano's superb hand-crafted wooden desk, a prestigious affair that had an integral cocktail cabinet. I thought I was being tasteful and fashionable when I filled my windowsill with a row of orange- and green-coloured plastic potted plants. I also thought it was trendy of me to take on an American, one Jo Bergman, as my first member of staff. Epstein told me not to buy any hi-fi gear because he'd get something sent down from one of his Liverpool shops. This turned out to be a pretty inadequate lo-fi system that stood unsteadily on spindly metal legs and still had a NEMS price tag attached to it that read: REDUCED TO £33.

Once I had The Beatles' new London press office up and running, the four boys became frequent visitors. Throughout the summer of 1963 they would drop in on us without warning or invitation and suggest lunch or after-work drinks. Paul in particular liked to surprise my secretary, Valerie Platt (née Sumpter), with a last-minute lunch date. We had a choice of good restaurants in the Monmouth Street area, including a superb little French place, Mon Plaisir, a few doors down from the office. Unfortunately, we weren't brave enough to try Mon Plaisir because of the daunting French-language menu in the window. Not daring to risk embarrassing ourselves, especially in front of Valerie, both Paul and I preferred to use an inferior steak house at the top of the street rather than putting our schoolboy French to the test. In the eyes of The Beatles, you knew where you stood with a well-done slice of sirloin and a generous serving of chips. John, George and Ringo also popped in on the spur of the moment and used to spend time with the girls who dealt with their fan mail. George used to have fun flirting outrageously with our female staff and they enjoyed it at least as much as he did in those good old pre-PC days!

Around this time I discovered that Paul had a special reason to be fascinated by the fact that we had taken over an office previously occupied by Joe Henderson. Some years earlier, when Henderson's popularity was at its peak and his 'Sing It With Joe' single had been high in the pop charts, Paul took an early hometown girlfriend, one he met at the Cavern and nicknamed "Harris", to see the keyboard player perform in person at the Empire Theatre on Liverpool's Lime Street. Paul embarrassed his date by singing along with the star at the top of his voice for her amusement. This was almost, but not quite, the end of a beautiful relationship. I didn't attempt to use this as the basis of a press story because (a) Brian Epstein hated to see anything about female friends of the boys in print and (b) I didn't think it would do Paul's image any good to be revealed as a closet fan of Mr Piano. "Harris", real name Iris Caldwell, was the sister of Rory Storm, who led a top Merseyside group called The Hurricanes, and to the envy of her Cavern mates went out for spells with both George and Paul, although neither relationship reached a serious stage. Later, Iris married Shane Fenton, the rock and roller who changed his name in the Seventies to Alvin Stardust and had a No 1 hit with 'Jealous Mind'.

In the Sixties it was much easier to keep unwanted stories out of the press than it would be today. In those days editors agreed that their younger readers wanted good news stories about their favourite pop stars so there was scarcely any of the nasty dirt-digging that goes on today. Fleet Street co-operated by simply not running the type of personal stuff that we wanted to play down. At Brian Epstein's firm insistence we were not admitting that John was married and, by May 1963, had a baby son named Julian. Even when people in Liverpool saw Cynthia wheeling her pram around the local shops quite openly, we had no comment for the papers and they made no great effort to uncover the facts. John had only himself to blame for bringing the Cynthia/Julian story to the boil. At the time of Julian's birth, instead of staying at Cynthia's side, he flew to Barcelona with Brian Epstein for a 10-day holiday. This raised eyebrows within The Beatles' circle. John dismissed all the criticism in one sentence: "I just thought what a bastard I was and went." We knew that Epstein had a serious crush on John and that he had been pestering the Beatle to come away with him for weekends to Copenhagen, Amsterdam and even Portmeirion in Wales, but for the pair to scoot off to Barcelona in the immediate wake of Julian's birth was a shock. In the privacy of our own clique John used to joke very openly about Epstein's advances and the joy he took in leading the poor man on only to rebuff him at the eleventh hour. John made it abundantly clear to me that there was no two-way traffic along this route, that Epstein did not stimulate him sexually to the slightest degree and never could. John told us that he knew that Brian was in love with him and in Spain he enjoyed watching Brian picking up boys in an attempt to make him jealous. After the holiday Epstein did what most of us would have done. To satisfy the nudge-nudge-wink-wink prying of his best mates, or at least those who shared his own sexual preferences, I don't doubt that Brian boasted of a successful sexual conquest with John. By way of broad hints and thinly veiled inferences to close pals he put across the message that he had started what promised to be a full-blown affair with John while they were away. I knew John's reputation as an intrepid explorer when it came to heterosexual affairs. I don't believe that the relationship between Brian and John became a physical one in Spain or elsewhere. I believe John's version, which was that he teased Brian to the limit but stopped short when they came to the brink. To John this must have been great fun, to Brian it must have been agonising frustration. John's insatiable appetite for stimulating adventure surely led him into every nook and cranny of his well-charted world of sex but on the question of homosexuality I tend to accept Paul's testimony. Having shared many hotel bedrooms with John over the touring years Paul swears that his fellow Beatle never made passes or showed any sign of being gay. Paul adds: "In all the years I was around him John never made any advances to me, but I did watch him chatting up dozens of girls."

As for the mythical Epstein/Lennon affair, matters came to a head in drunken circumstances during Paul's 21st birthday party on June 18 in a tent put up in the back garden of his Auntie Gin's house in Huyton. Cavern deejay Bob Wooler, a local hero with Mersey Beat musicians and fans alike, jokingly drew John into the trap: "Come on, John, come and tell us about you and Brian in Barcelona." A well-drunk John punched Wooler for taunting him about what had or had not gone on and I found myself talking to the Fleet Street news desks in the middle of the night to explain the attack. When I eventually reached a hungover John he told me gruffly: "Wooler was well out of fucking order. He called me a bloody queer so I battered him. It wasn't the drink that made me do it, I wasn't that pissed. The bastard had it coming. He teased me, I punched him. Of course I won't apologise." I trimmed and toned and spun John's response into a series of less belligerent quotes for the papers, but the stories they ran were still bad news. The *Daily Mirror* showbusiness specialist, Don Short, wrote: "Guitarist John Lennon, 22-year-old leader of The Beatles pop group, said last night, 'Why did I have to go and punch my best friend? I was so high I didn't realise what I was doing. Bob is the last person in the world I would want to have a fight with. I can only hope he realises that I was too far gone to know what I was doing.'." The warm-hearted Wooler readily agreed not to press an assault charge but took £200 from Lennon to settle the whole unsavoury affair. This was my first experience of getting John out of trouble but not my worst or last. What the episode brought home to me was just how shallow John's relationship with Cynthia was even in those early days of his first marriage. I knew few, if any, fathers who would prefer to swan off on a sunshine holiday for two with another man the moment his first son was born.

Having mapped out a media publicity campaign that would get The Beatles the maximum amount of editorial space in the newspapers and magazines, I worked the boys very hard that summer, grabbing them at every opportunity and hauling them into our new office for whole days at a time to do press interviews. I used to comb the date sheets sent down to me from the Liverpool office to look for the tiniest window between recording sessions or radio broadcasts where I could slot in a photo shoot or another batch of phone calls to provincial newspapers. I valued the provincial press highly, knowing that well over a million people read and trusted the *Liverpool Echo* each evening and millions more around the country spent more time looking at their local papers than the nationals. I tried to make the marathon phone sessions as comfortable as possible by laying on lavish amounts of liquid hospitality. Bottles of Coke were liberally laced with scotch. Pies and sandwiches were brought in for frequent snack breaks. Before the boys spoke to each provincial paper on the phone I dished out sheets of foolscap with the next journalist's first name written in big letters so that the boys could personalise the call. "Hi, Peter! How's the weather where you are?" "Hello, Annie, you've got a very sexy voice." As the day wore on, The Beatles would doodle on their sheets of paper while they did their interviews. I remember that John drew hideous little monsters, Ringo drew ships, George sketched the circular heads and curvy bodies of long-haired girls and

Paul liked to do landscapes. What happened to those drawings at the end of the day was little short of criminal waste. Imagine how much each sheet of original artwork by a Beatle might have earned at auction in today's memorabilia-mad world. Instead, the pages were crumpled up and binned by Valerie along with the empty (scotch and) Coke bottles and the curling sandwich crusts.

On the days when the boys came into my office I got them to sign a stack of autograph books and items such as concert programmes and album covers that fans had sent in. Paul and Ringo were the most helpful and would start signing stuff while they were doing press interviews over the phone. George was the slowest, taking ages to write his name. One afternoon I asked him: "How are you getting along?" Smiling, he replied: "I'm suffering in silence." John moaned at having to do such a repetitive task. He would sign three or four items and leave the rest. Ringo would go after him and pass the books and other souvenirs to the others until all four names had been put on every item.

Around this period we organised a tremendous amount of coverage in the teenage magazines, including Meet The Beatles competitions and numerous interview-based features that strengthened the link between the Fab Four and their youngest fans. Most of these magazines sent along pretty young girl reporters to see The Beatles, making the interviews a pleasant experience for all concerned. This helped us to gain the solid long-term support of the teen magazine sector and its many millions of adolescent readers which, in due course, helped to sell The Beatles' singles in the second half of the Sixties after the touring finished. I believe that this sort of heavy exposure in publications aimed at pre-teens and young teenagers actively helped to establish a faithful fan base that's still around today – many of them still keen to collect and treasure each new compilation CD that comes on the market.

The summer of 1963 also saw the launch of *The Beatles Book*, the only officially authorised monthly magazine devoted entirely to news and features about John, Paul, George and Ringo. Publisher/editor Sean O'Mahony negotiated the exclusive deal with Brian Epstein and myself. Epstein hoped to get a royalty for the boys; I was more interested in having a regularly published fan magazine that I could use for PR purposes. By a combination of professional wisdom and sheer good luck laced with a little foresight, O'Mahony achieved perfect timing with the launch of *The Beatles Book*. Within two months of the first issue, Beatlemania broke out in Britain and public demand sent the circulation soaring. I saw *The Beatles Book* as a wonderful way for the group to keep in contact with the fans without NEMS forking out for any additional fan-club printing and postage costs. My negotiations centred upon matters of editorial control and content and I gained the promise from O'Mahony that we could have at least two pages close to the front of each issue for a Fan Club Newsletter. By now we had established a national headquarters for the fan club above my press office at Service House, 13 Monmouth Street. Sean agreed to print this address in full each month along with membership details. In return for his valuable pledges *The Beatles Book* would be given regular access to John, Paul, George and Ringo for photography and interviews. I would provide the latest information on the group's current and forthcoming activities, including exclusive news items whenever possible. We established an excellent long-term working relationship and I found Sean O'Mahony totally amenable to all our requests. He also became a good friend and we socialised together in a foursome with our respective partners at various "off duty" dinners as well as showbusiness functions.

O'Mahony was only too willing to adopt a "good news" policy for *The Beatles Book* whereby he printed only the rose-tinted versions of any doubtful stories about the boys. We used his publication as a platform from which we could deny unsavoury rumours and dismiss tasteless gossip. We had one or two news pages each month which we used at least in part for propaganda purposes, publicising those aspects of the group's latest adventures that we wanted to put across to the fans for one reason or another.

In the first issue, cover dated August 1963, we ran profiles of each Beatle. George ("on Lead Guitar") said: "Now the money is coming in, I can indulge myself that bit more than before. But I'm not a big spender. I'd like to buy a big house somewhere quiet but for the meantime I just buy whatever I like in the way of clothes and records." John ("on Rhythm Guitar") said: "I must produce a stage musical one day. That's definite. It'd be a big challenge but I'd enjoy it." Paul ("on Bass Guitar") said: "Song-writing is very important to me. John and I work well together on this. We don't seem to have any shortage of ideas." Ringo ("on Drums") said: "I've built up my confidence over most things to do with drumming. But my main ambition now is to be able to play anything with either left or right hand. It's hard, needs plenty of practice, but it's coming along." A page of Letters From Beatle People (the name I coined for the group's fans) included this from Christine Kettle of Surrey: "I was pleased to hear that you were on Saturday Club today. I was in the scullery when I heard you singing 'Roll Over Beethoven'. I rushed to turn the radio up, tripped, lost my shoe and broke my toenail. Your autographs would compensate for my disablement." I contributed profiles of Brian Epstein ("Brian is calm, cool and confident by nature ...") and George Martin ("The recording of groups allows one to work very closely with the artists ... "). The Beatle News page reported that the boys loved their first week in variety at the Winter Gardens, Margate, and "many film producers have submitted scripts to manager Brian Epstein as they want to feature Britain's premier chart-topping and crowd-drawing group in their new productions to give them extra punch". In the third issue "Frederick James" wrote a profile of Neil Aspinall which included this: "Who supervises the plugging-in of the group's battery of amplifiers and the assembly of Ringo's precious drum kit? The busier-than-busy man responsible is Road Manager Neil Aspinall, 22 on October 13. Since May 1960 Neil has travelled everywhere with The Beatles attending to vital details ranging from passports and throat lozenges to rail reservations and hotel keys".

By mutual agreement between Epstein and O'Mahony, most issues of *The Beatles Book* carried little or no advertising except for O'Mahony's sister publications and a small range of "Nempix" – glossy fan photographs of The Beatles and other Epstein acts. The Beatles and their manager had decided that the fan club should operate as an information source, not a merchandising outlet, and this policy extended to *The Beatles Book*. By March 1964 Brian relaxed this rule to let his cousins, owners of Weldons of Peckham, sell an Official Beatles Badge ("top quality, two-tone, precision-finished embroidery in smart red and gold") through the magazine. This was followed up by Weldons' "high-fashioned black polo sweater in 100% botany wool designed specially for Beatle People", priced at 35/- (£1.75), which was modelled on the Fan Club Newsletter pages by bouffant-haired Fan Club girl Mary Cockram. When The Beatles disbanded,

O'Mahony reprinted his 77 issues with updated wrap-around pages at the front and back and then re-launched the publication in October 1982, to run for a further 20 years, all the way into the 21st century. The magazine worked very successfully both as a marketing tool and a popular source of news and features on the Fab Four. The first issue cost seven and a half old pennies in 1963; almost 40 years later the final issues were priced at £3.00.

Not all the names that appeared in *The Beatles Book* were real. Sean O'Mahony decided that he should have an Editor named Johnny Dean. Johnny did not exist but was an alias of Sean who did both jobs, penning a monthly editorial that was signed Johnny Dean and giving occasional media interviews under that name. I wrote numerous feature articles for the magazine including a few under my own name and some (at their own request) in the names of individual Beatles. For the rest I was Frederick James, my own middle names. The majority of the Fan Club Newsletters were signed "Anne Collingham", who did not exist either. The name covered the growing team of people, mostly young girls, who worked for me as fan club assistants at Monmouth Street. The main reason I instigated the use of the Collingham *nom de plume* was because both the press office and the fan club shared the same address and telephone number (COVent garden 2332) until March 1964 and it simplified things enormously if we could identify instantly which office people wanted to reach. If they asked for Anne they would never be put through to the press office.

We "back-room boys" were not the only ones to use false names when it suited our various purposes. The Beatles did the same thing when travelling, sometimes to avoid airline staff leaking details of their flight number and time, sometimes in the hope that a hotel would not find out who was coming and would be unable to publicise the band's arrival. For one memorable holiday trip John and Cynthia were Mr and Mrs Leslie, Paul became Mr Manning and Jane travelled as Miss Ashcroft, George took the name Mr Hargreaves and Pattie was Miss Bond. Ringo became Mr Stone and Maureen was Miss Cockcroft.

After the spread of Beatlemania in the last part of 1963 the pressures on The Beatles' time grew rapidly, national fame turning to planet-wide popularity in a matter of months. We outgrew the one-and-a-half rooms the press office occupied in Monmouth Street and moved to more spacious accommodation next to the London Palladium in Argyll Street. The days when The Beatles could give me a full day at a time for press interviews in the office were over. By now, other artists on Epstein's swelling roster of talented Merseysiders were making chart headlines, led by Cilla Black, Gerry and the Pacemakers, The Fourmost and Billy J Kramer with the Dakotas. The question Brian Epstein never did answer was why on earth he wanted to manage any of these other acts if he truly believed that his "boys" were destined to become bigger than Elvis Presley.

3 | The Awesome Foursome

THE MOST FREQUENTLY asked question put to me over the years has been: "Which of the Fab Four was your favourite?" "Which of The Beatles did you like working with the best?" The truth is that it was by turn heaven and hell to work with The Beatles, who could be benevolent gods or malevolent devils according to their moment-to-moment mood swings. The good times far outnumbered the bad ones and for the most part I have fond memories of my global travels with the boys. As I got to know John, Paul, George and Ringo I found that each had something very memorable to offer, not only in the field of music but in the form of reliable friendship and good-humoured conversation. Individually, the nature of the friendship on offer differed and even shifted over the years, but in all cases I discovered that it had to be earned. Most important was that you were not a close buddy of The Beatles until you proved yourself to be. Your membership of their elite inner circle came at a price. In their unique and vulnerable position they couldn't afford to welcome newcomers into their tight little entourage without first vetting them and obtaining what the boys considered to be satisfactory proof of reliability and trustworthiness.

At the peak of Beatlemania, a favourite question that journalists put to The Beatles was: "How do you think you've changed since the Liverpool days?" The boys used to claim that they hadn't changed much at all, but that those around them had. It is true that many of their closest and longest-serving aides and business associates were speedily overwhelmed by the group's fast rise to fame. They reacted by becoming servile, constantly telling the boys how wonderful they were and competing with one another to obey their every command.

My own aim was to maintain an open, candid and honest working relationship not only with the Fab Four, but also with the dozens of other top international show-business celebrities I worked with or came across throughout my career in PR. I think the main change in The Beatles between, say, 'Love Me Do' in 1962 and 'Paperback Writer' in 1966, was in the way they learned to wield the new-found power that accompanied their rise to the top. In the early years as recording artistes they allowed their producer, George Martin, to show them the ropes. They were content to be the master's eager pupils. They took in everything he told them about studio technology and recording techniques. They looked and listened intently and didn't question Martin's superior expertise. By 1966, their relationships with both Martin and Brian Epstein had altered. They no longer bothered to say "please" or "thank you" but expected everything from the trivial to the impossible to be done for them automatically. The Beatles were no longer under management control and now took most of their own decisions. Success had brought them an immense amount of influence and a greater degree of respect from their competitors and peers and they took maximum advantage of their new status.

Paul

When McCartney met Lennon for the first time one afternoon in 1957 at a mid-summer church fête there was no doubt about who was in charge. It was the loud-mouthed, well-built guy, a bit older than Paul, who was yelling too loudly at the rest of the band about what to play next. Paul's first impression of John's Quarry Men was that they looked like a unruly, disorganised and drunken bunch. "Oh dear. Not very cool," Paul recalled many years later. "They were having a few beers and stuff. I thought John was a bit of a slob, with boozy breath, you know." As soon as he heard the band begin to play, Paul reversed his first unfavourable reaction. He found John's large personality on stage, his singing and playing, all instantly impressive and decided he would like to join their line-up. If there was a moment in time when the Lennon and McCartney songwriting team was conceived this was it – Saturday July 7, 1957, in the grounds of

St Peter's Parish Church in the leafy up-market Liverpool suburb of Woolton.

By the time I met The Beatles in 1962 at the Devonshire Arms there was nothing obvious to show who was the leader of the group. Lennon was still the foul-mouthed, loud and blustery one with the sharpest tongue. McCartney was the one I homed in on because I found him so co-operative to work with. It was easy to imagine Paul putting on a professional smile even when it hurt and pulling out the stops for the press even when he was fed up with doing a marathon series of interviews. He was Mr Geniality with a very neat line in socialising to order. When Brian Epstein introduced me to "the boys" Paul stepped forward at once and pumped my hand energetically. Visibly oozing goodwill he asked what my wife and I would like to drink. Leaving me with John, he whisked around the group taking their orders, muttered something like, "We'll make them all doubles … " and shot off to the bar with his list well-memorised. Admittedly he turned the bill over to Brian for settlement but the basic generosity of the gesture was noteworthy. Paul had "got a round in", not bought it, but certainly got it in.

On that first ice-breaking evening in the pub Paul slipped easily into the role of party host, almost monopolising the conversation. Epstein stayed in the background and left the spotlight on Paul who clearly enjoyed being the centre of attention. He relished recalling details of The Beatles' recent adventures in Germany for my benefit. Aided by frequent and enthusiastic interruptions and reminders from the others, particularly John, he reeled off some jaw-dropping tales of backstage mayhem, madness and excess. Then, and on later occasions, the others contributed their own pungent recollections of hilarious intimacies with a happy bunch of friendly hookers in Hamburg's clubland who became not only The Beatles' playtime partners but also the washers of their underwear, seemingly over-coming or simply ignoring language and culture barriers. These were the same working girls who helped the boys to acquire whatever pills they needed to stay on their feet and work such long hours – uppers, downers, whatever it took to keep them awake on stage or grab a bit of sleep between sets. The constant aim of the Hamburg club bosses was to sell more beer so The Beatles were urged to act like fairground barkers to fill the room with fans who would buy drinks. The group faced a nightly challenge to pull in more and more casual customers off the street by making their stage show as sexy and wild and physical as possible. Everything they did on stage had to be larger than life, whether it was the music or the fooling around between numbers. Leaving as little as possible to the imagination, Paul demonstrated for me John's crude antics during the shows, everything from Nazi-style goose-stepping to his cruel impressions of the disabled, always favourite figures of fun for Lennon.

Paul was the first Beatle I got to know well, not simply because of his great entertainment value in the pub but because he turned out to have such a natural flair for public relations. He seemed to know instinctively how to work the media to the best advantage. I soon discovered that Paul was born with the distinctive DNA structure of a master showman, all the way from his bone marrow to his fingertips. Paul was the one-man Barnum & Bailey Beatle. He was then and is now incurably addicted to the adulation of an audience. He was and is a fervent believer in himself. Paul will be a pop megastar forever, always avidly feeding on the approval of his public. His body and his mind are custom-tailored for the job of standing in the full glare of powerful limelight – I can think of no other reason why this many-times-over multi-millionaire should continue to criss-cross our planet regularly to satisfy the demands of his concert-going fans in these, his golden bus-pass years. Macca is an unstoppable workaholic. He was also a self-taught expert in an art we used to call gamesmanship, which was all about staying one step ahead of the competition.

Paul has always insisted that he wants to keep his personal life totally private and "ordinary" but for most of the time he enjoys being in the public eye. When he married for the second time, taking the incredibly resilient former model Heather Mills for his new bride, he was following in the footsteps of his father, Jim, and in those of the three other former Beatles, all of whom had married more than once. Through the decades Sir Paul did not remain quite so baby-faced as Sir Cliff Richard but nor did he lead the same sheltered existence as his fellow knight. In PR terms Paul's special helpfulness to me in my new job as The Beatles' Press and Publicity Officer was that he would kick-start the dullest photo shoots and bring moments of interest to an otherwise mundane interview or press conference. Once in a London hotel lobby I remember a photographer who was trying to get a lively shot as we left but it was early in The Beatles' day and they were struggling to keep their eyes open. It was Paul who rallied the rest: "Come on lads, pick up a case or something. Let's all be walking towards the door." That was typical of Paul. He wanted everything to be just right. And he was the one who would take a last look in the mirror before the photographer snapped the pictures.

He came across in 1963 as a fun-loving, footloose bachelor who turned on his charm to devastating effect when he wanted to manipulate rivals, colleagues or women he fancied. Even at that early stage in his career he could be up-front and blunt with aides and associates in private, but he was often less candid and open in public. From the beginning, Paul put himself in sole charge of his own destiny. He was a smooth operator, as he is to this day. Metaphorically, he still takes that last look in the mirror. He had enormous powers of persuasion within The Beatles. He would get his own way by subtlety and suaveness where John resorted to shouting and bullying. John may have been the loudest Beatle but Paul was the shrewdest. I watched him twist the others round to his point of view in all sorts of contentious situations, some trivial, some more significant, some administrative, some creative. George told me that when he joined Paul and John in the line-up of The Quarry Men in 1958, Paul was already acting as though he was the decision-maker in the group. According to George: "I knew perfectly well that this was John's band and John was my hero, my idol, but from the way Paul talked he gave every indication that he was the real leader, the one who dictated what The Quarry Men would do and where they should be going as a group." This made sense to me because, from what I saw for myself in1963 and later, Paul's opinions and ideas tended to prevail with The Beatles, particularly on matters of musical policy such as whether a new number was worth recording or whether the running order for the group's stage show needed altering slightly. I didn't see any of the others resist him. They seemed to welcome Paul getting his way by winning arguments with John. When Paul wanted something badly enough from Brian Epstein he would speak softly, wooing the man rather than intimidating him. Epstein's defences would melt away as Paul looked him straight in the eye. In terms of song lyrics, Paul's idea of romantic was 'Michelle', John's was 'Norwegian Wood'. When Lennon and McCartney decided to write nostalgic songs about their hometown of Liverpool, John's came out as 'Strawberry Fields' and Paul's as 'Penny Lane'.

At the extreme, Paul could appear as a conceited, self-centred control freak. But as one half of the world's most brilliant songwriting team and with that sort of credential under his belt, any superficial shortcomings were to be written off as the eccentricities of genius. Unlike John and Brian Epstein, Paul did not appear to have any half-concealed demons to deal with. What impressed me most about him, apart from his exceptional talents as a composer and performer, was his determination. In his eyes, nothing was out of reach. Whatever he set his heart on had his devoted attention for as long as it took to score the goal, win the argument or complete the task. If a new song he believed in didn't work out at the first attempt he would stick with it. 'Yesterday' was a classic example, starting as a haunting tune without proper words and finishing up many months later as Paul's most recorded and most performed composition. John didn't have the patience or concentration span to write a 'Yesterday', so he openly criticised Paul's best-ever ballad. Paul set himself impossible targets and achieved them without apparent strain. He expected the same unquestioning effort and dedication from all those he worked with and still does today. I used him to influence the others, because that's what Paul himself would do all the time anyway.

I made the same early mistake as George Martin, advocating that one group member's name should be put in front of "The Beatles" (as in Buddy Holly and the Crickets, Cliff Richard and the Shadows, Gerry and the Pacemakers, Brian Poole and the Tremeloes even). I suggested to Brian Epstein that the group should be re-named Paul McCartney and The Beatles, to provide a more personal focus for the fans. Epstein brushed the idea aside, saying this was a democratic group and that he wanted the attention to be spread equally across all four. I came away with the impression that if I'd suggested John Lennon and The Beatles he would have at least discussed the proposal rather than dismissing it so absolutely. But of course Paul would never have let Lennon's name go in front like that. In recent years, Paul has become increasingly sensitive over the who-wrote-what question, seeing it as only fair that his name, not John's, should come first in composer credits for songs that John had little or nothing to do with. From the outset, everything either of them wrote was labelled a Lennon & McCartney song, partly to simplify the finances and provide both parties with equal publishing income, but Paul's recent stance was that history should reflect the facts more accurately. He wanted some credits reversed to read McCartney – Lennon and others amended to simply McCartney. I imagine he was not pleased when Yoko Ono hijacked his 'When I'm 64' and used the title of this well-known McCartney novelty number to sell an exhibition of John's artwork in New York, intended to mark what would have been her husband's 64th birthday in 2004. Yoko further inflamed the ongoing war of words between her and Paul at the end of 2004 when she claimed that 'Yesterday' was not a Paul McCartney song but belonged in The Beatles' songbook, meaning that she refused to give her blessing to the use of the title in a compilation of McCartney recordings.

I saw from the start that Paul was almost obsessively ambitious, where John was relatively laid back and lazy. John wanted to be successful as a music-maker and songwriter as long as it didn't involve too much actual effort. He quite liked the thought of becoming a big star and being rich and hugely famous, but Paul made stardom not merely his ultimate goal but his all-pervasive lifestyle. Paul admitted to me he had told Brian Epstein bluntly at the time The Beatles signed their first management contract that if for any reason the group's career failed to take off he wanted to go ahead on his own, which indeed he was destined to do with considerable ongoing success and extraordinary longevity after 1970 when the Fab Four disbanded.

Only on rare occasions did any of us have a chance to watch the actual Lennon & McCartney songwriting machinery in action. It was not the scenario that most outsiders imagined. As a rule John and Paul worked on their own. In the early years, they were more likely to rush off a No 1 hit on a tour bus or in a dressing room than at any formal songwriting session. Occasionally, they would come together if an urgent deadline was looming for new material, maybe a film soundtrack album or a pre-Christmas single, but neither one enjoyed sitting down together at a pre-arranged time in a pre-planned place to come up with new songs. A remarkable chemistry sparkled and crackled between the two songwriters and they worked best under high pressure. The competitive spirit between them often became ferocious. They were rivals who brought out the best in one another.

Like two brothers they fought extensively over everything, particularly their music, each determined to top the other's efforts. But the bond they formed through their songwriting was even stronger than brotherly love. I realised quite early on that The Beatles existed in order to serve the richly-talented Lennon & McCartney partnership. The band was not in reality a four-man co-operative but a delivery vehicle for the material that John and Paul were writing. Put another way, The Beatles could have continued to write their own material, perform it and record it with substitutes to replace George and Ringo, but the whole machine would have broken down in disarray without the vital songwriting input of Lennon and McCartney. This was a fact of life in the Fab Four and it meant that George Harrison's songs were relegated more often than not to album tracks. George didn't understand why he couldn't get his compositions on the A-side of any singles. The contest was between Lennon and McCartney; George was never in the running, with the result that his excellent songwriting abilities languished in the shade for much of the time that The Beatles were together. George was very frustrated by this. Had he been the sole songwriter in this or any other band I am sure that his career as a top of the pops tunesmith would have flourished long before he had a mega-hit with 'My Sweet Lord'.

Paul would promise people the earth and leave me or someone else to mop up the mess when he wouldn't or couldn't deliver. His endless endeavours to please his public caused me many a headache. He would promise a journalist an interview knowing his diary was full for weeks ahead and leave me to sort it out with minimum loss of goodwill. He would give in to the tearful pleas of a teenage fan who couldn't get concert tickets, telling her it would be OK and all she had to do was see me: "Tony will get you a couple of comps. Enjoy the show!" And Paul would be off with a broad smile for the grateful fan and a wink in my direction. With every seat and standing-room space sold out for most Beatles concerts, I was left either to let the girl down or to re-allocate a couple of press tickets and hope that some journalist would fail to show up.

When the other Beatles rang the office it might be to fix holiday flights or find a plumber. If Paul rang he was more likely to want help in tracking down a painting he wanted to buy or a sculptor he was keen to meet. His interest in the arts went wide and deep. From the spring of 1963 onwards, Paul's five-year romance with the stylish, attractive, flame-haired London actress Jane Asher afforded him the opportunity to share her high-echelon contacts in the capital's arts world. The daughter of a Harley Street doctor, Jane was talented and intelligent but one of her most precious attributes from Paul's point of view was her celebrity, which helped her to mix easily with the capital's most fashionable and beautiful people of the early Sixties. Paul enjoyed the idea of fast-tracking himself through the ranks of London's society scene with Jane on his arm. Attending premieres and first nights, gallery openings and gala events together, the pair gave media photographers plenty of material to work with. John and the others didn't fancy any of that. Until he bought his own house in Cavendish Avenue, St John's Wood, Paul stayed at Jane's place, enjoying the comfortable surroundings and happy to find himself welcomed into her warm and secure family circle. In time, John, George and Ringo moved out of their centrally-located London apartments to buy luxuriously appointed country mansions on exclusive estates in Surrey. But Paul stayed in town, living within a stone's throw of both the Abbey Road Studios and the West End. He liked to live over the shop.

George

I found George the easiest-going and most amiable of The Beatles. When we first met he smiled a lot and was a good listener – the least self-indulgent of the four, showing a genuine interest in what other people had to say. In social settings this was endearing and in media situations it was particularly useful. Journalists on a second or third interview with George felt they knew him as a friend. He remembered their names, their partners' names, and could recall exactly what they'd talked about the last time they had met. He was patient and good-humoured with inept interviewers and kept his cool when asked stupid questions. Within the group George was the Beatle who kept an eye on the money. He would go to Epstein on a regular basis to check where they stood financially. He knew how much was due from EMI in royalties and wanted to know when the cheque would arrive. He was the first to point out to Brian Epstein that the way the group's income was split sounded unfair. While the management held on to 25%, each Beatle was left with less than 20%. "How can that be right, Brian? We're doing all the work for 18.75% each while you're getting 6.25% more than we are!" Epstein, who was absolutely straight with the boys in all their financial dealings, patiently explained that 25% was not his personal wedge of The Beatles' income but had to cover extensive management and agency overheads, including the not inconsiderable cost of my recently launched Press and Publicity Division. George politely withdrew his complaint but successfully requested a copy of all future interim accounting concerning The Beatles so that he could "tell the others when we become millionaires".

With his romantic image and bedroom eyes Paul may have held the reputation as the group's most prolific womaniser, but in reality that title surely belonged to George. The faithful fans in Liverpool were not the kiss'n'tell type and most of The Beatles' earliest girlfriends and lovers have kept their lips sealed. Otherwise a number of juicy tabloid stories might have revealed all about the amorous George's teenage escapades in his hometown. The youngest Beatle used the oldest pulling trick in the book, appearing to be a little shy and naive. This, combined with a nicely dry sense of humour, worked wonders. George's jokes were often surreal but they were gentle compared to some of John's. Fun-time George made a lifestyle of flirting, always in an entertaining manner, sometimes unwittingly, seldom seriously. When Georgie kissed the girls they never cried. Most women on the receiving end of his advances reportedly enjoyed the experience and didn't feel at all threatened or pressured. At our first meeting he flirted with my wife, Corinne, and she enjoyed it immensely. On another occasion he playfully chatted up the wife of Sean O'Mahony, publisher and editor of *The Beatles Book*, without realising whose partner she was. One of George's few failures in the Liverpool days was Mersey Beat fan and Cavern regular Pauline Behan who dumped him to marry Gerry Marsden, leader of Gerry and the Pacemakers. According to Pauline, George warned her about Gerry: "He's a flirt, you know." The words "pot" and "kettle" and "black" come to mind.

With both men and women, close friends and mere acquaintances, George had this interesting habit of moving in at extremely close quarters when he was opening even the most casual of small-talk conversations. He would stand face-to-face, eye-to-eye, often no more than a few centimetres from the other person, and he would talk ever so quietly which gave onlookers the distinct impression that he was sharing some secret information of great significance that required total confidentiality. He was more likely to be talking about his newest guitar or the next car he'd like to buy. On stage, he was generally less flamboyant than John and Paul. The main spotlights shone on either John or Paul while George stood back in the shadows either just in front of Ringo's drum riser or to one side of the lead vocalists. He would hang his head as he played, earning himself a reputation with some fans for appearing shy or sulky. The truth is that he was concentrating on his playing.

It was George who accidentally started the craze among British and American fans of throwing jelly-babies at The Beatles during concerts. He mentioned in a press interview that the boys were partial to the soft, sugar-coated candies and that was enough to spark off the whole messy business. Jelly-babies rained down on stages wherever The Beatles played, leaving a thick sticky carpet that had to be cleared off afterwards. This craze was quickly picked up on by the manufacturers, Bassett's, who decided to sponsor zany deejay Kenny Everett's daily coverage of The Beatles' 1966 US tour for the pirate station Radio London. With tongue in cheek George vowed: "Next time I'll try asking for a Mercedes".

George had a healthy following of fans on both sides of the Atlantic. For his 21st birthday he received some 52 Royal Mail sacks crammed full of cards, the inevitable packets of jelly-babies and silvery cardboard horseshoes and keys. In those days reaching your 21st birthday marked a move into full adulthood and traditionally meant that you got the key of the door – literally the key to the front door of your family's home. George celebrated by visiting the fan club offices to see London-based secretaries Mary Cockram (aka Anne Collingham) and Bettina Rose who looked after a lot of The Beatles' mail. They presented him with his most unusual birthday gift – a full-sized wooden door, which had arrived from a fan with the message: "Here's something to open with all your birthday keys."

When the pressures and stresses of Beatlemania began to bite, good-natured George was the first of the Fab Four to show signs of strain. Somehow he was less able than the others to tolerate the dangers and absorb the discomforts of touring the world on The Beatles' biggest concert tours. The onslaught of Beatlemania sent George's head spinning off to the other end of the personality spectrum, making him irritable and grouchy. He was no longer prepared to put up with banal inquisition by the press and to me was becoming more of a PR liability than an asset. He was increasingly withdrawn and defiant and the press were quick to notice this. He was accused by interviewers of sullen behaviour. I found a partial and temporary solution to this by limiting the range of most interviews he did. Knowing George's studious interest in musical technique and his fascination with the latest guitars to hit the market I gave him to specialist journalists and let him talk about instruments and styles of playing. In that context he was fine, but he continued to be unhappy about touring the world in limos and aeroplanes. Although he was developing decidedly awkward attitude problems, he remained reasonably pleasant and friendly with John, Paul, Ringo and the rest of us who worked around him, although all of us noticed a change in him, which we didn't like. I remember that he made it known to us at every slightest opportunity that he couldn't wait to end the painful pursuit of touring. He wanted The Beatles to concentrate on the more peaceful and creative business of making records. Of the four, George was the most dedicated musician, the one who would tune not only his own but the rest of the group's guitars during the final minutes before a performance. You wouldn't catch John, Paul or Ringo doing any non-essential rehearsing, but George loved to find out more about the instruments he played and he practised for pleasure rather than pure necessity. The Beatle who later made such an intensive study of the Indian sitar was also fascinated by the ukulele and listened to a lot of recorded Hawaiian music from the Thirties and Forties. He was a keen fan of British war-time ukulele player and singer George Formby and used to exchange vintage Formby recordings with fellow collector Joe Brown, the Cockney musician and entertainer.

In January 1966 George became the third Beatle to take a wife, the beautiful model Pattie Boyd, leaving Paul as the only remaining bachelor boy. George always went to great lengths to keep the personal and professional sectors of his life apart. He valued his privacy very highly and blamed Beatlemania for depriving him of it. He seldom allowed the media to question him on his love life or on family affairs so it came as no surprise when George tested my loyalty by swearing me to secrecy over the details of his wedding. The deal was that I would deny all knowledge of what he was up to until the very last moment. When the civil ceremony was actually in progress at Epsom Register Office in Surrey, I would phone around the press agencies and Fleet Street's national newspapers with a prepared statement on behalf of George and Pattie. In a gesture that surprised me George agreed to come in to my office with his new bride within hours of the wedding for an informal photo call. For the photographers, Pattie wore a new fur coat from Mary Quant, a wedding gift from George. A Fleet Street showbusiness news reporter, Mike Housego – a good friend of mine as it happened – stumbled on the Register Office booking 24 hours beforehand and went knocking on the door of George's Esher bungalow. Without showing embarrassment, a poker-faced, poker-voiced George flatly denied that he was about to marry and sent the reporter away. When the guy phoned me that evening my dilemma was whether or not I should leak the truth or respect George's wishes. Should the PR man remain faithful to his clients or his best press contacts? I could have given my mate Mike a valuable exclusive, but this would have brought a crowd of media people and well-wishers to Epsom the following morning, which in turn would have intruded upon George's privacy. And if George had discovered that I failed to honour our deal I think our working relationship would have been ruined. Then, as at other times when the same sort of choice presented itself, I decided that my loyalty lay with The Beatles because that was partly what they were paying me for. I owed my allegiance to those who signed my salary cheques. On the actual morning of the wedding, the same journalist returned to George's front door and asked the direct question again: "Are you getting married today?" I was pleased that George continued to dismiss the suggestion. A few days later, two handsomely wrapped bottles of Dom Perignon champagne were delivered to my office with a simple message: To Tony Marrow (*sic*) with Best Wishes from Mr and Mrs George and Pattie.

Although he was terrified of flying, George managed a laugh after a frightening incident during our US concert tour in August 1965. As our chartered aircraft approached Portland in Oregon, one of the two engines on the right-hand side of the plane caught fire, belching black smoke and trailing long-tongued flames. Paul, who was sitting next to me, said: "Do you see anywhere we could land?" I didn't; there wasn't. We were flying through a gorge with tall, rocky mountains reaching up towards the clouds on either side of us. Scary! The pilot and co-pilot knew nothing about this for some minutes because they'd set everything to automatic while they came back into the cabin for a chat with John and Ringo. Most of us thought we were living our final moments. We gripped the arms of our seats with whitened knuckles and sweated profusely. George's face turned a whiter shade of pale. To our profound relief, ten minutes later, fire still blazing from our faulty engine, we landed without accident in Portland, touching down onto a carpet of foam spread out for us by the emergency fire-fighting services. There was no chance of flying on to Los Angeles that night in the same plane so the charter company laid on an ancient Constellation instead. Inspecting the interior of this replacement plane before we took off, George came across a dusty rope coiled up in an overhead locker. "That's an escape ladder," our stewardess volunteered. "How long is it?" asked George. "About 12 feet." George kept a straight face as he said solemnly: "Then I trust we shall be flying at a steady 13 feet tonight!"

After The Beatles finished touring in 1966, George's temporary irritability disappeared and he resumed his former chummy and cheerful attitude to those around him. He was calmer, more introspective and more at peace with himself and the world than he'd been since I first met him. Within a year he developed a keen interest in Transcendental Meditation, taught by an evangelical little giggling guru called Maharishi Mahesh Yogi. With startling enthusiasm George explored the philosophies and musical heritage of India. He bought piles of fat books to teach himself about the area's religious beliefs and stacks of records featuring the sitar playing of Ravi Shankar and others. George never did things by half and he became a great salesman for all things Indian, from the Maharishi to the sitar. Despite earnest and prolonged lobbying he couldn't persuade me to share his great interest in Maharishi's work, but I needed to know a little about it in order to relay details of the Beatle's latest fad to journalists. Believing I wanted to study the whole subject for myself, George was pleased to load me down with weighty tomes about the merits of meditation, gurus, sitar players and India's cultural icons which he insisted I must read. I skimmed through a few for George's sake. In later years some called George a crank and a hermit, others a genius. Like many of his other former buddies, pals and mates, I left him alone in his last years to tend his garden and eat his whole-foods, but my lasting memories of the man are of the happy times we shared even when Beatlemania was at its peak. In August 1965 we rented a splendid villa in the Hollywood Hills so that the boys could take a mid-tour break. One evening, a resourceful friend at Capitol Records sent over a pre-release copy of the new feature movie *What's New Pussycat?* and, as we settled down to watch it, George beckoned me to follow him to his bedroom where we were beyond the watchful eyes of the Burns Agency guards hired to look after us. Picking out the necessary ingredients from a bedside drawer, George rolled me one of the fattest joints I ever saw. At the time I was a marijuana virgin but George insisted I should try this massively awesome smoke. Two puffs and I went coughing and spluttering back to my nice cool lager and filter-tipped Rothman. Reluctantly, George gave me up as a bad job in the reefer department.

Ringo

I could never see why some people called George "The Quiet One". I thought he always had plenty to say for himself. The one who deserved the title was Ringo Starr. The well-known British comic Eric Morecambe used to call him Bongo, his bank manager knew the first-born Beatle as Richard Starkey and to his nearest and dearest he was Richie. He was a smart dresser and wore an array of flashy rings on his fingers. Once, when asked by a reporter why the rings were there he replied: "Where else?" In his book, *A Cellarful Of Noise*, Brian Epstein called him " … a little bearded chap from Dingle". In August 1962, Ringo shaved off his surplus whiskers, combed his hair into a Mop Top fringe and voila! He became a Beatle. Ringo's role in the group was often as an observer rather than an orator. He let his backbeat speak for himself. In August 1962, after their successful test session for George Martin but before the recording of 'Love Me Do',

The Beatles changed drummers, ditching Pete Best and hiring Ringo. It seemed like a strange time to fiddle around with the line-up. I asked John to explain the difference between Best and Starr. He told me simply: "Pete Best is a great drummer. Ringo Starr is a great Beatle." The Beatles had little use for clever drum solos in the middle of their songs so Ringo's percussive abilities were seldom stretched.

When Ringo came into the picture, John, Paul and George had been together for near enough five years, a particularly long time where formative adolescent years are concerned. John was right – Ringo adapted to being a Beatle as if he'd been put on earth to do the job, but it was a skin-deep transformation that never made up for his late arrival. I think he worked hard to overcome his inferiority complex but worrying simply made it worse. Ringo tended to stay silent until someone spoke to him. Openly, in private and in public, the other three willingly accepted him as a full-blown buddy, pal and mate, treating him totally as their equal, but there was always the underlying feeling that an outsider had become attached to the original unit with ties that were never quite so secure as those that bound the initial threesome together. Ringo said to me: "I often think, what's a scruff like me doing with this lot?" Like the rest, Ringo was a fully dues-paid musician, reckoned by many to be the best drummer on the Mersey Beat circuit. Immediately prior to joining The Beatles, Ringo was with Rory Storm and The Hurricanes, a well-respected Liverpool group. It was Rory who persuaded Richie Starkey to take the stage name of Ringo Starr, giving him his own vocal feature spot, "Ringo Starrtime", in which he sang 'Boys'. The tradition of giving Ringo a singing spot both on stage and on albums continued when he joined The Beatles. By August 1962 he had played extensively in Liverpool and Hamburg but not with The Beatles. It turned out that he had spent some time in a skiffle group and taken part in a talent contest that I promoted at St Luke's Hall, otherwise known as Crosby's Hive Of Jive. His group came second.

Unlike the other Beatles he was unable to share memories of high and low moments in the group's earliest history and could never fully join in conversations about that period. When Ringo arrived there was a brand-new EMI contract on the table. He had missed all the hopes and heartaches that went into Brian Epstein's six-month search for a record deal. Adding to this was the knowledge that his predecessor with The Beatles enjoyed considerable popularity among the Liverpool fans. More than a few of Pete Best's followers resented the sacking of the sexy and self-assured drummer and didn't take readily to Ringo.

Childhood ill-health had limited Ringo's education and he felt academically inferior. He had been in and out of hospital for abdominal surgery, which caused him to miss a lot of schooling at a critical age. He believed that the others noticed this deficiency and probably looked down on him for not being as well educated as they were. Automatically, he put up his old classroom defence of silence. It was safer to stay out of the action rather than risk embarrassment. Frankly, I don't think under-achievement in the classroom or lack of success in examinations were at all important among the Fab Four compared to musical prowess, but I suppose Ringo's reactions as the only lately co-opted Beatle were inevitable.

Musically, Ringo really was the outsider in that as a rule a band's drummer is not required to take much of an active role until the final stages of preparing a new song for recording. At a typical Beatles' studio session, the other three would work out their vocals, try various different guitar effects and only at the eleventh hour bring Ringo in to talk about the tempo of the piece and tell him what they needed from him. He was not part of the main creative process, merely the guy who provided the beat, so Ringo spent a great deal of studio time in corners of the room playing poker or whatever with Neil Aspinall and Mal Evans. Waiting to do his bit, he would chain-smoke and drink tea. On stage, Ringo was also separated from the front-liners, usually perched high on his drummer's rostrum which was set well back from the rest. This left him quite literally out of the limelight for most of the show. Like John, Ringo married his hometown sweetheart, a hairdresser named Maureen, in February 1965. In the early days of their romance, Ringo told us that he had great ambitions on her behalf, promising to put her in charge of her own nationwide hairdressing business. Ringo was the most ordinary Beatle and Maureen the most down-to-earth of their womenfolk. The hairdressing empire never came to pass and, like Cynthia Lennon, Maureen had to content herself with being a Beatle's faithful housewife and dutiful mother of their three children Zak, Jason and Lee.

I discovered that Ringo would seldom initiate a conversation,

for Tony.   *Freeman '89.*

In 1989 Robert Freeman made this special print from one of his most famous shots of The Beatles – the one used on the front cover of the 1963 UK album *With The Beatles* – and gave it to me as a Christmas present. On the album cover the print was darker; on the photo he did for me you could see the boys' black polo neck sweaters and a little more of their four mop tops. Perhaps the best-known and most creative of the band's "official" photographers during the middle Sixties, Freeman did cover shots for several of The Beatles' albums for which I wrote the sleeve notes. Bob became a particularly close friend of John and Cynthia.
(THE TONY BARROW COLLECTION.)

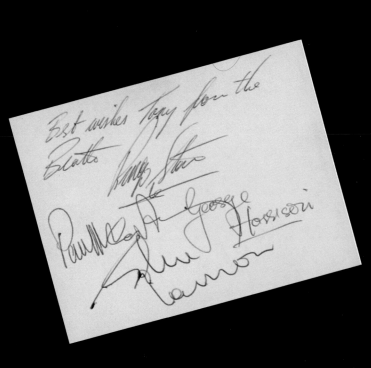

The autographed card that accompanied my personal Christmas gift from The Beatles in 1963. They gave me a handsome silver table lighter.
(THE TONY BARROW COLLECTION.)

Four young Beatles coming to
terms with fame, and the business
of giving interviews.
(THE SEAN O'MAHONY COLLECTION.)

Four young Beatles coming to
terms with fame, and the business
of answering fan mail.
(THE SEAN O'MAHONY COLLECTION.)

Record Retailer carries the story that I am leaving Decca. And in the same issue – on the same page – runs my ad for a secretary for my new office!

We established a national headquarters for the fan club above my press office at Service House, 13 Monmouth Street. The Fab Four were regular visitors, occasionally helping Fan Club organiser Mary Cockram, aka Anne Collingham, and her team answer fan mail.

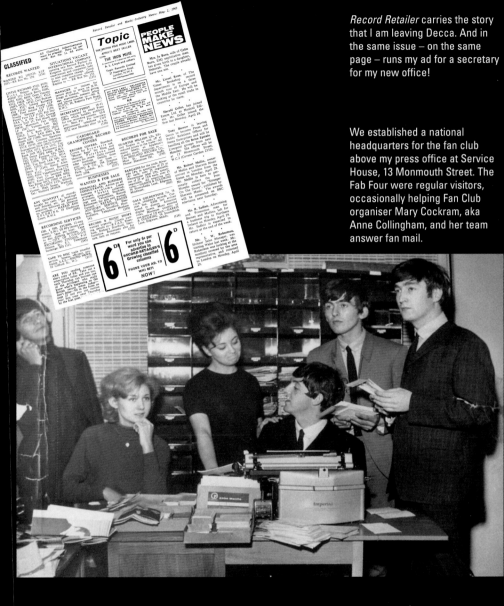

THE OFFICIAL

BEATLES SWEATER

Another number one hit!

HIGH FASHIONED BLACK POLO SWEATER IN 100% BOTANY WOOL. DESIGNED SPECIALLY FOR BEATLE PEOPLE BY A LEADING BRITISH MANUFACTURER. THE TWO-TONE BEATLE BADGE IS EMBROIDERED IN GOLD & RED. ONE SIZE ONLY—FASHIONED TO FIT THE WIDEST POSSIBLE RANGE OF AVERAGE-SIZED GIRLS.

35/- EACH   (POSTAGE AND PACKING FREE)

NOW AVAILABLE (MAIL ORDER ONLY) FROM:-

Department AC, WELDONS OF PECKHAM LTD.
144, Rye Lane, London, S.E.15

Weldons' "...high fashioned black polo sweater in 100% botany wool designed specially for Beatle People...", priced at 35/- (£1.75), modelled on the *Fan Club Newsletter* pages by bouffant-haired Fan Club organiser Mary Cockram.

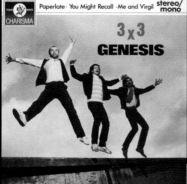

My sleeve notes for the 1963 EP featuring 'From Me To You', 'Thank You Girl', 'Please Please Me' and 'Love Me Do' in which I wrote: "The four numbers on this EP have been selected from the Lennon & McCartney Songbook. If that description sounds a trifle pompous perhaps I may suggest you preserve this sleeve for ten years, exhume it from your collection somewhere around the middle of 1973 and write me a very nasty letter if the pop people of the Seventies aren't talking with respect about at least two of these titles as 'early examples of modern Beat standards taken from the Lennon & McCartney Songbook'." Yes, I did get letters, in the Seventies and well beyond, reminding me of these words, but none of them was at all nasty.

In 1982 I received a phone call from Phil Collins. He wanted to talk about one of my sleeve notes for a Beatles EP. "Tell you what," said Phil, "Genesis is bringing out an EP called *3 X 3*. If I get Gered Mankowitz to do a black and white photo just like your Twist And Shout picture but with us three jumping in the air, will you do a spoof sleeve note in the style you used for The Beatles in the Sixties?" I thought it was a great idea and happily wrote a sleeve note that ended: "Prize this copy of *3 X 3*. Apart from being a fine item for any Genesis connoisseur's collection, these tracks seem to appreciate in audio value at each additional hearing." You see I hadn't lost the knack.

... Me, with back to the camera
facing Neil Aspinall as we discuss
a photo shoot with the boys. In the
third issue of *The Beatles Book*
I wrote – under my pseudonym
Frederick James – a profile of Neil
Aspinall which included this: "Who
supervises the plugging-in of the
group's battery of amplifiers and
the assembly of Ringo's precious
drum kit? The busier-than-busy
man responsible is Road Manager
Neil Aspinall, 22 on October 13.
Since May 1960 Neil has travelled
everywhere with The Beatles
attending to vital details ranging
from passports and throat lozenges
to rail reservations and hotel keys."
Even today Neil is my candidate for
the title The Fifth Beatle.
THE SEAN O'MAHONY COLLECTION.)

Ringo, George and John listen intently to a travelling reporter's question during one of many backstage interviews. In the background looking on … Me.

During interviews I had set up for the boys on tour and elsewhere, the others and I would hang around in the background and occasionally snap away with a Kodak Instamatic camera. Here Ringo is questioned while relaxing on his dressing room bed, ciggies always at hand.

John takes a short break between interviews. We expected all the local concert promoters to provide the boys with military-style iron-framed beds in our dressing rooms. The Americans called them "cots".

Paul spots the Instamatic camera while being interviewed by a US deejay from a travelling party of media people.
(THE TONY BARROW COLLECTION.)

Paul, George ... and Me, as a mid-tour press conference
is coming to an end. George is admiring a Rickenbacker
12-string guitar given to him by Minneapolis music store B
Sharp Music. The Rickenbacker 12-string sound became
a Beatles trademark in the middle period of their musical
development. (PHOTO COURTESY OF BILL CARLSON)

Sweet petite and perfectly formed model/actress Pattie Boyd,
most willful of The Beatles' early partners, sits at my office
desk in Argyll Street chatting with Brian Epstein shortly
before she married a totally besotted George Harrison.(THE
TONY BARROW COLLECTION)

The Awesome Foursome. The most frequently asked questions put to me over the years have been: "Which of The Fab Four was your favourite?" "Which of The Beatles did you like working with the best?" The truth is that it was by turn heaven and hell to work with The Beatles, who could be benevolent gods or malevolent devils …
(PHOTO COURTESY OF BILL CARLSON.)

unless it was to ask for a light or something equally trivial. On the other hand, if I took the trouble to start up a more meaningful dialogue he was perfectly capable of taking the challenge. I found him to be a cheerful drinking companion and I loved his low-key sense of humour. He used to come up with some remarkable one-liners and invented absurd catchphrases such as 'A Hard Day's Night', 'Eight Days A Week' and 'Tomorrow Never Knows'. My own favourite was the impromptu reply he gave to 'Ready Steady Go's presenter Cathy McGowan at the height of the Mods versus Rockers battle: "The Beatles aren't Mods or Rockers. We're just Mockers." All through the fiercely challenging Beatlemania years and well beyond, Ringo remained placid and kept his even temper. Towards the end of the Sixties, he was the one least involved in, or injured by, the deterioration of relationships within the band although he became so depressed by his own lack of progress and the increasing hostility between band members that he quit. To make it easy for him to return, the others almost ignored his brief absence, covering for him and almost kidding themselves that he was on an extended holiday. Ringo realised what he was missing and hastily rejoined the line-up.

In terms of management, Ringo avoided quarrels and put the people in the NEMS offices to the least trouble. He required the least hand-holding or ego massaging of the four of them and was extremely – and unnecessarily – grateful for the smallest job we did for him. His demands were never unreasonable and he was easily satisfied. His expectations were never over-the-top and he seldom used the celebrity of The Beatles to get special treatment. Of the four, he changed the least over the six years that I worked with The Beatles. At early media interviews with John, Paul and George, Ringo said little. But when eventually he did join in he could contribute some devastatingly funny punch-lines that topped whatever had gone before. Like John he loved to play around with words, although Ringo's vocabulary was relatively limited and his style of humour was fairly straightforward. His fixed, unsmiling facial expression often made him appear miserable, but he insisted he was perfectly contented and could not be responsible for his looks. His face simply didn't do happy: "My face may not look too chuffed, but the rest of me is." At one point he told me quite seriously: "I never realised I had a big nose until I was famous and a bloke from the *Jewish Chronicle* rang me up. I had to explain that I wasn't Jewish." Inevitably, Ringo received less fan mail than the others simply because fans didn't feel they knew him very well. This once actually earned him the sympathy vote when American girls took pity on "The Beatle At The Back" and rallied in support of Ringo, even turning a rubbish tribute record called "Ringo For President" into a minor Stateside hit.

During the summer of 1967 Paul persuaded The Beatles to sign a petition to say that the law against marijuana was immoral in principle and unworkable in practice. This was to be turned into a full-page advertisement in the *Times*. Signed by some 65 people, all of varying degrees of celebrity from diverse fields, the list was scheduled for publication on July 24. Days before this petition appeared in print the rest of Fleet Street got wind of the project and reporters called me about The Beatles' participation. They told me that John, Paul and George had signed but Ringo's name was missing. They asked: "Is there a split among the four mop tops over the pot-smoking debate?" I put the point to a shocked Ringo who stared back blankly: "What advert?" he exclaimed. "Nobody told me anything about it." Typically, Ringo was the last to learn about things, although none of us missed him out intentionally. His signature was hastily added to the others.

In March 1965 during the making of The Beatles' second feature film *Help!* on location at the Austrian ski resort of Obertauern, the Welsh actor Victor Spinetti fell ill with some debilitating flu-like bug that kept him in his hotel bed for some days. In turn John, Paul, and then George, sat at his bedside and one by one did their best to cheer him up. Each attempt was unsuccessful. Then Ringo arrived, took hold of the room-service menu and sat down close to Spinetti. Opening the menu, after a moment's silence, Ringo solemnly began to read: "Once upon a time there were three bears … ". Spinetti roared with laughter and later credited Ringo with speeding his recovery.

For a short time, Ringo had moderate personal success in movies, both with The Beatles and on his own, the humour in his screen roles relying more on silent slapstick comedy and miming sequences than on scripted lines. Ringo was no great actor but he had a flair for acting daft. I think he might have liked to emerge as a country & western singer later on but, typecast as a Beatle drummer, he would have found it hard to claim long-term credibility among the Nashville crowd. His career achievements were never as awesome or widespread as those of John, Paul and George. He was content with his drumming job but there was not a lot for him to do when the Fab Four disbanded. I rate Ringo second only to Paul in wanting to remain a bill-topping entertainer, a jobbing drummer in the public eye. Ringo is the one former Beatle who would turn back the clock to the high noon of Beatlemania and cheerfully do it all again. It did not surprise me to learn that he is sufficiently sentimental and nostalgic to have carefully cherished among his souvenirs the outfit he wore almost 40 years ago in The Beatles' musical comedy movie *Magical Mystery Tour*. And all through a divorce and many house moves, he kept a unique collection of more than 50 postcards sent to him by the other boys over the years from various parts of the world. These he collected into a book that was published towards the end of 2004 in aid of charities. I doubt if any of the others saved correspondence or other bits of personal memorabilia from the Sixties to remind them of the Fab years.

The songs The Beatles let Ringo sing were mainly lightweight little ditties like 'Yellow Submarine', which suited him well. He wrote a mere handful of songs and only one or two, primarily 'Octopus's Garden', achieved longevity. His has said that he contributed the Father Mackenzie bits to 'Eleanor Rigby' although I never heard Paul or John expand on this. Unlike George, Ringo never showed any signs of jealousy over the towering songwriting success of the Lennon and McCartney partnership. He was never as seriously rich as John and Paul who raked in hefty composer royalties in addition to performance fees and revenue from record sales. But since the disbanding of the Fab Four, Ringo appears to have enjoyed his combination of French Riviera playboy lifestyle and part-time musician, touring from time to time with his own All Starr Band and recording a number of unspectacular albums. Lately, his work has received greater respect and wider popularity among Americans than Britons. For all his problems, Ringo still enjoyed his eight stormy years with The Beatles at least as much as John and Paul and probably more than George. My feeling is that, coming face-to-face with celestial security at the Pearly Gates, Ringo would have to rely on using the words "Beatles' drummer" to get him into the VIP lounge of that great big starry night club in the sky. Those two words represent the only indelible credential on his CV. I can't see 'Thomas The Tank Engine' carrying much weight with the guardians of the Gate.

John

Initially I saw John as the rock-solid foundation upon which The Beatles were built – no Quarry Men, no Beatles. He seemed to have chosen and changed his early line-up wisely, holding the gang together through their tough, crazy and exhausting stints in Hamburg. Around him in the contemporary world of pop music he saw too many idols in gold-lamé jackets standing on high pedestals and he wanted none of that for The Beatles. In later years John openly acknowledged to me that some of his happiest times were spent in Liverpool at the Cavern where he never felt threatened because he knew he was among friends. On stage he was always visually compelling as a singer, standing with his legs well apart and his feet planted firmly on the ground, giving him an air of great authority. In the Cavern the casually leather-clad group could reach across the front of their tiny stage to touch the fans on the first row, grip their outstretched fingers, take little notes with requests and phone numbers on them, or accept half-smoked cigarettes and puff away on them, which sent the young girls crazy. Eat your heart out, Tom Jones, this was much more erotic for all concerned than having your followers chuck their knickers at you!

Leader of the group or not, John was the main reason for Brian Epstein's involvement with The Beatles and his becoming their Artists' Manager. On his first visits to Liverpool's Cavern, Epstein was definitely attracted to John's rough, tough and leather-clad image. Without that magnetic pull, Epstein might not have stayed long enough to appreciate the musical abilities of the group.

John was the last of the Fab Four that I got to know well. At first I found it impossible to establish any sort of rapport with this cocky guy who had such an inflated opinion of himself and who appeared to have such a low opinion of me. For months after our initial meeting most of our verbal contact was one-sided, with John constantly making cruel jokes at my expense. I felt he was not laughing with me but inviting the others to laugh at me. I found his acidic humour intimidating but, knowing that his temper had a short fuse and that he was handy with his fists when crossed, I didn't dare to retaliate in the same vein for fear of bringing out the worst in him. It was no comfort to watch him treat the sensitive Brian Epstein just as badly and worse, reducing the poor man to tears in front of the rest of us. Worst of all, I could find no good reason to explain his decidedly hostile attitude towards me. It was all done in the name of humour but I noticed that John was the only one laughing. I tried hard to avoid allowing this to damage our working relationship, but while I was bonding nicely with the others, forming friendships naturally and without conscious effort, it was impossible to break through the barrier that John set up between us. It took a long time for me to realise that the barrier was there for John's protection, not as a weapon but as a shield to hide behind while he checked people out. The truth was that John felt uncertain and insecure. Of course, the group knew this long before I did, perhaps that's why they ignored his frightful behaviour and left him alone to get on with upsetting and shocking people. In John's eyes I believe every new person he encountered was looked upon as an enemy until they proved otherwise. The blustering and the verbal abuse were his way of preventing the development of any relationship that might go sour on him. The name of the game was Get The Other Bastard Before He Gets You!

Some people in The Beatles' inner circle were sickened by his particularly cruel and crude imitations of the mentally ill and the physically handicapped. He would contort his face, twist his body and babble obscenities both in public and in private. He had been allowed (if not encouraged) to do this on stage in Hamburg and at the Cavern. Ironically, disabled, crippled and deformed children were brought backstage to meet The Beatles at many of the concert venues we played both at home and abroad. Ringo recalled in *The Beatles' Anthology*: "People would bring in these terrible cases and leave them in our dressing room to be touched by a Beatle. God help them. There were some poor little children who would be brought in baskets and some really sad Thalidomide kids with little broken bodies and no arms, no legs and little feet." A pitiful little line of these youngsters, some in wheelchairs, would wait outside the dressing room until they were allowed in for their brief moment in the presence of the Fab Four. Most of us found this ritual not only unpleasant, but revolting.

But we recognised that to turn these people away would be not only unkind, but also a dangerous act of negative public relations that would have brought the band unwanted headlines. John complained that The Beatles were being treated "like bloody faith healers". He added: "We're not cruel, we've seen enough tragedy in Merseyside. But when a mother shrieks, 'Just touch my son and maybe he will walk again' we want to run, cry, empty our pockets." Just before he let in each group of children, Neil or Mal would warn the boys with a cry of "Cripples". From this grew a routine that was brought into play to get rid of unwanted visitors. Whenever a "guest" outstayed his or her welcome in a dressing room, one of the boys would yell "Cripples, Neil" or "Cripples, Mal" and the attendant roadie would usher the unfortunate one out through the door with all speed.

When Brian Epstein signed The Beatles he took a powerful line with John, demanding more acceptable behaviour from him, at least in front of outsiders. This reduced but did not entirely eradicate John's face-pulling and grotesque gestures behind people's backs, but the fact that John complied to a great extent and curbed the worst of his antics in public indicates the high level of respect he had for Epstein's management, at least in early days. This respect did not stop him verbally thrashing Epstein and occasionally attacking the man physically without provocation. I was having a meeting with Epstein one day in his office when John walked in unexpectedly. Beaming broadly he came towards me and shook my hand, an unusual thing for him to do. Then he walked over to Epstein and it looked as though he was going to repeat the formal hand-shake routine. Brian smiled and extended his hand in readiness but at the last moment John's hand plunged down to Epstein's groin and he grabbed hold of his testicles and held on tightly. Epstein involuntarily gasped in pain and my eyes watered in sympathy. Still grinning broadly and gripping relentlessly John simply said: "Whoops!" I was shocked and disgusted by this degrading spectacle. This happened in 1964 at a point in time where John and the other Beatles still seemed to have a great deal of respect for Epstein – far too much, I thought, to do something like this to him, especially in front of any third party. My initial instinct was to hurry off and tell all my colleagues what John had done, but I realised that I would only have been adding to Brian's embarrassment if most of his staff finished up sniggering about the incident behind his back and I didn't feel that he deserved that. Afterwards, I found myself wondering why John had done this and decided that it was specifically to humiliate Epstein in front of me, one of his staff. If I had not been in the room I don't think he would have bothered. John found deep joy in hurting people both physically and mentally and on this occasion he had done both – and embarrassed me into the bargain, as the only witness to this sadistic act. For a fleeting moment I wondered if what John had done might be turned into an anecdote for *The Beatles Book* monthly magazine, but I found myself laughing inwardly at my own naivety even as the idea passed through my mind. Even if I could have adapted the story to make it less offensive this was the sort of stuff that both publisher Sean O'Mahony and his alter ego, editor Johnny Dean, would have turned down flat as thoroughly unsuitable fodder for the fans!

Much of John's music was as controversial as his lifestyle. Only John could have written 'I Am The Walrus'. He was one of the era's most adventurous composer-lyricists, probably a full decade ahead of himself. I believe he would have been completely at home as the raucous-voiced leader of a London punk rock band at the end of the Seventies had he not been otherwise engaged with Yoko in New York. The combination of opposites in his make-up confused even those closest to him. Even his wedding to Cynthia was part-fantasy and part-sham in that John admitted to me that he would metaphorically shut his eyes and think of some movie star, probably Brigitte Bardot. Cynthia wasn't what John was looking for but she was willing to change for him. I asked John the crucial question: "If Cyn had not been pregnant in 1962 would you have got married?" He thought for a long time and then replied: "It's a hypothetical question after the event but I don't think so." I was left with the impression that John was never truly in love until he met Yoko Ono. He was much misunderstood but mostly through his own fault. He put up his brick wall of sheer bravado to screen off a chronic fear of inadequacy. He claimed that he was not a cruel person but I for one found his humour very painful on a number of occasions. Those around him, from the roadies to his lovers, had the same stark options – shrug off the sudden attacks of bad temper and the cutting remarks or simply leave Lennon alone. He said what he thought and he meant what he said. Then he'd hurry on to something new for fear of boring himself. If, as I did, you stayed around long enough to find out, you discovered that when he was not bullying or bellowing, John could be exceptionally considerate. There was a truly gentle side to his nature. He was a hard nut to crack but once you got through that protective shell there was a good-hearted fellow hiding within. There was also a streak of the philosopher in him. He told me: "We don't die completely until the last person on earth who remembers us has also died." If original, that was a pretty profound comment. I saw John as a belated teddy boy and a premature punk rocker, but throughout my early years with him in the mid-Sixties I did not notice any evidence to suggest that he would turn into a preacher of peace and a lecturer on world love in the Seventies.

I can remember the specific occasion when I "got through" to John for the first time and his long period of unexplained antagonism towards me ended. By chance we found ourselves left alone late one night in a fashionable West End club called the Speakeasy, in Margaret Street, near Oxford Circus. Reached through a coffin-shaped entrance door "The Speak" was a favourite haunt of pop and rock heroes of the day from The Bee Gees and Jimi Hendrix to The Rolling Stones and Lulu. This was the place where we first heard 'A Whiter Shade Of Pale' and Paul persuaded club boss Roy Flynn to book Procol Harum to play live for us.

On the evening that John turned nice on me, the other Beatles had gone home and he was waiting in "The Speak" for his driver to arrive. For no good reason that I can recall the two of us were in the mood to get drunk and a second bottle of Jack Daniels had been delivered to our table. As the alcohol oiled our nerves and loosened our minds we stopped talking shop and moved on to more personal affairs – our respective wives, the burdens of our mortgages, the attractiveness of those two nubile Asian girls who had just walked in. John admitted that night that he had to bluff his way through a lot of things. He even asked: "Do I come over too arrogantly? Am I too pushy and aggressive?" He said he felt a constant need to refresh and confirm his image as a leader and remind others of his powerful strength. Surprisingly, he also worried about his lack of bonding with his young son, Julian, and saw himself as a "bad father". I told him he had only himself and the success of The Beatles to blame. That was one of the few times when John opened his heart to me and it marked the beginning of a friendship which I valued and I believe he did too. I was never again made to squirm by being a target for his singularly vicious style of "good fun", although I did continue to watch him hurt others in this way. Beneath the bullet-proof exterior I had found a pitifully insecure man who doubted his own abilities and couldn't concentrate long enough on his songwriting to complete more than a fraction of his best work. He had heaps of unfinished songs surrounding him throughout the time I knew him best in the Sixties. But in the process John had become my good friend, probably the most reliable buddy, pal and mate of the four over the years, even if I did have to dig him out of one or two particularly sticky situations with the media before my six-year stint with the Fab Four came to its natural end.

4 | The Nemperor

BRIAN EPSTEIN WAS the saddest and yet the most successful businessmen I have ever known. He was the living – and dying – proof that money can't buy you love. His inability to form any lasting and loving relationship left him miserably unhappy. Instead, his lust for rough sex led him into brief sexual encounters with dangerous characters, heartless men and boys who took advantage of him, hurt him, robbed him and left him helpless.

Epstein was a failed actor who lacked the stamina to stay the course at drama school. But for five glorious years afterwards he played the role of personal manager to the world's most famous pop group that incorporated the 20th century's greatest songwriting team. In the eyes of The Beatles, for at least the first few of those crucial years, "Eppy" was a brilliant manager, a well-respected role model, a wise mentor and a good friend. They trusted him absolutely. They had a blind faith in his business acumen as well as his abundance of social skills. When he started to manage The Beatles, Epstein was totally lacking in professional experience in this sector of the entertainment industry, as were most of the people he hired to form his initial team of executives at NEMS Enterprises. We turned our ignorance into a viable asset rather than a liability by bringing our own fresh ideas to a stagnating music business that was crying out for creative refurbishment among both artists and administrators. At the outset, Epstein wanted me to stress the comprehensive service that NEMS offered its rising stars – management, direction and promotion. Few managers or agents covered all these three areas. It was clear to me that Epstein was not embarking on the business of representing pop singers and rock'n'roll bands simply as a means of making a fast buck. His heart was in his work and his aim was to build and sustain the careers of his stars.

The myth that spread far and wide at the time Epstein signed up The Beatles was that he discovered the group as unknowns and recognised the true extent of their talent before anyone else. The truth is a little less breathtaking in that The Beatles were already the most popular local band on Merseyside by the time Brian Epstein took an interest in them at the end of 1961. Announcing the results of *Mersey Beat* magazine's 1961 Popularity Poll, published at the beginning of January 1962, the editor, Bill Harry, declared that readers had voted The Beatles No 1. He added: "The Beatles have been regarded as a top group throughout 1961". What Brian Epstein did was to become manager of a group that was already massively popular in the northwest of England. Because The Beatles rose to such great heights so phenomenally fast, Epstein found himself wheeling and dealing with some of the fattest cigars in show business, while still lacking the experience to do so. There was a massive difference between selling Top 20 records at retail level and selling dates for Top 20 recording stars to television producers and venue bookers. He covered his inexperience by bluff. A top business mogul would offer a specific fee for The Beatles to do a summer week at a seaside theatre or a particular television special and Epstein wouldn't have the slightest idea if this was a good or bad deal. So he'd stall by promising to come back with an answer the following day. Meanwhile, he'd seek the expert advice of his new London lawyer, David Jacobs, who would probably confirm that the fee was fair and should be accepted. At the same time, Mr Fat Cigar would worry that he was losing The Beatles simply because he hadn't offered enough money and so he would phone through a higher figure first thing the next morning. Delighted by the easy result, Epstein cultivated this way of doing his business, turning his own professional weakness to advantage. He used to boast to us: "I never take the first fee I'm offered, there's always a better one to follow." Equally, he wouldn't go back on a done deal. Each time The Beatles shot to the top of the pop charts with a new hit single or an album their earning power went higher, but a club booker or concert promoter who had made his deal with Epstein well in advance was never asked for the extra cash. Gazumping was not Epstein's style and agents throughout the business grew to respect him for this. His inscrutable business methods, the sleek sophistication projected by his public persona and his worldly image among the young Liverpudlian musicians that he managed added up to a strikingly different strain of manager/agent in London showbusiness circles during the middle Sixties.

Having launched NEMS Enterprises at first exclusively as a management vehicle for John, Paul, George and Ringo, Epstein proceeded to sign up other acts at an alarming rate. He gave the impression of wanting to put the cream of Merseyside's pop music talent under contract before anyone else could get to them. I was never sure how much of this was a flamboyant ego-trip for Epstein, snatching the most popular Mersey Beat bands from under the noses of would-be rivals, and how much he really valued the artistry of the bands and singers he brought under our control. We had substantial success with a handful of his early post-Beatles signings, Cilla Black, Gerry and the Pacemakers, Billy J Kramer with the Dakotas and later on with Cliff Bennett and the Rebel Rousers and The Scaffold. Others, including The Fourmost and Sounds Incorporated, became reliable second-on-the-bill concert and club attractions. One of Epstein's earliest failures was an exciting and most promising Liverpool group called The Big Three who had a fat sound and a vast following of fans on Merseyside. Unfortunately, the sheer brute force of their stage act didn't transfer onto their records and after mild success with 'Some Other Guy' their career as recording artists fizzled out. Epstein also satisfied his unpleasant passion for the "sport" of bullfighting by signing up an English bullfighter, Henry Higgins, who enjoyed moderate fame in Spain for a short spell but never to my knowledge generated any income for NEMS or even repaid the generous advances Brian made to him. Boyish singer Tommy Quickly was an ordinary Northern lad who took Epstein's fancy, a one-hit wonder whose relationship with NEMS came to an abrupt end when Epstein announced in March 1966: "We have mutually agreed to relinquish our obligations to each other." With unbelievable generosity towards his former manager the unfortunate Quickly added: "There is no ill-feeling. Brian did a tremendous amount for me." In the same springtime clear-out NEMS ditched a singer named Michael Haslam and a group called The Rustiks, who were signed on a whim when Epstein joined the panel of judges at a Westward Television talent contest at Paignton in Devon and couldn't resist offering the winner a management contract. The career of The Moody Blues simply stood still for the brief period when the group came under NEMS management and a number of other acts, including Paddy, Klaus and Gibson, The Remo Four and The Silkie, never enjoyed more than the slightest smear of fame or fortune. Some of these acts accused Epstein of ineptitude, neglect and bad management. Others accepted that there were limits to the magic NEMS could do for a mediocre performer.

Jealousy broke out regularly among the acts and Epstein was always being accused of devoting an unfair proportion of his time and attention to The Beatles. Some of the lesser talents on the Epstein roster had good reason to criticise him on grounds of neglect, but I was surprised to find that the jealousy thing actually worked in both directions. The Beatles complained when they thought he was spending too much time with Cilla or when he accompanied Gerry or Billy J to America for television dates or the opening of concert tours. The boys would ask: "Who is looking after us while Eppy is hanging out in New York? What deals are we missing out on because he's not at his desk in London?" This last question was to take on particular relevance during the final year of Brian's life.

While his relationship with The Beatles was at its best, Epstein dangled the incentive of a Lennon and McCartney composition in front of new and rising acts he hoped to sign, telling them that he would have John and Paul pen a custom-tailored song just for them. In almost all such cases these turned out to be pre-existing songs discarded by The Beatles for one reason or another or used by them as "fillers" on albums. Although he deliberately gave the impression to outsiders that he had absolute control over The Beatles and that they did what they were told, this was never really so. John, Paul, George and Ringo expected Epstein to ask their approval of everything he was doing on their behalf, and he usually did. However, some of their most stormy exchanges were the result of Epstein going ahead and committing the group to projects without their prior knowledge and permission.

Born on Yom Kippur, September 19, in 1934, Brian Samuel Epstein was brought up in a well-heeled Liverpool retailing family that owned several city and suburban furniture and electrical shops. He was a problem child who attended a total of nine schools ranging from a wartime nursery school at Prestatyn, north Wales, and Beaconsfield Jewish prep school in Sussex, to the relatively prestigious Wrekin College, a minor public school in Shropshire. He was called up for National Service and was conscripted into the Royal Army Service Corps (not his choice, he hoped to join the RAF) where he worked as a documentation clerk at Regent's Park Barracks. He was discharged on medical grounds after 10 months in January 1954. His final personnel report from the RASC described Private Epstein as of smart appearance, sober habits and utter trustworthiness. The first, and the last, of these attributes stayed with him until his untimely death several weeks before his 33rd birthday in 1967.

At the time of his 22nd birthday in September 1956, he began a course at Britain's most famous drama school, RADA, but quit after less than a year. Deciding that the arrival of rock'n'roll from America was going to revolutionise the UK music scene, Brian persuaded his father to expand the record departments in the family's stores. Brian was put in charge of the NEMS outlet at Charlotte Street in Liverpool's city centre and, later, the new flagship store in Whitechapel. He put in ridiculously long hours, working from 8am until well into the night. According to his book *A Cellarful Of Noise*, ghost-written for him by the former *Daily Express* feature writer Derek Taylor and re-named *A Cellarful Of Boys* by John Lennon, the pop record side of the business was "running like an 18-jewelled watch" by autumn 1962. Brian had cultivated an extraordinary flair for spotting the next No 1 hit at first hearing, a talent which he thought of as a huge plus when he moved on from record retailing into artists' management. His fervent wish to become an actor may have made Epstein a more sympathetic manager because he could appreciate the viewpoint of the performer as well as his own. His approach to business was scrupulously open and painstakingly meticulous. He looked after the interests of his singers and musicians to the best of his ability and with complete honesty. Being a workaholic with no romantic relationship to steer him off course he devoted his entire attention to looking after the acts on his management roster and providing them with the best possible environment in which to enhance their careers. He bathed in the reflected glory of The Beatles and his eyes shone with sheer love-light whenever he stood in the wings watching the Fab Four perform. I suppose all of us who worked with the group for any length of time liked to share in their fantastic success and claim some minuscule portion of it for ourselves, but with Epstein it went much further. His proud attachment to John, Paul, George and Ringo was passionate, fanatical, obsessive and all-pervading. Their management, done Brian's way, left little room for leisure pursuits, which is the way he liked it. He took responsibility for their every fresh achievement and adopted a ferociously possessive attitude when anyone got too close to the boys. At least one top NEMS executive, Derek Taylor, his ghost-writer who was later appointed as his assistant, fell by the wayside solely because he became too friendly with the group for Epstein's liking. Although Brian had worked happily and closely with the easygoing former journalist when *A Cellarful Of Noise* was being written, the rot set in for the unfortunate man when he accompanied The Beatles to America in 1964 and made the big mistake of jumping into limousines with the boys ahead of Epstein.

As The Beatles' fame spread, Epstein became one of the entertainment world's best-known "back-room" boys, probably second only to Elvis Presley's mentor and minder, Colonel Tom Parker. He himself was the first to recognise his new-found status. When the demand for autographed publicity pictures of The Beatles grew to huge proportions I realised that photographs crudely and obviously rubber-stamped with four reproduction signatures were a bit of an insult both to the group and the fans. I found a supplier who had perfected a marvellous new technique where celebrity autographs could be imprinted on glossy photographs leaving visible and touchable indentations that closely resembled those created by a ballpoint pen. Finding a pile of these on my desk, Brian was much impressed and said: "How quickly can you get me a few thousand signed pictures like this? You know I'm off to New York next week." When I said innocently that we had about 5,000 in stock that he could take with him, Brian reacted sharply: "I don't mean pictures of The Beatles. I want some of me. I want my own publicity photographs for all my fans and it would be lovely to have them signed like this to save me the trouble of doing them all by hand." And he wasn't kidding! From then on, my press office kept a stock of fan pics signed by Brian Epstein alongside those of The Beatles, Cilla, Gerry and the rest. When word-wizard and Cavern Club resident deejay Bob Wooler jokingly nicknamed him "The Nemperor", Epstein was greatly chuffed. He went on to use the word Nemperor as the telegraphic address of NEMS Enterprises in London and as the name of his New York company, Nemperor Holdings. Eventually, the NEMS office at 3 Hill Street in Mayfair was named Nemperor House. It was impossible to flatter Brian Epstein because he did that so capably for himself; he was his own most ardent fan. As he saw it, his status in the business rose ever higher with each new success of The Beatles and he was quick to upgrade his material possessions accordingly, switching from a smart Knightsbridge flat to a smarter Belgravia house and from a Bentley to a Rolls Royce.

It did not take me long to discover that beneath the superficial veneer of charm and self-importance Epstein had a filthy temper which he made no attempt to keep in check. All his toys, from the dummy to the rattle, would come flying out of the pram when he didn't get his own way. He treated some members of his staff, notably the mild-mannered office manager Alistair Taylor, like a door mat, walking all over them, firing them on the slightest pretext and hastily re-hiring them the next day, sometimes with a lunch or dinner invitation that he saw as the furthest he ever needed to go by way of apology for his shabby behaviour. Luckily for Epstein those of Alistair's ilk found their work at NEMS so attractive that his childish tantrums were tolerated and forgiven. I think he knew that one or two of us would not have stood by him for long if he had treated us with such disdain, and that if he valued our services there needed to be a two-way exchange of polite respect. But it was the lowest-ranking members of staff, particularly the young girls who had followed him down to London from the Liverpool office, for whom I felt most sorry. Afraid – if not unable – to answer back when they found themselves on the receiving end of a tongue-lashing from Epstein, they put up with his rudeness like reprimanded school girls, bowed their heads low and got on with their job. The only women Epstein got along with were those for whom he had special respect; the rest he seemed merely to tolerate for their usefulness. Working with Brian Epstein was a little like spending time alongside Dr Jekyll and Mr Hyde. I found it hard to accept that the obnoxious Mr Hyde was the same man who could be such a wonderful host on socio-business occasions. When Epstein sat down at a dinner party with a few of his senior staff and maybe one or two of his favourite stars, he changed from a bad-tempered boss into a sparklingly entertaining conversationalist. He was witty, charming and in all respects a generous host. Equally, outsiders who did any business with NEMS always found themselves dealing with the affable and agreeable Dr Jekyll, never the verbally abusive Mr Hyde.

Curiously enough, when a serious need arose to fire someone (as against the frequent overnight sackings and re-hirings that were commonplace at NEMS), Epstein chickened out, using any possible pretext to shift the responsibility onto a subordinate. In all other situations he found it difficult to delegate, but sacking someone was a task he loathed and tried his hardest to avoid. Within less than a year of signing up The Beatles, Brian was faced with the major problem of dumping the group's drummer, the popular and accomplished Pete Best. His departure would not be welcomed by Merseyside fans, so there was a damage limitation element for Epstein to consider. With the group's recording debut on Parlophone little more than six weeks away this was no time to invite adverse media publicity, so The Beatles had to get rid of Pete with the minimum unpleasantness. Put simply, the other three Beatles did not feel that Pete fitted in. They claimed it was a personality thing, that Pete was "too conventional" and this had nothing to do with his undoubted prowess as a drummer. Perhaps the poor guy was too popular with the Cavern fans for his own good. With his dark good looks Pete oozed sex appeal and physically matched up to Paul's attractiveness so far as Cavern-goers were concerned. In this respect, Paul must have seen Pete as something of a threat to his popularity with the girls.

In recent times Paul has played down Pete's role in the group's early evolution, indicating that the drummer was brought in mainly for several Hamburg bookings and that The Beatles never did feel they had a complete, final and permanent line-up until Ringo replaced him. In Paul's own words: "You could say that it was after Hamburg that The Beatles were born, when we got back to Liverpool and we got with Ringo. We had seen Ringo and really admired him. We thought Ringo was the best drummer in Liverpool." There were other complications. Although Pete's employment had been brief – two years almost to the day – his links with The Beatles involved a tangle of personal and professional relationships. For several years Pete's mother, Mona Best, had run a coffee club called The Casbah in the basement of her home in West Derby. This place had served as a cosy meeting-room and convenient rehearsal space for the boys and Mona had taken an increasingly close interest in the general management of their affairs, booking them for gigs at The Casbah and at a variety of other local venues, advancing them money, allowing them to store their stage gear at the club and acting as their confidante. Pete was recruited in a hurry in August 1960 when The Beatles had to add a drummer to their line-up as a contractual necessity for a trip to Hamburg. When Brian Epstein came into the picture about 15 months later, his arrival created a potentially dangerous triangle with him in one corner, Mona Best in another and The Beatles in the third. Epstein admitted to me later that he saw this as an instant threat to his control of the group but he still agreed to meet the boys on Mona's home ground, The Casbah, for their first in-depth management discussion. Even if Epstein had taken a less possessive stance over his management of The Beatles he would have found it difficult to work with Pete Best's enthusiastic and ambitious mother breathing down his neck, and it was unlikely that Mona would withdraw from the scene while her son was the group's drummer. Adding another dimension to the dilemma, roadie Neil Aspinall was in a relationship with Mona, which led to the birth of a son on July 21, 1962. The Best family kept this quiet since there was some stigma attached to having a child out of wedlock in the Sixties and they were keen to avoid a scandal. The Beatles wanted Mona's son to be sacked without sacrificing their friendship with Aspinall who was already shaping up as a useful roadie and who had become a very close friend of John, Paul and George. When I talked to Pete at a US Beatlefest convention in Chicago many years later, he denied that a clash between his mother and Brian Epstein played any part in his sacking or that it might have proved detrimental to The Beatles. I disagree. Mona Best was a strong-willed and determined woman and Brian Epstein wanted sole control of the group and would not have been prepared to consider any joint management set-up with the drummer's mother.

Epstein confessed to me that his sacking of Best left him in an appalling position in Liverpool. Overnight, he became the most disliked man in the city. He had the support of The Beatles who were still Liverpool's darlings, but the fans wanted Pete and there were unpleasant scenes. Epstein also claimed to have the support of George

Martin who was said to be underwhelmed by Pete's drumming and had "decided his beat was wrong for their music". As news of the change spread across the city, gangs of angry young girls gathered in Matthew Street outside the Cavern and chanted: "Pete for ever! Ringo never!" The Fan Club secretary Freda Kelly did not agree with this minority element among her members. She was perfectly happy about the change and told me: "Ringo brought out the motherly instinct in me. I was glad when Pete went. He had no personality. He never looked as though he was enjoying himself. He looked sideways while he played. Ringo faced his audience, for a start! You could see that he fitted in just by looking at him. He looned about and actually enjoyed himself on stage." A Cavern regular, Laurie McCaffrey, who later became chief telephonist/receptionist at the NEMS London office, took the opposite view: "There was a great deal of bitterness about Pete Best being thrown out. He had broody James Dean good looks. There was a strong fellowship within The Beatles. Pete never thought they'd get rid of him." For some unknown reason it was George who found himself the target for the fans' anger at the height of the Best battle. Once, George arrived on stage with a bruised cheek and blacked eye. Ringo was also victimised physically and arrived at the Cavern with a bleeding nose as a result of a fan's attack in the street. But the protests of a few hundred, hometown fans failed to influence the unstoppable progress of The Beatles, who played and sang their way into millions of new hearts up and down the country in the wake of Ringo's arrival.

Much has been made of Brian Epstein's inability to keep an adequate eye on the merchandising of souvenir products associated with the Fab Four during the Beatlemania years and beyond. He has been blamed for denying the boys many millions of dollars that they might have earned quite effortlessly from sales of mop-top memorabilia, such as wigs, Beatle boots, beakers and scores of other lines, if he had employed reliable specialists to negotiate sensible percentages and watertight deals at the outset. I have to say that I defend him here. For one thing he was acting on an informal verbal agreement made with John, Paul, George and Ringo, who told him they wanted to make the maximum amount of money from their music but did not wish to cheapen their brand name by selling stuff that had no connection with their core business. It was well-known to those of us in The Beatles' entourage that they didn't mind items being sold that were directly associated with their concerts and records – tour brochures and programmes, posters and photographs – but they did not want to be seen as wholesale rip-off merchants out to bleed their younger fans dry by selling extraneous goods simply because they could. The boys were happy to let Brian authorise a limited range of relevant items regardless of whether or not they made a profit, but all such goods had to be credible accessories to the group's musical image and quality was to rank way above making money.

Merchandising by pop and rock stars was in its infancy – T-shirts and the rest were of the Seventies, not the Sixties. Probably the only existing example of large-scale international souvenir merchandising in the entertainment industry was that set by Walt Disney's people with the successful retailing of cinema cartoon characters. Between 1964 and 1968 just about anything with the name "Beatles" on it would have been snapped up by fans around the world and, in the absence of any coherent policy for official franchising, unauthorised production went ahead unchecked on both sides of the Atlantic. While Epstein and the rest of us concentrated on the concerts, tours and record sales, merchandising enquiries were forwarded to Brian's solicitor David Jacobs where they were dealt with amateurishly by inexperienced members of his staff who did their best to cope with a situation that had already gone spinning way out of control. Belatedly, more suitable arrangements were made with a specialist firm that traded as Seltaeb (Beatles backwards) in the US, but the initial percentages agreed by Epstein were the reverse of what they should have been with a ludicrously low 10% coming to The Beatles and an unbelievable 90% being swallowed up by a top-heavy network of middlemen, licensees, manufacturers, distributors and retailers. Even when the figures were revised in time to catch the majority of sales during the peak of Beatlemania in 1964 and 1965, the boys continued to receive less than 10% each after NEMS had deducted its 25% commission. This was only the tip of the iceberg. Duplication of licences for certain products, overlap of territorial franchises, and complaints from unhappy licensees led to a massive tangle of litigation that brought about one successful claim for five million pounds against NEMS in the New York courts. In his specialist book on the business side of The Beatles' history, *I Should Have Known Better*, Brian Epstein's director and chief administrator of NEMS Enterprises, Geoffrey Ellis, winds up a section on The Beatles' merchandising with this: "All the proceedings were eventually settled. Accountings were made, damages assessed on both sides and a balance was struck. By then, claims had mounted to a sum approaching 100 million dollars, but the balancing-out resulted in our paying to Seltaeb Inc. less than £100,000. As for the costs on our side, Brian insisted on paying them out of his own pocket since he felt personally responsible for the mess." Ellis agrees that The Beatles lost out on the huge amounts that could have been earned by properly controlled merchandising. In his mind there is equally no doubt that Brian was deeply scarred by the experience and that this helped to lead to the depression and dependence on drugs, which were coming to dominate his private life at this time.

Epstein's homosexuality had been burdensome to him since his teenage years in Liverpool. Until 1967, the year of his senseless death, homosexual activities were illegal in the UK so Epstein had to hide his loves away. The young girl typists in the NEMS Liverpool office were not even sure what it meant to be homosexual, or "queer" as the slang of the time would have it. Apparently, John Lennon was delighted to explain things to them in graphic detail. One thing was for sure – gay was the last word anyone would have applied to Epstein's situation. For most of his adolescent and adult life he was an unhappy, confused, lonely and pessimistic person. The biggest problem lay in the fact that Brian was not even a "straight" gay and never enjoyed a loving relationship with a long-term partner. His peculiar sexual preferences brought him into contact with the darkest and most unpleasant inhabitants of a violent underworld peopled by fly-by-nights, thieves and rogues. The phrases used constantly about him among NEMS artists and staff was that he "couldn't resist his bit of rough" and that he "liked to get knocked about a bit". This meant that Epstein was threatened with knives, beaten up and robbed at his own bedside or that of an unwisely selected partner, the culprit fleeing without risk of arrest or punishment since the victim was unable to reveal the circumstances to the police. When blackmailed he simply paid up and moved on, accepting such treatment as part and parcel of his unhappy lifestyle. The care with which Epstein was forced to conceal details of his sex life made him paranoid about press stories involving The Beatles' lovers and wives. He felt that not only their one-night-stands, but also their fully-fledged romantic affairs had to be hidden from the media. He impressed this on all the singers and bands he signed up although the same rule applied a hundred times over in the case of The Beatles. He was furious when John flouted his instructions and insisted on taking Cynthia with him to America. It didn't matter that John and Cynthia were not merely lovers but properly married and had a young son. As far as Brian was concerned any news item that mentioned their marriage and/or their offspring would be damaging to the image of The Beatles. I thought this was a preposterous stance to take. His fear was that young females would fall out of love with John if they found out that he was a married man. My view was that in the Swinging Sixties an increasingly number of teenage fans would find John all the more interesting when they knew he had a wife. Here was an additional challenge of the forbidden fruit variety!

To my knowledge Epstein only once came even close to having a satisfactory one-on-one relationship and the guy in question let him down pretty badly – but Brian came back for more. He was an aspiring actor named John "Dizz" Gillespie, described by one of Brian's more cynical but realistic business associates as "a rather good-looking, sophisticated male hustler from the American mid-West who seduced Brian into thinking that he really cared about him". Epstein was so besotted that he gave Dizz a management contract with NEMS and a weekly retainer. At the end of 1964, there was a press release to announce that Gillespie was the "first straight actor" to join the Epstein roster of artists. Straight? There was no follow-through PR campaign and I had no discussions with my boss over what he planned for our latest acquisition. Apparently, Dizz was bisexual and was unfaithful to Brian with women as well as other men. The buzz among those of us who worked closely with Epstein was that when the Dizz affair came to a stormy climax, Brian was threatened at knifepoint with blackmail. Dizz demanded a lot of money to disappear. Clearly, Epstein was well rid of this predator, but he didn't see it that way and seemed to have lingering feelings for the man that went on for several years.

*

Epstein compensated vigorously for the lack of a contented love life by working harder and longer than was necessary, often on tasks which could have been delegated, and by surrounding himself with talented and celebrated people, culled from the fashionable "in crowd" of London's West End. In business his strategy was to avoid using the power of The Beatles to swing deals for his other acts but in his private life he used them all the time to fill up his fabulous dinner parties with important and influential guests. His idea of the perfect party evening at his penthouse apartment near Harrods and, later, at his luxurious 19th-century London town house at 24 Chapel Street, Belgravia, involved the presence of one or more of The Beatles, maybe a couple of The Rolling Stones, certainly his only female star, Cilla Black, and a scattering of social "celebrities" who would appreciate and be comfortable in the presence of his scintillating showbusiness guests. Visiting stars, colleagues and relatives alike were suitably impressed by the presence of Lonnie, his tall, black, statuesque valet, a strangely colonial touch. Epstein thought it prestigious to employ a black manservant. When there was a party, his small team of servants, headed by a Spanish butler in a formal dark coat, would fetch out fine vintage champagnes and chilled caviar and Epstein's joy would be unconfined. Sometimes we would ask each other the purpose of this or that party. Then we realised that the real motive behind most of Brian's lavish hospitality was to surround himself with fashionable people who acted as an antidote to his otherwise lonely social life. The sheer elegance and richness with which he entertained top pop people and their beautiful partners was in contrast to the sleaziness and dirtiness of his sexual encounters.

One of his most memorable and glittering "At Home" parties took place on August 12, 1964, four months before Brian upgraded to the mega-luxury of his Belgravia house in Chapel Street. He was still in a smart penthouse apartment at Whaddon House, William Mews, on the borders of Knightsbridge and Belgravia, located between ultra-fashionable Sloane Street and mega-expensive Belgrave Square. Each of us received a most impressive, formally-worded invitation card, all beautifully engraved and gilt-edged: "Buffet Supper 9.30pm, Informal Dress". Brian's stated reason for the event was to mark the imminent departure of John, Paul, George and Ringo on their first full-blown concert tour of North America. To underscore the significance of the tour, he arranged for copies of the current New York *Saturday Evening Post* to be scattered around the apartment. There was a front-cover picture of The Beatles and a lengthy interview-based article by Al Aronowitz, who helped to bring Bob Dylan and the Fab Four together at a New York hotel room meeting that particularly impressed George Harrison. For this eve-of-tour party, Epstein's invitation list exceeded in sheer star power all his previous London bashes to date. Headed by a last-minute addition, his heroine the legendary Judy Garland, the guests included The Beatles and Cilla Black, Brian's other favourite female singer Alma Cogan, Rolling Stones Mick Jagger and Keith Richards, the duo Peter and Gordon, The Searchers, Tommy Steele, Lionel Bart and three top deejays of the day, Alan Freeman, Pete Murray and Brian Matthew. Dusty Springfield also popped in that night; she was a popular party animal who was to be spotted at most "A"-list parties in the Swinging London of 1964. The matriarchal First Lady in Brian's life, his mother Queenie, travelled from Liverpool for the glittering occasion. She attended few of his parties as a rule and Brian was exceedingly happy to see her. A large white marquee was erected on the roof where tables were set out for dinner and guests could gaze out across south-west London through plastic windows. There were beautiful candelabra and thousands of carnations. "Buffet" was an inadequate word for the spectacular display of food on offer, from fillets of beef to slices of duck, from chilled lobster to all manner of other seafood delicacies and baskets laden with exotic fruits. The amazing array of refreshments included a special selection of kosher foods, which obviously pleased Queenie. A small crowd of stargazers built up in the private mews outside Whaddon House who were to witness a most embarrassing scene involving the late arrivals Judy Garland and her current escort, Mark Herron. They were being refused entry because they were not named on the guest list. Swaddled in an eye-catching mink coat she was pleading desperately to be admitted, saying: "This is awful. We met Brian with Li (Lionel Bart) in a restaurant and he asked us to come along." When Brian heard what was happening he turned a brighter shade of pink and spluttered: "What a catastrophe!" His idol and her boyfriend were hastily fetched inside and she was plied with compliments to massage her over-heated ego. She refused champagne but knocked back glass upon glass of orange juice. The previous evening, Brian had dined at one of his favourite haunts, the Caprice restaurant, and found himself seated close to Judy Garland. Of course, he couldn't resist inviting her verbally to come and meet The Beatles at his party but her name was never added to the official list. My wife, Corinne, spotted Garland a table or two away across the crowded candlelit dining room and noticed that she was making no attempt to hide the evidence of recent injury to both wrists. Garland looked pale, weak, ill at ease and a million miles from the effervescent personality we'd seen so many times on the cinema screen. Despite her worrying appearance she was bouncing off the walls and gabbling away to her host. By and large The Beatles took little notice of her, preferring to stay with members of the Rolling Stones and the Searchers. Of the four, only Paul bothered to get into conversation with her. They went into a close huddle and could be overheard discussing stage musicals in general and Lionel Bart's *Maggie May* in particular. This led to a leaked press story that McCartney might be collaborating with Garland on some spectacular theatrical vehicle for staging on New York's Broadway and in London's West End. For the next 24 hours I took calls from most of Fleet Street's show business editors asking for more information, but all the concerned parties claimed that the reports were totally inaccurate and no such show would be going on.

Judy Garland's misfortunes continued when she found no place setting in her name. A lot of whispering and shuffling around went on and suddenly she was seated with Lionel Bart. A little later during this eventful evening Garland disappeared into the toilet for some time. We might not have noticed the abnormal length of her stay in there if Corinne had not been at the head of a queue of other guests waiting to use the convenience. At first even banging on the door was ignored and, remembering the unsightly state of her very slender wrists, we were becoming genuinely concerned that she might be harming herself behind the locked door. Herron gave nothing away, simply saying: "She has been sick today." When eventually she emerged, Garland was perspiring profusely but remained artificially perky.

The noise from Epstein's rooftop party wafted out across the nearby apartment blocks and around midnight we had a visit from the local police. It wasn't a raid exactly, they merely relayed a number of complaints phoned in to their station rather than issuing any formal warnings. Alistair Taylor assumed his usual NEMS role of

"Mr Fixit" and went downstairs to sweet-talk the cops. Corinne and I saw him pick up an unopened bottle of champagne and jokingly asked him where he was off to with that. Alistair explained that it was a peace offering. At this moment Brian appeared from nowhere, asked Alistair the same question and got the same answer. "Oh no, you don't," said Epstein without a hint of a smile or good humour in his voice. "If anybody's going to give away my wine it's going to be me." With that he snatched the champagne from Alistair's hands and stomped off. While Alistair, Corinne and I stared at one another in disbelief, Epstein came back, obviously having reconsidered his position and decided that he couldn't be bothered leaving the party to deal with the police in person. Speaking less aggressively now, he said: "Alistair, give this champagne to the police with my compliments and in future please make sure you ask me personally before you shower my hospitality on outsiders." This was a half-hearted apology for such a display of rudeness, but Alistair brushed off the reprimand and trotted off obediently to do Brian's bidding without another word.

That evening Epstein and Bart hatched a plan to present Garland in a West End concert. Pressed for an answer on the spot she agreed to appear for them but that event, like the rumoured McCartney-Garland theatrical co-production, never came to fruition.

Epstein's happiness in playing the role of party host to the stars was matched only by his addiction to gambling. Not your amusement arcade or bingo-hall stuff and not bookies either but the ultra-exciting, gold-plated, big-money, high-rolling type of gambling that took him into the smart casinos of Mayfair where all the rich folk threw dice, played cards and bet on roulette wheels. I never accompanied him to any of these places in London but, when I went on a quickie trip to Las Vegas with several American friends at the end of The Beatles' 1966 US tour, we bumped into Brian and I watched him lose thousands of dollars at the Caesar's Palace gaming tables in a matter of minutes. Whether in London or Vegas such hefty losses didn't make much of a dent in his multi-million-pound bank balance, but they pinpointed another weakness in the Epstein character, one that he was just as incapable of curing as his addiction to unusual sexual practices. In his final years he added drug- and drink-abuse to his list of unhealthy habits and these were the two cravings that brought about his death in 1967. At first, when he sampled some illegal drugs it was because he wanted to be one of the boys, his boys. They were moving on from pot to experimenting with LSD and Epstein felt peer pressure to join in the mind-blowin' head-splitterin' fun. He took to holding lavish weekend house parties down in the country at his house at Kingsley Hill, Sussex, with guests ranging from Lulu to the deejay Kenny Everett. The completion of recording sessions for the new *Sergeant Pepper* album provided the ideal excuse for one particularly colourful party. The Beatles reported that this was a truly wild affair at which most guests, Lulu excluded, took copious quantities of drugs, particularly some highly-recommended LSD straight from San Francisco. According to the boys, Brian's depression seemed to have lifted somewhat and he was enjoying playing the grand host again at Kingsley Hill. His mistake was to imagine that he could resume the mixing of prescribed drugs with a cocktail of illegal pills and powders on top of vast amounts of booze. I have never believed that he intended to commit suicide but, if I had been asked how long I thought he had to live, given the type of lifestyle he was leading by 1967, I'd have said: "I believe he'll be dead within five years at the most."

Unlike Brian Epstein, I found it possible to work closely with The Beatles without sharing their drug-taking habits because, although they frequently offered, they never tried to persuade me to do anything I didn't want to do. The most adventurous was John, the least involved was Ringo. Only one of the Fab Four, John, became seriously addicted to dangerous drugs while the others used their chosen stimulators and comforters for what they called "recreational purposes" and swore they never came close to any sort of serious addiction. One main way in which I avoided being sucked into that scary side of their lives was to draw a line between work and play, business and pleasure. In the world of entertainment I often found only the flimsiest of boundary fences between the territory where I did my job and where I did my socialising after I left the workplace. Partying used to pick up where the working day left off. I think I enjoyed a friendly and mutually rewarding professional relationship with The Beatles and all my other celebrity clients but I took due care to separate the different sectors of my life and keep my business and private activities within their own well-defined perimeters. I had my own very happy family life to live, a lovely wife and two infant sons with whom I wanted to spend time, so the clients were made to feel close enough but were kept at an arm's length from what went on in our home. Equally, I seldom visited the boys in their homes and I never, ever went to any of Epstein's house parties in the country. This strategy was not intended to keep me off drink or drugs but most of us chose one or the other in the Sixties; many of those in our circle of friends who went for both and became hooked died prematurely. If you didn't heed the warnings in time you paid the price sooner or later. I stuck with the bourbon and Seven Up during my first decade in PR, moving over to fine white wines by the later Seventies and beyond, having taught myself to recognise the substantial difference between Portugal's Mateus Rose, Germany's Liebfraumilch and the wonderful French wines of Burgundy. Staying off non-prescribed drugs was never a moral or even a health issue with me but a matter of personal taste. I got all the highs and kicks I wanted from booze and tobacco rather than mind-bending hallucinatory drugs. I've kicked the smoking but please feel free to crack open another bottle of Chablis Premier Cru to share with me at any time you like.

In 1966 and 1967 I watched Brian Epstein destroy himself. With the help of his doctor he tried from time to time to clean himself up, even checking into The Priory, the rehab clinic at Roehampton recommended by many stricken celebrities. His stars noticed the decline in Brian and tried unsuccessfully to sort him out. Fearing that his diminishing sense of responsibility would become damaging to her career, Cilla Black started to make alternative management arrangements for herself. Epstein appeared less and less frequently in either of his two London offices, in Argyll Street and Albemarle Street, and failed to turn up for an increasing number of essential business meetings. He let it be known to his staff that he was "working from home", which meant from his house at Chapel Street, but he was difficult to reach there and responded to fewer phone calls and hand-delivered memo messages. His hard-working assistants and secretarial staff came under a horrendous amount of pressure, trying to put people off with plausible excuses for his failures and no-shows. This was the first time that colleagues and competitors had been given cause to question Brian's reliability and integrity as a businessman. He was unhappy and depressed to the point of contemplating and even attempting suicide.

He was sinking ever deeper into a mess of drink and drugs that were damaging both his body and his mind. He was impossible to work with in this sad and sorry state. Eventually, after many attempts, I would manage to reach him on the phone and ask for his decision on something. He would answer positively without the slightest ambiguity or hesitation and I would go ahead with the project, pleased to have his unconditional OK. Then I would get an irate call: "What did you do that for? I told you not to, I said I didn't agree, you had no right to go ahead!" He became so unreliable that I stopped taking his word for anything and demanded answers to everything in writing. I used to send him written messages with boxes that gave him multiple-choice options and were captioned: "Yes, I agree", "Please Discuss ASAP", "No".

In the last part of his life, Brian brought two new high-echelon executives into NEMS along with the stars they represented. It was relatively simple to see why he took over The Vic Lewis Organisation. Vic's Mayfair-based booking agency had the type of clients that NEMS lacked – prestigious and stylish talents ranging from the balladeer Matt Monro to the lyricist Don Black, and via his association with the General Artists Corporation of America, he had access to other world-class acts for European tours. It was less obvious to any of us why he brought in the Australian Robert Stigwood, the flamboyant manager behind The Bee Gees and Cream. Without warning his artists or his staff what he was up to, Epstein laid plans to hand Stigwood a majority interest of 51% in NEMS Enterprises. The arrangement was that only the personal management of The Beatles and Cilla Black would stay in Brian's hands while Stigwood slipped into the driver's seat to run the rest of the operation. We were appalled by this move because neither The Beatles, nor Cilla Black, nor the NEMS staff had much time for Stigwood's business strategies. In general, our artists had no intention of letting anyone new meddle in their management and this applied equally to Stigwood and Lewis. Epstein did not get on well with Vic Lewis, they disagreed violently on matters of policy and, although Brian was a friend of Robert Stigwood and mixed with some of his cronies in private, there was a clash in their professional personalities because their business methods were poles apart. We were baffled by Brian's behaviour as we could not understand why he would want to give away his sole control of NEMS.

For me, the arrival of Lewis and Stigwood made little difference to the running of my Press & Publicity Division, although I did not always approve of the nature of Stigwood's PR stunts for his Bee Gees, which I had to handle through my office – although I got on exceedingly well with the friendly young Gibb brothers and the rest of The Bee Gees band. The only consoling thought was that in abdicating the majority of his management responsibilities, Brian might calm down, come to his senses and improve his quality of life. He did not. Meanwhile, his other recent ventures, including the short-lived take-over of the West End's Saville theatre in Shaftesbury Avenue, the presentation of all-star Sunday concerts in the West End and his production of unsuccessful theatrical shows such as *Smashing Day* and *On The Level*, not only lost money but also increased Brian's own mounting sense of inadequacy.

None of us ever found out what was behind Brian's rapid downfall but we made our guesses. First and most obvious was his inability to handle the dire combinations of alcohol and abusive drugs with which he was slowly poisoning his system. Then there were his fears that he was losing The Beatles. He was extremely upset when they refused to do any further concerts after August 1966. He had mapped out the next UK tour and shown me a list of possible venues and dates but the boys were adamant that there were to be no more gigs. The time when they would simply do as they were told had passed. Brian became aware of their covert plans to set up a massive group of self-management companies under the umbrella of Apple Corps. He did not expect to be asked to play any part in the running of Apple and he became increasingly convinced that The Beatles would not re-sign with him when their current contract ran out in 1967. On the personal side, Dizz Gillespie had come back into Brian's life at the time of The Beatles' final concert in San Francisco, but it was to taunt and extort, not to love and cherish. The grim truth that he had less than a handful of true friends and scores of unreliable acquaintances dawned on Brian during the winter of 1966. He died alone in his bedroom at 24, Chapel Street, during the August Bank Holiday weekend in 1967, bottles of prescribed drugs and a variety of pills strewn around the place. Ironically, there were some signs that he was pulling himself together. Resigned to the facts that The Beatles did not intend to tour again and had planned to look after their own business affairs, Epstein was looking forward to several new business projects of his own, including the opportunity to present a music television show in Canada. For this and other similar reasons, I do not believe he intended to die as he did. I think it was a case of fatal carelessness, not suicide. He drank a lot of alcohol, took sleeping pills and in a hazy and confused state took some more. Surrounded by indifferent acquaintances and fair-weather friends, Brian was as lonely in death as he had been in life. Although there was an unseemly scramble to seize control of the Nemperor's business properties, there was an even more unsavoury tussle behind the scenes to grab his personal possessions. One man who liked to be known as one of Epstein's closest friends looked through the dressing table drawers in his bedroom and pulled out a pile of expensively hand-made silk shirts, each monogrammed with Brian's initials, B.E. Then he asked without a trace of emotion, let alone grief: "Do you think I'll be able to unpick these initials?"

Neil Aspinall

Brian Epstein was considered by some to be The Fifth Beatle, but I never considered our Nemperor to be a serious contender for that title. Epstein liked to send out signals that he and The Beatles were together constantly and enjoyed one another's company, but this was not so even when we were all on the road. During tours he often broke away from the main entourage and travelled off in a different direction to the tour. Occasionally, this was to pick up cash sums due to The Beatles, but mostly it was to visit friends in New York or Los Angeles. Between tours, Brian was not a regular visitor to any of their homes and they came to his place in town only for rare business meetings and on the occasions of his star-studded "At Home" events. They were poles apart intellectually and shared few or no interests outside show business. The same applied in the case of George Martin, their closest colleague and guru in the recording studio, but not outside it.

In my view The Fifth Beatle's throne has been occupied, quite rightly, for the past 45 years by Neil Aspinall, the one they called "Nel". Since the break-up of the Fab Four in 1970, Aspinall has almost single-handedly run the worldwide business of The Beatles. He is Apple.

Neil was born in October 1941 in Prestatyn, north Wales, where his mother had moved from Merseyside during World War II. Returning to Liverpool he studied Art and English at Liverpool Institute alongside Paul McCartney. His first encounter with George Harrison took place behind the school's air-raid shelter: "This great mass of shaggy hair loomed up and in an out-of-breath voice requested a quick drag of my Woodbine. It was one of the first cigarettes either of us had smoked. We spluttered our way through it bravely and gleefully. By the time we were ready to take our GCE exams we added John Lennon to our mad-lad gang – he was doing his first terms at Liverpool College of Art which overlooked the Institute playground." Neil took nine CGE subjects and passed all but French. From 1959 he studied accountancy with a Liverpool firm of chartered accountants, augmenting his salary of £2.50 a week by driving The Beatles around the Mersey Beat circuit. His eventual choice to dump accountancy in favour of working full-time with The Beatles brought him a career that offered "a rewarding mixture of excitement, fun and very hard work".

Faithful, careful and honest way beyond the call of duty all through the years, he has continued to collect royalties and revenues on behalf of the surviving Beatles and the estates of those who have died. He has waged a never-ending war against copyright infringements, pulling back into the safe custody of Apple's domain many thousands of photographs and other unique scraps of the group's history which outsiders had managed to get their hands on. Some years ago after recovering from an illness Neil confessed to me over lunch that the entire sprawling business machinery of The Beatles would grind to a halt, at least temporarily, the moment he died because the group insisted that he did not delegate any portion of his exclusive management of their affairs. It is no exaggeration to say that Neil devoted his life to looking after the Fab Four. Having started by running the group to and from early gigs on Merseyside and collecting and counting their cash before they left each venue, he moved on to accept the job of road manager. When they came to sign up with Brian Epstein, The Beatles made it clear to their new manager that Nel came as part of the package. Later, he drove them further afield – to and from London for instance – and fed them with supplies of hot dogs and Coke in their dressing rooms. Until the arrival of the gentle giant Mal Evans, who became Neil's much-needed assistant, he also looked after The Beatles' stage outfits, the shirts and suits and boots, made sure all the guitars and amplifiers were set just where the boys wanted them on the stage and made sure that Ringo's precious drum kit was assembled correctly. But Aspinall's greatest value to The Beatles was not as a gofer and a shifter of gear, a cash collector or refreshment delivery man, but as their most trustworthy ally who has never did let them down in 45 years and served their interests until his death in March 2008 at the age of 66.

I reckon all this more than qualifies Neil for the honorary title of The Fifth Beatle.

5 | The Birth Of Beatlemania

I CAN PINPOINT the birth of Beatlemania quite precisely. The date was Sunday, October 13, 1963.

By September many of the interviews and photo shoots we did with the teenybopper magazines during the summer were beginning to appear in print. I had not been able to get quite as much editorial exposure for The Beatles in the UK's national newspapers but there had been a handful of good stories. In July the *Daily Mirror* described The Beatles as "one of the biggest disc properties in Britain" and in September the *Daily Herald* said the "cult" group had caught up with Elvis and become the "highest paid property in British showbusiness". On September 10 the *Daily Mirror*, Britain's top-circulation tabloid in those days, published an eye-catching two-page feature by the celebrity columnist Donald Zec headlined: FOUR FRENZIED LITTLE LORD FONTLEROYS WHO ARE EARNING £5,000 A WEEK. In 1963 five thousand was a big deal and the figure was an exaggerated one even if you included possible Lennon and McCartney writing royalties from the group's recent best-selling records. So far in the UK during 1963 these had included the singles 'Please Please Me' (January), 'From Me To You' (April), and 'She Loves You' (August), the EPs 'Twist And Shout' (July) and 'The Beatles' Hits' (September) plus the album *Please Please Me* (March). In his typically wry writing style Zec declared The Beatles to be "as nice a group of well-mannered music makers as you'll find perforating the eardrums anywhere" and described them as "four cheeky-looking kids with stone-age hair styles, Chelsea boots, three electric guitars, and one set of drums, who know their amps and ohms if not their Beethoven". Coming from the acidic pen of the widely-read Zec this was high praise! Frankly, if Zec had said a lot of lovely things about The Beatles I would have liked his story less. The fact that his piece did some sneering at their expense was good publicity in my view because, if Zec had loved John, Paul, George and Ringo in his piece, it would have put teenagers off! So far as the size of the story was concerned, it was quite unusual for Zec to give any pop or rock band such a big spread. I felt it was no coincidence that the *Melody Maker*, a magazine within the Mirror Group, was about to announce its 1963 pop poll results, which revealed The Beatles as Top British Group.

When Brian Epstein blocked off great chunks of September in his office diary and scrawled across the pages: BEATLES ON HOLIDAY–ON NO ACCOUNT BOOK!!! he had not reckoned on the *Melody Maker* win and the consequent wave of media interest. One by one, journalists I had contacted earlier to push the boys came back to me to say their editors were having second thoughts and they'd like to write something. But at the very moment when my hard work might have paid off handsomely and turned into valuable column inches, The Beatles were out of the country and unavailable to me.

In October we were scheduled to vacate our tiny Monmouth Street offices and had already allocated the space on two floors at Monmouth Street to new national headquarters for The Official Beatles Fan Club. Brian was bringing his Liverpool management operation to London – along with some of the more adventurous members of staff – and we were all to be housed together in more spacious premises in Argyll Street, next door to the London Palladium theatre. Golden-voiced Laurie McCaffrey, in charge of the telephone switchboard at the Liverpool office, was one of Brian's staff who would make the move to London. Unfortunately, the fan club secretary, Freda Kelly, had to stay at home for family reasons. I was looking forward to the move, because it was becoming impossible to deal with not only the Fab Four, but also Cilla Black, Gerry and the Pacemakers, Billy J Kramer with the Dakotas, The Big Three and The Fourmost, in such cramped office accommodation. On days when we were holding press interview sessions the place was like a busy doctor's surgery with journalists queuing alongside artistes to await the opening of their particular window of opportunity. Even without the added congestion caused by visiting artistes, my office saw the sheer madness of Brian Epstein working on one end of my desk and sharing my one telephone line whenever he was in town. I'm not sure which one of us was less amused by the news that the big move would have to be postponed until the spring of 1964 (something to do with delays in putting in partitioning) and that we were destined to spend the winter in Monmouth Street, surrounded by growing mountains of mail awaiting the attention of the fan club staff who had by now taken over the floor above my office. In the middle of all this mayhem I was working flat-out to launch the recording career of Priscilla Maria Veronica White, aka Cilla Black, the carrot-red-haired young songstress from Liverpool's notorious Scotland Road, who had just released her first single, featuring Lennon and McCartney's 'Love Of The Loved'.

If we take the release date of 'Love Me Do' as the time of conception, there was a 12-month gestation period before the birth of Beatlemania. London fans of The Beatles had not seen their fave, rave Fab Four, singly or collectively, for a while. John and Cynthia had been on holiday in Paris, celebrating a belated honeymoon and spending their first quality time together since baby Julian's arrival. For these fleeting moments in the romantic environment of the French capital it is likely that the couple were as close to one another as they would ever get. And then, would you believe it, Brian Epstein joined them there at his own invitation, doubtless reviving sour-tasting memories of Barcelona in Cynthia's mind. John decided that Paris was "one bloody big night club", which meant that he approved of the place, and he told me so on the back of a holiday postcard. Paul and Jane went to Greece with Ringo and Maureen and they toured the sights of Athens with their new movie cameras, while George flew to America to visit his sister, Louise, in Benton, Illinois. Next to nobody knew about The Beatles in Benton, which suited George perfectly.

On their return the group did several one-night-stand concert dates in Scotland and a couple of radio and television recordings in London, but these were not widely publicised and few fans realised they were back from their travels. Then came the weekend of television's 'Sunday Night At The London Palladium'. At the last minute the boys realised they should put in a spot of rehearsal prior to such an important appearance. By the time they asked us to find them a rehearsal room in central London for Saturday evening all the usual places were already booked. Finally they came to Monmouth Street and used my office as a makeshift rehearsal studio. I remember they used several of my treasured plastic plant pots as ashtrays.

The Palladium, known in the Sixties as the world's greatest variety venue, had a very special theatrical charisma about it. Made by Associated TeleVision (ATV), the top-rated hour-long prime-time variety show went out live on the ITV network, usually at eight o'clock, attracting an average audience of up to 15 million viewers. Iconic American entertainers regularly headlined and rising comedians often had to wait years to earn a brief, but precious slot further down the busy bill. The sound quality for any musical act was dreadful, largely due to insufficient sound-checking time and badly-balanced voices and instruments, but everyone recognised that, if a singer or band landed a guest spot on the show, record sales would surge spectacularly and shows sell out faster. For a pop group there was also a valuable upward shift in status to be gained from a Palladium TV appearance because the viewing audience was from a much wider spread of the population than that of your average pop music programme, bringing an act to the attention of some millions of people who would not normally take much notice of the latest new group from Liverpool, or buy chart records.

By the autumn of 1963, having notched up three consecutive chart-topping singles, to follow the initial success of 'Love Me Do', The Beatles were creating such a good buzz that they were fast-tracked to the top of the Palladium television bill for Sunday, October 13, with all the attendant pre-transmission publicity that went with the booking. They were top of a bill that also included American balladeer Brook Benton and British entertainers Des O'Connor and Bruce Forsyth. Fans all over the country saw countless on-screen trailers in the days leading up to that Sunday and, when the day arrived, as many as possible flocked to central London and filled Argyll Street in the hope of catching a glimpse of John, Paul, George and Ringo arriving for afternoon rehearsals at the Palladium. Some had managed to get free tickets for the evening, the rest were there simply to give noisy support to the Fab Four from outside the venue.

As a rule, Sunday was a notoriously quiet day at the news desks in Fleet Street, a day when publicists knew they stood the best chance of getting weaker showbiz stories and pictures into the following morning's papers. To put it another way, Monday was the morning when the nationals were most likely to run that mythical old news story about the dead donkey. Fleet Street's national papers habitually sent photographers and reporters to Palladium rehearsals to take early pictures of the stars. That afternoon they must have said to their picture desk people: "Have someone nip down and get rehearsal shots of those Liverpool lads on the stage in time for the first edition." So when fans of The Beatles began to scream and shout in the street outside the theatre that afternoon representatives of the full range of British dailies were on hand to hear and then see what was happening. The newsworthiness of the scene was enhanced by the arrival of policemen from the nearby West End Central police station. The crowd suddenly shifted its focus from the theatre's front entrance in Argyll Street to the stage door in Great Marlborough Street. Were The Beatles arriving? Leaving? No, it was nothing more exciting than the arrival of roadies Neil and Mal carrying cardboard boxes of Cokes and hot dogs bought from a Carnaby Street café to feed their four masters. The crowd surged back round the corner into Argyll Street where energetic reinforcements of cops stopped them short of the Palladium steps and in doing so provided the ideal photo opportunity. The cameras flashed and the kids opened their mouths and yelled their heads off. The reporters collected quotes from a few fans to accompany their pictures and because this was the hardest news around that night the dead donkey was dropped yet again and Beatlemania was splashed across the front pages of Monday morning's editions. One paper called it "Beatle Fever!" and the *Daily Mirror* coined the term "Beatlemania". The story was also included in Sunday's late-evening news bulletin on ITV.

As the guy responsible for the group's publicity I would love to claim that I engineered the whole scenario, that I put together a suitably photogenic riot outside the Palladium, but the truth is that the birth of Beatlemania was not artificially induced; it was a completely natural affair. This was a spontaneous display of loyalty, affection, devotion – adoration even – on the part of the fans, the first of many that occurred wherever The Beatles appeared in public. Most aspects of the group's career relied on their natural abilities rather than invented publicity puff or stunts. My role in The Beatles' progress was to keep the media informed of plans and achievements and to project the most positive parts of the group's story, not to peddle sheer fiction. I knew very well that it was not necessary to pour any layer of manufactured hype on top of four such rich and colourful characters.

What the Fleet Street editors didn't seem to realise was that Beatlemania had been creeping up on us, and them, for months. What happened outside the Palladium in October had been happening on a smaller scale outside provincial theatres and hotels for most of the summer. In my view Fleet Street was always appallingly late in latching on to the latest new stars of the pop and rock music scene. Equally, they were writing about over-the-hill has-beens for ages after the teenage press had moved on. Undoubtedly, my job with The Beatles changed dramatically after the emergence of Beatlemania. Most of what I had done before would be classed as pro-active and promotional. Strong elements of protection and careful selectivity now came into my strategy. I began to be highly selective over what The Beatles did for the media, choosing to work only with those publications, those photographers and those writers who would do us the most good. As pressure on The Beatles' time increased, they became less available to me and I had to turn down more and more proposals of valuable and attractive feature articles or photo spreads on the accessibility factor alone. The snowball gathered momentum – more fame meant more gigs, more gigs left less room for me to negotiate windows for media activities.

I remember one occasion when The Beatles were doing a guest spot for a BBC radio show, probably 'Easy Beat', at the Playhouse Theatre, Charing Cross, and I managed to clear time between the programme's rehearsals and the actual recording for them to do some press interviews. I had a long list of outstanding requests from significant magazine and newspaper feature writers, many of them Fleet Street celebrities in their own right that I pruned down ruthlessly to about half-a-dozen key journalists from the most prestigious and/or largest-circulation publications. These people deserved – and as a rule would have demanded – exclusive one-on-one interview time. Instead, all those on my chosen shortlist had to make do with a shared 45 minutes in cramped and uncomfortable working conditions in an airless and poorly-lit basement room beneath the auditorium at the Playhouse. I asked the journalists to spread themselves out into a large circle, each with a spare chair positioned to one side or in front.

Then we played a sort of musical chairs game. I brought in the four boys, did a hasty round of introductions and offered each of the first four journalists one Beatle each. After about seven or eight minutes I moved each Beatle one place on in the circle and the interviewing resumed. For such important Fleet Street personalities this would have been unacceptable treatment in less fraught circumstances but all of them gratefully took advantage of my emergency arrangements because they were so desperate to write about The Beatles now that Beatlemania was out in the open. At the time I didn't think for one moment that I could get away with such an unsatisfactory way of dealing with top-echelon writers on a regular basis but the format I devised for the Playhouse actually became my template for many similar "musical chairs" interview sessions in the future. The idea of settling a group of international media people, a combination of magazine and newspaper writers plus deejays from top radio stations, into a circle and bringing them a Beatle, one at a time, became part of a standard format I used very successfully in places all around the globe.

With the benefit of hindsight it may seem insane now that I even considered handing over the routine part of my work as Beatles' Press Officer to anybody else, but this is precisely what happened as the demands of Beatlemania grew more pressing. I found myself involved in some really negative conversations where I would be hard-selling the talents of, say, Cilla Black to a journalist and suggesting ideas for interview-based features on our one and only female singer, only to be faced with replies like: "OK, Tony, of course I'll do something for you on Cilla, but first what about that interview I asked you for weeks ago with Paul McCartney. When can I do that?" Yes, you could call it a mild form of blackmail but that was the way it worked in the wonderful world of PR.

Becoming thoroughly frustrated at having to turn down so many requests from different sectors of the media, I tackled Brian Epstein about the possibility of bringing an extra person into the Press Office who would be exclusively responsible for dealing with the day-to-day PR affairs of the Fab Four. He could be the bad man who almost always said "No!" After all, I argued, Brian would be making better use of whatever positive talents I had developed as a PR man if I concentrated on launching and sustaining the careers of his other promising acts rather than repeatedly turning down people who wanted to write about John, Paul, George and Ringo. Brian promised to discuss my situation with The Beatles. The outcome was that Brian told me they agreed to have a new Beatles' Press Officer to travel about with them but they and he wanted me to stay in overall control of the group's media and publicity affairs. Epstein said: "We're thinking particularly of America, which is the boys' most important project for 1964. Even if we have a new man on the road when we're touring, I want you to co-ordinate our whole US launch campaign, plan the press conferences, work with the people at Capitol Records and liaise with the local concert promoters. Can you do all that from a desk in London?" I assured him that I could.

A mere matter of days after this meeting, Epstein announced that he had found the ideal man to look after the boys; an old pal named Brian Sommerville. A former Lieutenant Commander in the Royal Navy, he was a little older than Epstein and had an air of military authority about him. He never actually joined the Press Office staff but was hired as an outside consultant on a retainer. I was not convinced that he had the right temperament to be The Beatles' PR man and I felt that Brian Epstein had hired him on the strength of an old friendship without weighing up his professional credentials. Sommerville had no problem dealing with the growing waiting list of journalists. He simply struck most of the names off his list, regardless of priorities. From the outset I thought his relationship with the group, George in particular, was uncomfortable and strained. He used to talk down to them in a dominant parental way and tried to bring a little more discipline into the way they approached their press appointments. From what I saw and heard, Sommerville was unduly harsh in his dealings with the press and quickly lost their goodwill. Certainly, he damaged a number of good contacts that I had taken time and effort to build up. All through my 20 years in PR I tried to maintain good relationships between myself and each journalist even when I couldn't satisfy their immediate and specific needs. Such relationships didn't seem to matter to Brian Sommerville. He took an equally hard line with The Beatles, which irritated them and made them less amenable to him. They gave him the nickname of Baldie and set about taunting and teasing him in every conceivable way. As early as January 1964 there was a trivial but nasty incident at the

George Cinq hotel in Paris when George refused to jump to it and see a journalist when suddenly asked to do so. In the brief and bitter exchange that followed, a glass of icy-cold breakfast juice was poured over Sommerville's shiny pate and George took a retaliatory punch to the side of his head. An exasperated Sommerville claimed: "I don't have any trouble with the press. It's just the boys. I need complete control but I get no support from Brian." From my personal experience before and after the Sommerville episode I know that dealing with The Beatles was a job with more pitfalls than perks and I had to teach myself to treat them with great care in order to keep a good working relationship between us. In his own way I believe that Sommerville thought that he dealt efficiently with an increasingly difficult job but he soon outlasted his welcome with the boys and left the job before his contract was due to expire.

His successor, the former Manchester-based *Daily Express* journalist Derek Taylor, was at the opposite end of the personality spectrum. Dry-humoured and affable, Derek got on exceedingly well with The Beatles, George in particular, but his fatal mistake was to get too chummy with them. He strove hard to be "one of the lads" and he succeeded in winning their affections, but in doing so he earned a hefty black mark from Brian Epstein. Brian's jealous, possessive nature made him mistrust the motives of anyone who developed a close personal relationship with his boys. This was something I realised very soon after I went to work with him. Derek was a good writer and a kind, considerate and even-tempered person, but he lost Epstein's support by taking too many matters into his own hands and failing to keep his boss posted on what he was doing. The friction between the two men grew hotter and their ferocious arguments became an everyday occurrence, witnessed by everyone from the boys themselves to the office clerks and receptionists. Eventually, both parties admitted that they could not go on working with one another and Taylor's professional connection with The Beatles was severed, although his friendship with them survived.

It was clear that too many changes of press agent might be unsettling for The Beatles, damaging to their relationship with the press, and might attract destructive rather than constructive comment from newspaper columnists. The outcome was that I got a direct and strongly worded request from John, Paul, George and Ringo to resume my hands-on handling of their PR and to get back on the road with them for what turned out to be their biggest-ever world tours. By then I was beginning to realise that only an absolute fool would have volunteered to stand down as I had done for even one moment from a unique job that involved close and personal contact with history in the making. So I made up for my mistake by leaping back into the Eppycentre of the action where I remained until 1968. Although our basic approaches to the business of PR differed widely, I had a lot of time for Derek Taylor who moved on to open a successful PR consultancy in California until returning home to the UK to work at Apple in 1968, the year after Brian Epstein's death.

Three days after the group's appearance on 'Sunday Night At The London Palladium' came the announcement that The Beatles had accepted an invitation to line up alongside Marlene Dietrich, Sophie Tucker, Max Bygraves, Maurice Chevalier, *Half A Sixpence* star Tommy Steele and the singing piglets Pinky & Perky in the 1963 Royal Command Variety Performance. The event took place at the West End's Prince Of Wales theatre with the Queen Mother and Princess Margaret in attendance. Meeting the group after the show, her Queen Mumness asked where The Beatles were due to play next. Told that they were resuming their autumn tour the following evening at Slough, she remarked: "Oh, that's near us (at Windsor Castle)." Despite the star-stacked cast, it was John who raised the biggest laugh and captured the best headlines for The Beatles with his cheeky request to the audience that those in the cheaper seats should clap their hands while the richer and posher folk in the front circle and stalls rattled their jewellery. To Brian Epstein's immense relief he deleted a shocking expletive he had threatened to put between "their" and "jewellery".

Together, the publicity from the Palladium and the Royal Command Variety Performance amounted to an unstoppable barrage of press stories that immediately broke out beyond the boundaries of Britain and brought the first headline news about The Beatles to Americans across the Atlantic. The timing could not have been more perfect. We were already planning to take The Beatles to New York in the early part of 1964 and these stories in the US newspapers paved the way for Brian Epstein to firm up top-level negotiations for the trip. The Beatles were now poised to move up the ladder of fame from being the UK's favourite new group to the then-rare ranks of international pop superstars. And all this spectacular progress had taken place more or less within a year of 'Love Me Do'.

Although this was one of the busiest periods in The Beatles' sensational – albeit short-lived – career as a working band, they found time to go and see their most admired competitors in concert whenever possible. A veritable wish-list of the Fab Four's favourites toured UK theatres and cinemas together in one fantastic package show during the autumn of 1963. Headlined at the last minute by the king and queen of rock'n'roll Little Richard, with heavyweights The Rolling Stones, The Everly Brothers and Bo Diddley, plus songstress Julie Grant and Mickie Most in support, this was one concert The Beatles were determined not to miss and they managed to catch a performance on the eve of their own autumn UK concert tour. The group heard the irrepressible Richard assure his audience in his usual shy way: "I taught The Beatles how to rock!" On November 1 at the Odeon, Cheltenham, The Beatles began a strenuous 33-stop series of one-nighters designed to coincide with the release of their fifth single, 'I Want To Hold Your Hand', and their second album, *With The Beatles*.

When tour tickets ran out before box office queues did, theatres around the country became the settings for explosive demonstrations. Six hundred fans waited all night outside the ABC cinema in Carlisle. Impatient to unveil a darker face of Beatlemania, one press story reported that, "in bigger towns and cities the casualties ran into hundreds as shop windows were smashed". The *Daily Telegraph* ran a lead piece criticising the hysterical outbursts of the fans but the *Daily Mirror*, knowing upon which side its bread was buttered countered with: "You have to be a real sour square not to love the nutty, noisy, happy, handsome Beatles. The Beatles are whacky. They wear their hair like a mop but it's washed, it's super clean. So is their fresh young act. They don't have to rely on off-colour jokes about homos for their fun…Good Luck, Beatles!" Clearly the man from the *Mirror* hadn't heard John's off-stage off-colour jokes. After the Royal Variety gig it seemed that Beatlemania had a By Appointment seal of approval. An increasing number of media commentators started coming out in favour of everything the Fab Four sang, played, said or did.

Meanwhile, The Official Beatles Fan Club was in crisis. The extraordinary speed with which the group's fame and popularity had grown brought a huge swell of public interest in fan club membership, which was up to 30,000 and would eventually peak at 80,000. In no time, the hitherto adequate full-time staff found themselves drowning under a deluge of unopened mail bags. One piece of incoming mail that by chance did get opened promptly was a fan's letter from America addressed to The Beatles c/o HRH Prince Philip, Buckingham Palace, London. Before forwarding it to Monmouth Street, some palace mailroom flunkie had written across the envelope: NOT KNOWN AT BUCKINGHAM PALACE which gave the boys a laugh in view of their very recent Royal Variety Performance in front of prominent Family members! Just as bizarre was the letter from Australia that had no writing whatsoever on the envelope but simply a drawing of four mop-top fringes. But, thanks to the ingenuity of someone at London's West Central post office, this was delivered without delay to the fan club offices.

I could see a PR disaster looming as impatient fans began to complain about unanswered letters and unacknowledged subscription postal orders. I knew that I had to come up with a damage limitation plan that would turn thousands of disgruntled would-be fan club members back into being our new best friends. My solution was 'The Beatles' Fan Club Christmas Record'. My thinking was that the most beloved possession of any Beatles fan was the group's latest record and if we produced a special recording that was exclusively available to Fan Club members we would be creating a precious souvenir that people would show off to envious friends and probably prize for a lifetime. No other pop or rock stars had given away a gift like this so we could bank on favourable publicity all round. I also decided that in future press releases and fan club literature we should refer to the fans as Beatle People, a move which I thought might make the group's most ardent followers feel that much closer to John, Paul, George and Ringo.

When I gave Brian Epstein an outline of my idea for a Yuletide flexi-disc his inevitable reaction was to reject it out of hand at once on grounds of cost. He said he knew the club was intended to be a non-profit-making affair but there was a limit to the extent he was prepared to subsidise its operation out of his management commission. So I went to John, Paul, George and Ringo and they loved the concept, saying they would get George Martin to make the recording on the end of one of their scheduled sessions at EMI and that I should set to work on writing the script. Script? I hadn't thought of that! Epstein's budget-conscious objections were swept aside and I was able to explore the logistics of the project in proper detail. The actual record closely resembled the flexible seven-inch promotional discs widely distributed to the public via mail shots from *Reader's Digest* to promote new album sets. The satirical magazine *Private Eye* also produced similar flexi-discs, which they attached to special issues from time to time. Both sources used Lyntone Records as their supplier and I tracked down the label's boss, Paul Lynton, who conveniently headquartered his business a mile or two from my office in Monmouth Street.

When I drafted a script for The Beatles to follow I was relying on them to mess around with my words and make them funnier. They didn't let me, or themselves, down. Although part of their Christmas message was a genuine "thank you" to fans for buying their records, joining their fan club and coming to their concerts during the year, the rest of the material I gave them provided ample scope for plenty of clowning around, far more than we needed to fit on our flexi-disc. The recording took place on October 17 at Abbey Road after The Beatles had taped 'I Want To Hold Your Hand'. I took the finished recording to Paul Lynton's place and we edited it to fit on one single side of a seven-inch flexi-disc. Crazily, when I say "edited" I mean we actually cut the tape recording with scissors, patched the pieces together and let the discarded bits drop to the floor. In doing this we destroyed a master tape that at some future date might have raised many thousands of pounds at auction as a unique piece of memorabilia – particularly with all the unused bad language left in!

Lyntone's staff pulled out all the stops to produce some 31,000 copies of the edited disc and we got this eagerly awaited Christmas present in the post just in time to beat the seasonal rush. Epstein's grudgingly given budget for the venture left us with little cash to spend on a conventional EP-style cover or sleeve to house the disc. We had to make do with a cheap, vomit-yellow-coloured container, overprinted in black and made of an inexpensive cross between paper and board. It was put together with staples that came open too easily. This was the one part of the product of which I felt ashamed. Otherwise, the record did the damage limitation job for which it was intended, and much more.

The following year it was the boys themselves who prompted me into continuing the tradition. "When are we doing this year's Crimble record?" they asked me. They also wanted another script. I knew they needed my words simply as a security measure in case they dried up. In the event they made everything I wrote much funnier by their distinctively zany, Goons-style presentation. I had never thought of the "Fan Club Christmas Record" as being an annual Christmas gift from The Beatles to their most faithful fans, but the 1963 product was destined to become just the first of a series that we made and distributed throughout the UK each December between 1963 and 1969. At one stage a rumour circulated suggesting that my inspiration for the records was the Queen's Christmas Day message to her subjects. "Presto!" I was supposed to have said. "Why not have The Beatles do the same and send out a record to their fans just before Christmas?" Well, I have to admit that this sounds like a good spin-doctor's version of events but it's completely untrue. My sole object in creating the "Fan Club Christmas Record" was to revive the club's reputation among members. In supervising fan club affairs as a small but integral part of my over-all PR responsibilities I was acutely aware that, while 30,000 – 80,000 record buyers might never turn a sub-standard single into a No 1 hit, the same number of votes in a newspaper or magazine popularity poll could turn a loser into a winner!

In the autumn of 1963, to the surprise of all of us at NEMS including Brian Epstein, EMI's Beatles very kindly provided Decca's Rolling Stones with their first Top 10 hit single! The myth that did the rounds at the time was that John and Paul actually wrote 'I Wanna Be Your Man' especially for Mick Jagger's mob. The truth is that this very simple up-tempo ditty was intended all along to be a vocal showcase for Ringo and it was custom-tailored to fit his special talents in that area. Along the way a casual and unplanned meeting took place on a West End street between John and Paul and Andrew Oldham, the publicist who had become The Stones' manager. The two Beatles had been to a pleasantly boozy Variety Club luncheon at the Savoy where the Prime Minister Harold Wilson handed them a Top Vocal Group Of The Year award, which John referred to in his acceptance speech as a "purple heart". Memories of what happened that afternoon after John and Paul left the Savoy have blurred with the passage of time. Paul told his biographer Barry Miles that he and John were leaving the offices of the music publisher Dick James at the corner of Denmark Street and Charing Cross Road when Mick Jagger and Keith Richards came by in a taxi: "We were each other's counterparts because they became the writers in the (Rolling Stones) group. We bummed a lift off them." In his autobiography, *Stoned*, Andy Oldham claims that he was the one in the passing taxi, not Mick, not Keith: "They (John and Paul) looked like they'd just stepped off the stage of the London Palladium, their casual charisma was very much in evidence, and they seemed slightly embarrassed to be caught wearing such finery in broad daylight. John and Paul were fabulous in their three-piece, four-button bespoke Dougie Millings suits. With Paul in lighter and John in darker shades of grey, their gear was a Mod variation of the classic Ted drape jacket, set off by black velvet collars, slash pockets and narrow plain-front trousers." Nothing hazy about the Oldham memory of who wore what, but then Andy was always meticulously concerned with male fashion. Whoever it was in the taxi, Andy on his own or Mick with Keith, what nobody argues about is that Oldham half facetiously demanded a Lennon & McCartney number for his band because they were taking too long to come up with a single of their own to follow up and cash in on the minor chart impact made by 'Come On' several months back. He took John and Paul to the 51 Club in Great Newport Street, a jazz place owned by bandleader Ken Colyer, where Mick, Keith and the rest of The Rolling Stones were rehearsing fresh material. Here Andy repeated his plea for a song in front of the group. Neither embarrassed nor fazed, the two Beatles went into a huddle and emerged with 'I Wanna Be Your Man'. "All yours!" they said to Andy, Mick and Keith. The inference was that they were generously donating a newly completed but unassigned number, but in fact The Beatles were already planning to record this title themselves at Abbey Road the following day! Paul said later that The Stones "Bo Diddleyed it up a bit", a good way of putting it, while John admitted the song was "a throwaway", adding: "We weren't going to give them anything great, right?" Apart from giving The Stones their biggest best-seller to date, the song also went into The Beatles' repertoire as one of Ringo's popular speciality numbers.

Several extraordinary events in The Beatles' 1963 calendar took place during the final months of the year, including a couple of Fan Club Conventions, one in the North, one in the South, a very special edition of BBC Television's 'Juke Box Jury' and The Beatles' first Christmas Show staged at London's Astoria cinema in Seven Sisters Road, Finsbury Park, later to be renamed The Rainbow.

The fan club events were part of my ongoing public relations campaign to pacify as many previously disgruntled fans as possible. The strangest of these occasions was the Southern Area Fan Club Convention on Saturday, December 14. In a never-to-be-repeated marathon flesh-pumping experience The Beatles shook the over-heated hands of almost 3,000 Beatle People in the space of a few hours. We took over Wimbledon Palais – probably the best-known ballroom in London in its heyday – for the event, and filled the place with invited club members chosen at random. The Beatles stood for several hours behind the ballroom's long wooden bar, leaning across to be kissed by their fans or to sign autograph books. Considering the high excitement of the situation, the fans were well-behaved. Neil and Mal acted as security guards, keeping the seemingly endless queue moving along and occasionally untangling a Beatle who had become hopelessly enmeshed with an over-excited fan. After these close encounters with the Fab Four, the fans were treated to a special stage show in the main ballroom area where an over-protective Palais management had constructed a high-walled metal cage inside which the group were to perform on an extended makeshift stage beneath a huge banner that screamed: WIMBLEDON PALAIS WELCOMES THE BEATLES. Welcomes? The cage didn't make it look like that! In my lengthy preparatory discussions with the Palais people they had seriously understated their plans to surround The Beatles' stage with metal barriers for the protection of both the boys and their fans. When we saw the reality of the monstrous structure we were furious. The Beatles threatened at first to walk out unless the whole intimidating barricade was demolished and there were mutterings about "prison conditions" and "more like a zoo than a dance hall". Eventually, for the sake of their fan club members, they went on and gave an enthusiastic mini-concert. During this, as the crowd surged forward pinning those with a place in the front row against the cage, John remarked in a loud stage whisper: "If they press any harder they'll come through as chips."

The previous weekend in Liverpool the Northern Area convention had been almost as unusual in its way. In the Empire Theatre on Lime Street, BBC Television devoted an entire programme in its 'Juke Box Jury' series to a Beatles Special, all four boys making up the panel to judge a dozen or so of the week's newly issued singles under the chairmanship of deejay David ("Hello there") Jacobs. As usual,'Juke Box Jury' had a second panel on hand to decide any unresolved "hit" or "miss" votes in cases where the main panel expressed equally divided opinion. For this special edition of the show, three of our Official Fan Club secretaries formed the second panel – Anne Collingham (aka Mary Cockram) and Bettina Rose from the London office and Freda Kelly from Liverpool, representing the club's Northern Area section. Waiting for the lighting and camera people to set everything up, The Beatles were having a laugh with the three girls. Mary / Anne told me recently: "They had new movie cameras which they were using like mad to film us girls backstage. They were like kids with new Christmas presents! Paul in particular took lots of pictures of me, some on my own, some with the other boys. I wrote not so long ago to ask him if there was any chance of getting a copy of the stuff he took of me, just for my own personal use and to show my partner, but I had a letter back telling me it was too difficult because Paul was so busy."

Voting Liverpool's The Chants and 'I Could Write A Book' a unanimous hit, George said, "Enough plugs and they've got a hit." Listening to Elvis Presley's new 'Kiss Me Quick', Paul commented: "What I don't like about Elvis are his songs." Other releases they heard included Chan Romero's 'The Hippy Hippy Shake' covered over here by well-respected Mersey Beat outfit The Swinging Blue Jeans (a unanimous hit) and Paul Anka's 'Did You Have A Happy Birthday?' (a unanimous miss). Then, in front of the same fan club audience and under infinitely superior staging conditions than those we would encounter at Wimbledon, the BBC went on to make a half-hour Concert Special entitled 'It's The Beatles', which was transmitted the same evening. For this, their set consisted of 11 titles including 'I Want To Hold Your Hand, 'Twist And Shout' and 'Roll Over Beethoven'. The third and final element of this Saturday afternoon session of BBC recordings took the form of a brief radio interview to air on Christmas Day in a special show, 'Top Pops Of

1963', presented by Alan Freeman, for what was quaintly called in those pre-Radios 1 and 2 days the BBC Light Programme. With mock sincerity, George whispered to me: "You're listening to the BBC, the Beatles' Broadcasting Corporation."

All of this represented just the first half of the band's work that day. That evening, they resumed their UK tour of one-nighters with a pair of concerts at the Liverpool Odeon. The move between venues was uncomplicated enough because the Odeon was/is located in London Road, just around the corner from the Empire. The police closed the back street that ran behind the Empire and down the side of the Odeon and, with the boys in their stage suits, we made a dash between the two buildings, drawing a riotous burst of screams from the thrilled crowd which consisted of the exited afternoon Empire audience plus early arrivals for the first of the two evening shows at the Odeon. Ironically, the paying customers at the evening concerts saw a slightly shorter set (one or two songs lighter) than Beatle People had seen for free in the afternoon.

Only two weekends later, on Sunday December 22, the boys were back at the Liverpool Empire to preview their Christmas stage show prior to its London opening at Finsbury Park. This was one of two such provincial previews (the other was at the Gaumont in Bradford), which were seen by sceptics as "fast buck" money-spinners for the show's promoter and headline stars. In truth they were simplified concert versions of the full London production and they acted as last-minute rehearsals for all concerned. I think we were to be congratulated for mounting a theatrical Christmas show that tried very hard to be something more than a pop concert. For example, The Beatles dressed up in Victorian melodrama costumes for one comic sketch in which they did their best to be heard above the continuous shrieking of their audiences. All that mattered in the end was the musical bit of the show, a 25-minute set at the end of the second half. Capacity crowds totalling around 100,000 saw the 30 London performances of The Beatles Christmas Show, creating a massive public demand for another similar production the following Christmas.

At the beginning of 1963 in *The World's Fair*, the trade paper for fairground showmen and Britain's amusement industry, I wrote a guest article, which included my predictions for the year in terms of the pop charts. In style I suppose this was an extension of the stuff I was used to writing for album sleeve notes: "Now, in 1963, there are plentiful signs to suggest that the emergence of Liverpool's leading groups on record could trigger off and then go on to dominate a national trend towards homespun but slickly presented group hits with enough built-in pop power to outsell the streamlined Stateside combos. First off the mark is the North West's favourite vocal/instrumental quartet, The Beatles, who scored with some force last autumn with their first Parlophone single, 'Love Me Do'. They look all set for even greater things with their second single, 'Please Please Me'. Behind The Beatles is an astute, energetic young manager named Brian Epstein. He's a director of NEMS, one of Liverpool's largest disc retailing concerns, and he's a director of NEMS Enterprises Ltd., an organisation that handles the cream of Merseyside's local talent in allied capacities of management, direction and promotion. The success of The Beatles has brought him a sort of local Larry Parnes reputation, and he has already placed two of his other groups with major record companies. One of them, The Big Three, will record for Decca next month, and another, Gerry and the Pacemakers, will be at the EMI studios a few days later. Epstein's latest signing is an exceptionally good-looking singer named Billy Kramer. It would not surprise me if the Epstein stable of youthful but explosive new stars took control of the British vocal group scene within the next 12 months."

I wrote this piece in December for January shortly before I agreed to join NEMS Enterprises so it wasn't a matter of sucking up to my new boss – and, incidentally, I hadn't even met Billy Kramer at the time of writing so the description "exceptionally good-looking singer" was in reality a direct quote from Epstein. By December 1963, The Beatles had notched up five best-selling singles in the UK, including four chart-toppers. Gerry and the Pacemakers had No 1 hits with their first three singles, an industry first. Between May and November Billy J Kramer with the Dakotas released three singles that became Top 5 best-sellers. The Fourmost made their debut in September and enjoyed Top 10 chart success with Lennon and McCartney's 'Hello Little Girl'. Even The Big Three went into the charts twice between April and July. Please feel free to write off my above predictions for 1963 as nothing more than publicist's hype, or say to yourself "Well, he would say that, wouldn't he?", as it's true, I was about to be a full-time employee of The Beatles and Brian Epstein. But whichever way you look at it, astounding perspicacity or PR man's puff'n'stuff, I got it right!

Elsewhere, eminent Fleet Street journalists closed 1963 by writing pieces full of praise for the awesome foursome. In the *Times* dated December 27, William Mann wrote: "The outstanding English composers of 1963 must seem to have been John Lennon and Paul McCartney. The songs are the most imaginative and inventive examples of a style that has been developing on Merseyside…They have brought a distinctive and exhilarating flavour into a genre of music that was in danger of ceasing to be music at all." Two days later in the *Sunday Times* Richard Buckles wrote that Messrs McCartney and Lennon were "the greatest composers since Beethoven" which must have made Beethoven roll over in his grave. When the *NME* published its end-of-the-year poll results The Beatles were placed first in the World's Top Group section. In Britain, at least, Brian Epstein's boys were now bigger than Elvis.

John was asked by one reporter: "What's the secret of your success?" He replied: "We have a press agent." Thank you, John.

6 | American Dream

"WHO IS GLORIA STAVERS?" Brian Epstein asked as he glanced at the piece of paper I had passed across my desk to him with her name and New York phone number on it.

I told him: "I'd like you to wine and dine her while you're in New York. She's an exceedingly influential lady with a lot of power in the teenybopper magazine field." Epstein was flying to New York immediately after The Beatles' appearance on the *Royal Variety Show* and the time was right for him to consolidate the groundwork I had recently laid with Gloria Stavers.

Towards the end of 1963, when our planning for The Beatles' imminent invasion of the USA was in its early stages, I hoped to make Gloria Stavers my secret weapon by persuading her to spearhead the battle with a big burst of editorial coverage. She was editor-in-chief of *16* magazine, arguably America's strongest monthly publication aimed at youthful pop fans. Unlike many of her competitors, Stavers seemed to take an almost sisterly interest in the stars she promoted on her pages, often personally writing her own interview-based feature articles on the ones who impressed her most.

Stavers was tall, attractive, elegant, dynamic and sophisticated. She was not the sort of Gloria you would dream of calling Glo. As we got to know one another, I saw her as the archetypal New York businesswoman of the day; sexy, in total control, accustomed to living splendidly, working hard and getting her own way. She had zero tolerance for incompetence and carelessness, frequently yelling the "f" word at blundering staff who made grammatical errors or failed to check facts – in an era when few women swore so colourfully. The word her French publisher used to describe her to me was *formidable*.

As I got to know her I discovered that Gloria had a heart of gold that could turn to steel in an instant if she felt threatened or betrayed. She was a sort of grown-up supergroupie who had her own idols, heroes and heroines – and enemies – in the entertainment world. She became the very close friend of stars she admired, but she quickly dropped those who fell from public favour.

Gloria's offices were at 745 Park Avenue, not a million miles from the plush Plaza Hotel where so many of New York's visiting stars used to stay. Born in North Carolina she gave up a well-paid model-ling career to work as a subscription clerk at *16* magazine where she rose to become editor-in-chief in 1958. Her special flair was to pick out and nurture the careers of new names, rising stars who were mostly dishy male teenagers. She would predict fame for her latest favourites and then help them to achieve it by giving them valu-able ongoing publicity via the photo and feature pages of *16*. She demanded that her "discoveries" should be talented, ambitious and good-looking. After that, once she believed in the potential of a band, a singer or a TV newcomer, she could work wonders for them by giving them the type of concentrated editorial exposure that money can't buy. I knew from my research that past issues of *16* had given plentiful picture publicity to bare-chested beefcake including Paul Revere and the Raiders, Paul Anka, Bobby Vee and Bobby Rydell, as well as the obvious names like Elvis Presley and Ricky Nelson. Stavers used just the right approach to beguile her adolescent male interview subjects, flirting with them to precisely the right extent but no more. Her enemies called Gloria a ruthless prima donna, but with a monthly circulation usually exceeding a million copies, and a read-ership of young and impressionable female fans, Gloria Stavers was someone whose friendship any wise PR man would wish to foster by all means.

When I first phoned her from London a haughty-voiced aide told me firmly: "Miss Stavers doesn't take calls from publicists she doesn't know. May I give you to one of her assistant editors?" Refusing to be put off, I persevered: "Please tell Miss Stavers that I'm ringing from London and I represent The Beatles." Seconds later the lady herself came on the line: "Congratulations on your success at the London Palladium." Only days earlier The Beatles had scored their publicity triumph when Fleet Street announced the outbreak of

Beatlemania in the wake of the group's well-received appearance on ATV's *Sunday Night At The London Palladium*. That Gloria Stavers had picked up on our London newspaper coverage so quickly imp-ressed me. It confirmed my feeling that the woman was extraordinarily professional at her job, keeping her eyes on the international pop scene as well as home-grown US talent, and I was pleased to know that our press stories on the birth of Beatlemania were reaching the right people on the far side of the Atlantic. It emerged much later that Gloria was friendly with a New York showbusiness and divorce attorney named Nat Weiss, who represented the London impre-sario Larry Parnes and was to become Epstein's friend and business partner in Nemperor Holdings in 1965. I imagine that she used Weiss as her eyes and ears on what was going on in the European enter-tainment industry. "I hear some good things about your four boys," Gloria went on, giving me the perfect opening. "Then let me tell you a lot more."

She said: "You have a cute English accent but it's not Liverpool." I replied: "It is, you know, I was born and raised on Merseyside, but much of the accent has worn off since I came to live in London." I had intended to make this a short introductory phone call but we talked for well over 30 minutes. She asked about each of The Beatles in turn, about Brian Epstein and about the so-called Mersey Beat sound. I promised to airmail a press pack to her containing our latest set of photographs, a bundle of recent press cuttings including show reviews and a pile of biographical data on John, Paul, George and Ringo. My way of wooing Gloria Stavers was not merely to ply her with publicity materials, but also to offer her exclusive articles from time to time, each by-lined by a Beatle or one of the group's two road managers. We agreed to stay in touch and I arranged to keep her posted regularly with news updates on the group, especially their first visit to America. She said: "I'd like to meet you all when you're over here." I told her that Brian Epstein would be in New York quite soon, bringing his new signing, Billy J Kramer, with him and staying at the Regency Hotel on Park Avenue. She said: "What a good choice!"

I believe that the substantial volume of editorial space Gloria Stavers gave the Fab Four to coincide with their US launch was of significant help to us and to Capitol Records, assisting us to fast-track the group to the top of the charts after the initial success of the single

'I Want To Hold your Hand'. Having helped to speed up the group's widespread acceptance by the American public, her fanzine's heavy-weight coverage over the following several years sustained their peak popularity in the long periods between their annual coast-to-coast summer concert tours. Under the signatures of Neil Aspinall and Mal Evans, and with their collaboration, I wrote numerous columns for 16, billed as "exclusive from Liverpool, England", during the touring years and afterwards and we kept the publication well supplied with the newest and often exclusive photographs. Stavers produced special issues to mark each of The Beatles' feature films and she was given VIP media treatment as a photo-journalist during the shooting of *Help!* on location on New Providence Island in the Bahamas. At her first interview with the boys she breezed into their room like an eagerly-awaited Hollywood celebrity and announced: "Hi! I'm 16." Although she was clearly thirty-something, Ringo replied: "You don't look 16, you look much younger."

Under Gloria's charismatic control, 16 retained a marvellous Peter Pan-like disregard for the adult world, seeing everything through the rose-tinted spectacles of a pony-tailed teenage girl – Bobbysoxers, as the Americans used to call them. While its readers reached and passed through adolescence, 16 was the perennial teenage publication waiting to serve the next generation of pony-tailed pop fans. Paul McCartney was aware of 16 even before The Beatles went over to America and he knew it had a good reputation among US Beatle People: "We knew we needed to be in it although we thought of it as Cutesville on ice." Paul remembered Gloria as being very digni-fied, very professional, and totally businesslike. He said: "She inspired respect from us all." Once The Beatles' image outgrew its "cutesville" period in the post-touring period, 16 moved on to cuddle a fresh set of boy stars, including The Monkees.

Apart from support from America's teenybopper press, including the rivals of 16, a number of key coast-to-coast news syndication sources and the news departments of the NBC and CBS television networks picked up on the recent swell of editorial coverage we were getting from Fleet Street. Valuable stories appeared not only in the *New Yorker*, but also in *Time*, *Newsweek* and other respected magazines. In the *New York Times*, Frederick Lewis wrote: "The Beatles' impact on Britain has been greater than that of any other exponent of popular music. There has been adulation before but no one has taken the national fancy as they have. Beatlemania, as it is called, affects all social classes and all levels of intelligence." Under the headline "Beatlemania", the *Newsweek* piece began: "They wear sheepdog bangs [fringes], collarless jackets, and drainpipe trousers. One plays left-handed guitar, two have falsetto voices, one wishes he were a businessman, and all four sing. They are The Beatles and the sound of their music is one of the most persistent noises heard over England since the air-raid sirens were dismantled. Their leader is John Lennon, a Liverpudlian like the others, and the only one of the group who is married. He writes most of their songs in collaboration with Paul McCartney. The guitarist is George Harrison who claims to be a Segovia fan and the drummer is Ringo Starr, nicknamed for the four rings he wears." I was pleased to notice that most of this story so far was lifted directly from publicity material I had written and sent to *Newsweek*. The article went on: "Beatle music is high-pitched, loud beyond reason, and stupefyingly repetitive. Like rock'n'roll, to which it is closely allied, it is even more effective to watch than to hear. They prance, skip, and turn in circles. The Beatles have even been known to kiss their guitars. The style, certainly, is their own." *Time* headlined its story "The New Madness" and said that the group's raucous big-beat sound made their performances "slightly orgiastic", and added: " ... but the boys are the very spirit of good clean fun." The *New York Times* magazine said: "To see a Beatle is joy, to touch one paradise on earth, and for just the simplest opportunity of this privilege, people will fight like mad things and with dedication for a Great Cause, like natural survival."

Capitol Records, whose headquarters were in Hollywood, had first option on EMI UK products, which included The Beatles' earliest singles and albums on the Parlophone label. At first, they decided not to exercise that option because there was "little interest among American fans in recordings from England", with the result that the single 'Please Please Me' was released in America in February 1963 via the R&B and Gospel music specialist Vee-Jay Records, a Chicago-based independent label. For a while Vee-Jay persistently mis-spelt the band's name as Beattles in their publicity for 'Please Please Me' and even on the actual record label. But by May, when they brought out 'From Me To You', they'd got it right. After this, in September 1963,

Philadelphia's Swan Records came into the picture by picking up 'She Loves You' for US release. In January 1964, within ten days of one another, Vee-Jay put out the album *Introducing The Beatles* and Capitol weighed in with *Meet The Beatles*.

Coming soon after the assassination of President Kennedy, such lively new sounds might have been seen by many young Americans as welcome light relief amid the all-pervading air of doom and gloom that hung over the whole continent in the wake of the Dallas tragedy. In my opinion, some commentators have grossly exaggerated the connection between Kennedy's death and the remarkable speed with which Beatlemania took off in the US. Network television, particularly 'The Ed Sullivan Show', which was America's equivalent of the UK's 'Sunday Night At The London Palladium', gave The Beatles a terrific popularity boost and broadened their fan base on their initial arrival on American soil in February 1964. Various American and British agents, from Vic Lewis, who represented the giant American talent agency General Artists Corporation in London, to New York's Sid Bernstein, who promoted The Beatles at Carnegie Hall and later at Shea Stadium, have claimed a share of the credit for getting the boys onto Sullivan's primetime Sunday evening show and breaking the group in the US. Probably the most valid claimant must be the London entrepreneur Peter Pritchard who was employed by the *Sullivan* show as its European coordinator and talent scout, but the truth is that in the end it was Brian Epstein's impressive demeanour and polished powers of persuasion that did the trick. On occasions like this, Epstein's smart appearance and almost aristocratic air of authority played their part in his successful negotiations with Americans on behalf of The Beatles. Pulling out all the stops during his New York visit, Epstein was the epitome of traditional English charm. On the strength of his vivid description of the group's recent UK successes, backed up by our ever-thickening file of press cuttings, Epstein landed, not just one but a series of three Sullivan guest spots for the boys on consecutive shows in February – two live and a third taped. This does not mean that Sullivan's production people were a soft touch. The price Epstein paid was in hard cash; he virtually gave back the appearance fees, agreeing to a nominal amount of less than $700 per Beatle per show. When I, and others, back home at NEMS Enterprises questioned the sense of valuing The Beatles at such a low figure, Epstein reasoned that he would have been willing to pay Sullivan's producers for such a priceless television showcase with such an enviable rating in terms of viewers. He told me: "My negotiation was not about the money but the appearances. It's unheard-of for a new band to get three bookings in a row without a string of hit records." In his first US magazine interview, for the *New Yorker*, Epstein repeated almost verbatim the well-rehearsed pitch that he'd given the Sullivan people: "The Beatles have broken every conceivable entertainment record in Britain. They are the most worshipped, the most idolised boys in the country. They have tremendous style and a great effervescence, which communicates itself in an extraordinary way. Their beat is something like rock'n'roll, but different from it. They are genuine, they have life, humour and strange, handsome good looks."

Before The Beatles, very few British pop stars or rock'n'roll groups were successful in America. To the majority, the notion of having a hit record in the US was a dream but for most it remained no more than that, an American dream. There was plenty of traffic in the opposite direction and, ever since the establishment of sales charts for singles in the UK during the Fifties, recordings by American artists had shown up strongly among our bestsellers. There were also many cover versions of American hits recorded by British singers and bands, which meant the same song title often showed up more than once in any given week's Top Twenty, a phenomenon that phased itself out in the Sixties when more singer-songwriters appeared on the scene and more hits were performed by their own composers, as was the case with Lennon and McCartney and The Beatles. The Beatles broke with established tradition by invading the US music scene so forcefully in 1964, not only scoring consecutive hits with their singles and albums but also opening the floodgates so that others could follow and keep the tide running high. Until the arrival of The Beatles, British artists copied the recording styles of their most successful US counterparts. After The Beatles, American acts copied what The Beatles were doing. This dramatic sea-change meant that, for an increasing number of British artists, their American dream was realised. Regardless of what part of the UK they came from, some British groups were advertised in America as "Direct from Liverpool". Among those who achieved lasting success were The Rolling Stones, The Dave Clark Five and

Herman's Hermits. Apart from Gerry and the Pacemakers and, to a lesser extent, Billy J Kramer, Brian Epstein's other acts did not feature prominently in the British invasion of the US pop scene.

I was always convinced that neither verbal nor written descriptions of The Beatles could possibly do justice to their vibrant visual and musical attributes and that one had to watch them in action on a stage to gain a full impression of their strength. Norman Weiss, a top agent at GAC's New York headquarters, saw The Beatles in their Paris season at the Olympia Theatre in January 1964. The French audience was not so rowdy as those we saw in the UK and elsewhere in the world. There was a larger-than-usual proportion of male fans who listened rather than screamed, a great advantage according to George, who told me: "This was good for the audience and good for us. It was what happened occasionally in Hamburg when our audience happened to contain a majority of appreciative local students and not drunken tourists. They actually listened to what we were singing and playing. We like to play to this type of crowd." The *New Musical Express* took a more pessimistic view: "Beatlemania was not visible in Paris when Les Fabs attempted to impress unimpressionable L'Olympia patrons on the first night of a three-week variety season." Certainly the relatively calm environment of the Olympia helped GAC's Norman Weiss, who was there to visit his client Trini Lopez, assess The Beatles' stage performance and get a full flavour of their talent as entertainers. This led to GAC becoming The Beatles' US agent, dealing with the booking of their concert tours in that part of the world from 1964 until August 1966 when the touring came to an end.

One of Norman's part-time colleagues at GAC was the agent/impresario Sid Bernstein, who went ahead on his own and fixed directly with Brian Epstein the Fab Four's very first concerts in New York at the hugely prestigious Carnegie Hall on February 12 – a national holiday in the US for Lincoln's birthday. For this pair of concerts Bernstein paid The Beatles more than Sullivan gave for the three television appearances. The first public announcement of the Carnegie Hall gig was made in New York newspapers on Sunday January 26 and every seat was sold within six hours of the box office opening. During the visit The Beatles would undertake just one other concert date, on February 11 at the Coliseum in Washington, DC.

One of our most useful contributions to the US launch campaign was to talk Capitol Records into establishing a massive $50,000 budget to publicise the arrival of The Beatles. As part of the label's crash programme, every radio station across the US got a goody bag of Beatles' material including BE A BEATLE BOOSTER badges. Millions of posters saying THE BEATLES ARE COMING went up at prominent sites in towns and cities. Two days into the group's Paris season we heard that 'I Want To Hold Your Hand' had shot to the top of the American singles charts. By way of celebration, The Beatles stayed up all night and got well and truly drunk. The US music industry trade paper *Cashbox* announced that it wouldn't be long before "every group with long hair will be sought by American companies". Capitol Records reported that "fan clubs are sprouting like crabgrass and Beatle wigs are the rage on high school campuses. Beatle buttons, Beatle sweatshirts and even Beatlenut ice cream are being readied for the marketplace." In private, Paul was the most cautious of The Beatles, asking openly: "What have we got to give a country like America? Yes, I know that we've got a record at the top of the charts, but that doesn't mean they'll go for us personally, does it?"

In the weeks before The Beatles travelled to New York on February 7 1964, my press office went into overdrive, co-ordinating the media side of the visit by distributing bundles of press material to hundreds of US newspapers and magazines and arranging a limited number of transatlantic phone interviews for individual Beatles during the group's seasons at London's Finsbury Park Astoria and the Paris Olympia. We recorded a spoken-word album for Capitol Records carrying a specially prepared open-ended interview that was distributed to radio stations so that deejays could drop in the questions and add links between The Beatles' answers. For this pre-packaged all-purpose radio guest spot, taped in London at EMI's Abbey Road studios a month before the US trip, we "bent" bits of the group's history in several trivial ways in order to say what we wanted the Americans to hear. Brian Epstein insisted that we should ignore the group's first UK single, 'Love Me Do', which had been unsuccessful in the US on another label. On the interview LP, George said: "We made our first record at the beginning of 1963 and we had a hit with that." We didn't want to go into all the intricate details of how the group's trademark haircuts evolved, the influence of existentialist students with whom the boys had become friendly in Hamburg and so forth. Asked about which one of the guys thought up the mop-top haircut, Paul facetiously gave his dad the credit: "He said: 'You know, Paul, it's a bit square, this', the haircut I had, you know, short back and sides. 'Why don't you get a Beatle Cut, son?'"

During the first weeks of 1964 a seemingly endless number of draft press releases were rushed to and fro between Capitol's Hollywood headquarters and my office in London where the wording was either amended or approved. One release put out by the CBS Television Network said: "The Beatles count among their fans Queen Elizabeth and Princess Margaret." I could have reminded them that it was actually Queen Elizabeth The Queen Mother and not our reigning monarch who attended the Royal Variety Performance, but I didn't. Elsewhere, someone at Capitol got a Beverly Hills hair stylist to create a new Beatle cut for women and arranged for the wife of the Hollywood actor Steve McQueen to model it for press pictures. The efforts of Capitol's album merchandising manager, Paul Russell, were incredible. He sent his sales executives Beatle Booster buttons and told them: "Have all of your sales staff wear one." He followed up with Beatle Wigs, ordering that "as soon as they arrive and until further notice you and each of your sales and promotion staff are to wear the wig during the business day". Was this man for real? I asked myself. Sid Bernstein remarked: "This isn't just showbusiness, it's history." Yes ... and a whole lot of hastily put together and highly-expensive US marketing hype!

We continued to do our bit from the London end. With the blessing of both The Beatles and Brian Epstein, I wrote a number of pre-packaged interview articles in which John, Paul, George and Ringo replied to some most frequently asked questions and these went to editors who could not be given personal interviews but who nonetheless deserved our special attention because their publications were important and/or their circulations were significant.

Fleet Street reported that an estimated 4,000 fans were on hand at Heathrow to wish The Beatles well in America as Pan Am's Boeing 707 jet flight to New York City taxied down the runway and took off. At New York's John F Kennedy International Airport another 3,500 teenagers gathered to greet the boys, many waving banners and flags with WE LOVE YOU BEATLES slogans given to them by busy promotion people from Capitol Records. The American kids had been waiting many hours on a chilly, winter morning, cheered up by regular radio reports on the progress of the Jet Clipper Defiance, aka PA 101: "At WMCA New York it's twenty minutes past the hour Beatle time and the downtown temperature in Manhattan is 34 Beatle degrees. Current estimated time of arrival for The Beatles' flight at JFK is 1.20pm and this is their smash hit single, 'I Want To Hold Your Hand'." Competitors tried to outdo one another to claim special affinity with the Fab Four: "You're listening to Ten Ten WINS New York, your official Beatle station." Deejay Murray (The K) Kaufman went the extra mile by informing WINS listeners precisely where fans could find the boys: "They're staying at the Plaza Hotel right by Central Park, folks." Then, if not sooner, the conservative Plaza management must have started to doubt the wisdom of having accepted the group's booking. We had been uncommonly candid with the hotel's reservation department, using the real names of all four boys – Lennon, McCartney, Harrison and Starkey – to book their rooms, although we did fail to add (oops!) that collectively these were The Beatles and, without this final detail, I don't believe the Plaza knew just what they had let themselves in for. Staff controller Hilary Brown put up a warning on the staff bulletin board: "During the stay of The Beatles at the Plaza Hotel I want extreme caution by all elevator operators as to the type of people you take upstairs to the 12th, 13th and 14th floors." Obviously, craftier fans were trying to make themselves less conspicuous by asking lift attendants for one of the upper floors from where they would simply walk down to the Beatles Zone on the 12th floor!

I had briefed Brian Sommerville thoroughly about his first US press conference, but in the event there was sheer pandemonium in the airport press room, which was packed with some 200 representatives of the US and international media. Reporters and photographers heard Sommerville attempt in vain to follow the format we'd planned with such care for detail – photographers to have first priority followed by the main Q&A session between the boys and a hundred or more journalists. But the battery of noisy cameramen refused to budge when their allotted time slot ran out. "Would the photographers please be quiet now so the reporters can ask questions. PLEASE!!" Minutes later, his polite request still being ignored by the majority,

The Beatles shopping for postcards on a street in Paris at the beginning of 1964. There they played a short season at the Olympia Theatre, during which they were given the news that 'I Want To Hold Your Hand' had gone to Nº1 in the US in just three weeks. They couldn't have walked out like this on a London street, or in a major US city. Fans tended to leave them alone when they were out and about in Paris.
(THE SEAN O'MAHONY COLLECTION.)

At the end of 1963 BBC Television devoted an entire programme in its *Juke Box Jury* series to a Beatles Special, The Beatles making up the panel to judge a dozen or so of the week's newly issued singles under the chairmanship of deejay David Jacobs. For this special edition of the show, three of our Official Fan Club secretaries formed the second panel – Anne Collingham (aka Mary Cockram) and Bettina Rose from the London office and Freda Kelly from Liverpool, representing the club's Northern Area section.
(THE TONY BARROW COLLECTION.)

Beatle ladies in waiting – Ringo's first wife Maureen, and Cynthia Lennon. It was a common sight, various Beatle wives and partners gathering in canteens and bars waiting for the band to finish performing, rehearsing or recording.
(THE SEAN O'MAHONY COLLECTION.)

The Beatles spent much time together in hotel rooms
during the touring years, either waiting to go on stage or
hiding from hysterical crowds on the streets outside. Here
John and George play acoustic guitar while Paul provides
the percussion, Buddy Holly-style, slapping his hands
against his legs – a favourite percussion choice of Paul's
and used on a number of his post-Beatles recordings.
(THE SEAN O'MAHONY COLLECTION.)

The Beatles face the press, with Brian Epstein (behind Paul in
dark glasses) ... and Me. Throughout the touring years we gave a
major press conference in every town and city we visited.
(THE TONY BARROW COLLECTION.)

The Beatles on Broadway! During
a rehearsal for *The Ed Sullivan
Show* in February 1964, Sullivan
takes a moment during a break

1964 YOUR TOP DISC STARS ON PARADE EVERY FRIDAY IN THE new MUSICAL EXPRESS

THE BEATLES
CLIFF RICHARD • ELVIS PRESLEY

JANUARY

Sun.	Mon.	Tue.	Wed.	Thu.	Fri.	Sat.
...	...	...	1	2	3	4
5	6	7	8	9	10	11
12	13	14	15	16	17	18
19	20	21	22	23	24	25
26	27	28	29	30	31	...
...	...	...	...	...	...	...

In 1964 The Beatles still had to share some of the limelight with others – here in the *NME Calendar*, "Your Top Disc Stars" include British singer Cliff Richard, The Beatles, and Elvis.

ODEON HAMMERSMITH
BRIAN EPSTEIN presents
ANOTHER BEATLES
CHRISTMAS SHOW
1st Performance at 6-15 p.m.
TUESDAY, JAN. 12th, 1965
STALLS £1/-/-
Seat
Block
24 C 15
No ticket exchanged nor money refunded
THIS PORTION TO BE RETAINED

A seat at *Another Beatles Christmas Show* at the Hammersmith Odeon, West London, in January 1965, cost £1.00.

On the bill with The Beatles for their 1964/1965 Christmas show …
(THE PETER RHODES COLLECTION.)

BRIAN EPSTEIN Presents

ANOTHER BEATLES CHRISTMAS SHOW

THE BEATLES

FREDDIE and the DREAMERS

JIMMY SAVILE · SOUNDS INCORPORATED

ELKIE BROOKS · THE YARDBIRDS · MICHAEL HASLAM
THE MIKE COTTON SOUND · RAY FELL

DEVISED AND PRODUCED BY PETER YOLLAND

HAMMERSMITH ODEON
(Manager: Dennis Tapsell)

Thursday 24 December 1964 —
Saturday 16 January 1965

For Brian Epstein:
Assistant producer John Lyndon
Scenic Designer Andrew Drummond
Stage Director Johnny Gunn
Press Representative Tony Barrow

For the Rank Organisation Theatre Division:
Booking Controller George Pinches
Production Director Stan Fishman
Stage Director Bill West
Advertising & Publicity Michael Buist

Scenery made and painted by Stage Decor Ltd., Harold Fielding Ltd.   Additional lighting equipment by Strand Electric & Engineering Co. Ltd.
Costumes by Bermans Ltd., and Theatre Zoo   Additional material by Ireland Cutter, Peter Yolland and John Blythe   'Melinex' polyester film by I.C.I.

"Next question from over there please." The film distributors got a big plug for The Beatles' second feature film *Help!* at this press conference, by hanging a giant sign behind the band.
(THE TONY BARROW COLLECTION.)

Bess Coleman with John Lennon. Bess was part of the press office team at EMI Records when we launched The Beatles. Moving temporarily to New York, she worked with Derek Taylor during the group's 1964 US tour and reported on later Fab Four US trips for various radio stations and magazines. Returning to London after the NEMS era, Bess became a co-director in my independent PR and management companies during the Seventies.
(THE TONY BARROW COLLECTION.)

The "tour team" of 1965. The
Beatles and their entourage pose
with travelling media people for
a souvenir shot in a locker room
backstage at Chicago's Comiskey
Park. Back row: the media pack.
Centre row: George, Paul, John,
Ringo, Neil Aspinall. Front row: Alf
Bicknell (the band's chauffeur), …
Me, and Mal Evans.
(THE TONY BARROW COLLECTION.)

Paul ... and Me in dark glasses,
front centre. When Beatlemania was
at its peak I often had to double as
minder in situations like this where

The Presidential Suite at the Tokyo Hilton, The Beatles'
hideout while staying in the Japanese capital, 1966. Brian
Epstein (left), Paul McCartney, Rumi Hoshika, editor of
Japan's *Music Life* magazine … Me, Ringo Starr, and
concert promoter Tats Nagashima.
(THE TONY BARROW COLLECTION.)

… Me, Ringo, Rumi Hoshika, and John. Behind John can
be seen a painting on which the Fab Four collaborated
while we were "under hotel arrest" in the Tokyo Hilton. The
gracious Rumi gave me these photos to keep as souvenirs
of our visit to Japan on the second leg of the Beatles' final
concert tour in the Summer of 1966.
(THE TONY BARROW COLLECTION.)

Sommerville shouted: "This has got entirely out of control. Ladies and gentlemen, this is ridiculous. If you won't be quiet we'll just stand here until you are. Shut up! Just shut up!" Despite Sommerville's loss of control, from the utter chaos of that initial US press conference came some remarkably useful film footage that was seen by television news audiences on both sides of the Atlantic.

The boys' departure from JFK was as crazy and chaotic as the conference. Three Beatles leapt or were thrown into the leading black Cadillac limousine and Brian Sommerville pushed his way through the tight surrounding ring of cops to join them. Someone banged on the limo roof and yelled: "Go, go, go!" John was left on the sidewalk cursing loudly until he was pushed into the second of Capitol Records' Cadillacs. "Go, go, go!" This left an irate Brian Epstein to watch the little convoy of vehicles disappear rapidly in the direction of the expressway with NYPD sirens screeching in front and behind it. One airport official told the *New York Times*: "We've never seen anything like this here before. Not even for kings and queens."

Outside the Plaza Hotel lines of mounted policemen held back hundreds of screaming fans. In one of their bedrooms The Beatles watched the first television news reports of their airport arrival with the sound turned down so that they could also listen to WMCA, WABC and WINS radio reports that punctuated non-stop, round-the-clock plays of their records. I heard later from Brian Sommerville that at this point Epstein took the opportunity to get his revenge on Sommerville for stealing his place in the first of the airport vehicles with Paul, George and Ringo. Sommerville told me: "I couldn't believe it when Brian turned on me and complained about the cost of the meal I ordered for myself on room service. I'd been working hard for him since dawn and he was grudging me the only decent meal I'd had all day. It was only ordinary stuff off the menu but he called it a lavish feast. You'd have thought I'd ordered trolley-loads of caviar or something!" When I asked how the trip was going otherwise, Sommerville replied: "I've been fired by Brian a couple of times." So there was nothing new there. "But he's also going out of his way to make me look foolish in front of other people, which really is not on." At one point during the US visit, Epstein's personal assistant, Wendy Hanson, rang me: "Brian wants to know your thoughts on something. He thinks that Brian Sommerville is charging up far too much in expenses. Do you think we should put a cap on how much he's spending? Might we set a budget of so much a day perhaps? Brian says it's getting out of hand." I explained that, as far as I was concerned, any press aide working away from home was entitled to put in for all his out-of-pocket expenses for the duration of his trip and if I was working on location somewhere I certainly wouldn't be able to give an accurate estimate of my daily outgoings in advance. It was only much later, when everyone returned to London, that I discovered that one or more of The Beatles had made complaints to Epstein about Sommerville over some trivial matter and, instead of facing the man with the accusations, Epstein chose to give him a hard time generally, and over expenses in particular.

Soon after The Beatles arrived in Manhattan, the brothers Albert and David Maysles from Massachusetts were shooting first sequences for their "officially authorised" documentary on The Beatles, shown in various versions in the UK and the US under different titles, including *The Beatles In America, What's Happening!, The Beatles In The USA,* and *Yeah! Yeah! Yeah! The Beatles In New York.* This was a Granada Television co-production with the brothers' own filmmaking outfit, for which Epstein had negotiated personal editorial control. For the entire duration of The Beatles' two-week stay in America, the Maysles brothers stalked John, Paul, George, Ringo and Brian just about everywhere but the bathroom. Murray The K made great efforts to be within camera range for as many scenes as possible and even persuaded the producers to include his catch phrase "What's Happening?" in one of the finished programme's titles. George sarcastically referred to him as "The Fifth Beatle" and the deejay was too thick-skinned to realise that he didn't mean it. Murray immediately adopted this as his new nickname and turned up everywhere, even taking the boys to meet his mates The Ronettes at New York's self-styled "Temple Of Twist", the famous Peppermint Lounge, where Ringo twisted the night away with a vivacious club dancer named Geri Miller. Brian Epstein was happy to let Murray fix all this because he wasn't into clubbing himself. The Ronette Estelle Bennett came over to the Plaza the next day to see George, with whom she had already set up a close friendship when The Ronettes were in London. At one point in the film, Paul was seen lounging in the back of The Beatles' limousine listening to a radio station's promotional trailer for a programme which they were claiming would be heard later that day in which "The Beatles will be reading their own poetry for us". At this Paul's jaw dropped, his eyes opened wide and he said directly to the camera: "Oh really! We will?" The Beatles soon realised that a lot of what they heard on American Top 40 music radio was sheer fantasy punctuated by no more than a smattering of fact. One of the American artists The Beatles heard constantly on New York radio was Mary Wells, of 'My Guy' fame, a firm favourite with the Fab Four. The saturation airplay she was getting reminded the boys how much they liked her singing and they agreed among themselves as they cruised along in their limousine that they would ask Brian Epstein to book her onto their next series of UK concerts, scheduled to take place later in the year.

Taken as a whole, the Maysles brothers' film confirmed that Paul was the most animated of The Beatles, whether he was packing suitcases or feeding seagulls out of a Miami Beach hotel window. John came across as the most serious, Ringo as the zaniest and George as the least active. At the boys' personal request the pair of limousines taking them from the Plaza to the CBS television studio on Broadway did a considerable detour so that they could have a lightning tour of Harlem. This was one of the few sightseeing initiatives that did NOT involve the Maysles duo. Sequences set up specifically for the film showed The Beatles in Central Park, riding in a horse-drawn carriage outside the Plaza, fooling about on the train that took them to Washington for their first US concert and at play in Miami Beach in several photogenic situations. Throughout the US visit, the London-based Czechoslovakian freelance photographer Dezo Hoffmann – who took most of the group's earliest studio publicity pictures in London – was also shooting away with his stills camera. The showbiz veteran Hoffmann, a one-time clapper boy at the A-B film studios in Prague, probably took more shots of John, Paul, George and Ringo than any other photographer, largely because we readily gave him so much access to the boys during the first years we were in London.

Outsiders looking at the Maysles movie and Hoffmann's stills, most of which were made to look like happy and informal holiday snaps, might be forgiven for imagining that The Beatles had loads of free time in America and did a whole lot of sightseeing. The less attractive truth is that John, Paul, George and Ringo spent almost every waking hour working. Posing for publicity shots, sometimes even in the middle of meals or when they were dressing to go out, was an integral part of their job as superstars. On the initial US trip the boys did a major photo shoot for *Life* magazine around a private swimming pool in Miami Beach, they posed for cosy "at home" pictures with the family of their temporary bodyguard, police sergeant Buddy Dresner, went water-skiing, stood in snowy weather conditions in front of several Washington landmarks, even tried their hand at a spot of fishing and mocked up a fight scene with the boxing champion Cassius Clay (aka Mohammed Ali) who was in training for his showdown world-title bout with Sonny Liston. Believe me, these photo opportunities were at least as strenuous and tiring as giving full-blown stage performances or making new recordings in the studio. We were envied by friends who saw The Beatles' world tours as excuses for a succession of extended vacations in faraway destinations. Of course, we were fortunate to be visiting so many different places but as we criss-crossed the planet during the touring years, it never felt for even one moment as though we were on holiday. I must have been to scores of cities in exotic countries during my time with The Beatles but neither they nor I saw much of any of these wonderful places beyond an airport, an hotel, a concert venue and maybe the odd television or radio studio in each case.

Our relationships with freelance photographers during the Beatlemania years were often bittersweet affairs. It was very useful to have at least one friendly cameraman in tow when we went on the road. If we took an "official" photographer with us as part of The Beatles' entourage he would be on the spot to snap any unplanned drama that happened along the way. We would also use the same guy to do all our "candid" shots, the off-duty pics in places like hotel rooms and backstage areas where we wanted to limit media access while needing a pictorial record of what went on for future use. Over the years I often made mutually valuable deals with hand-picked photographers whereby I would give them special access to The Beatles so that they could shoot some specific set-up of their own in return for snapping off a new set of straightforward head-and-shoulder shots for publicity hand-outs. I was very careful in my choice of allies for this sort of work because in my eyes it was always of paramount importance that our handful of "official" photographers should have a friendly rapport with our stars. One of these was David Magnus, an extremely bright and creative young photographer who started his career as Dezo Hoffmann's assistant. Magnus got on well with The Beatles and most of the other top acts I represented during the Sixties and Seventies. He specialised in innovative and unusual sessions for leading magazines and newspapers and he was also my favourite photographer for shooting exclusive mother-father-and-baby pictures in maternity wards. As a whole range of my former clients from Ringo Starr to Cilla Black can testify, to have one known cameraman at mum's bedside was a much less daunting prospect for the star concerned than having the place invaded by a horde of Fleet Street staffers with unfamiliar faces. Magnus took one of the best – and sadly the last – recording studio pictures of Brian Epstein with The Beatles in 1967.

Unfortunately, relationships between The Beatles and their regular photographers seldom lasted very long. They tended to have "flavour of the month" choices, often basing their assessment on personality rather than professional ability. Some of their longer-lasting, and most talented, favourites were Robert Freeman, whose speciality was atmospheric album covers, Leslie Bryce, who worked for Sean O'Mahony, publisher of *The Beatles Monthly Book*, and Harry Goodwin, the BBC's 'Top Of The Pops' photographer. I do not put Bob Whitaker in this short-list of favourites because his position was different. Whitaker was discovered in Melbourne by Brian Epstein during The Beatles' 1964 tour of Australia and brought back to London to become the company's official staff photographer, managed by Epstein and on the payroll of NEMS Enterprises. During his two-year stay with us, his best-known and most infamous work was The Beatles' so-called "butcher session" in March 1966, of which more in a later chapter.

In the early days, and certainly in 1964 at the beginning of the group's first visit to America, it looked as though Dezo Hoffmann was shaping up well to earn his place on our initial list of longer-lasting regulars but he was dropped from the group's "in-crowd" largely because the role of a freelance photographer was not always fully understood by The Beatles. Hoffmann had his living to earn so, when we invited him to join the entourage for a particular trip, I expected him to be available to do special shots that I might ask for, but I fully understood that he would take as many other pictures as possible to sell to publications in the UK and around the world. Selling the rights to reproduce his prints, mostly in publications but occasionally imprinted in one way or another on merchandise, was what Dezo and every other freelancer did. Of The Beatles, John was the first to complain that Hoffmann was "making millions out of us". He said it to the photographer's face and to me. I tried to explain the way things worked and that what we got in good worldwide media publicity from Dezo's photographs probably matched what he got in hard cash, that the photographer and the group were making money out of one another. John was particularly touchy about pictures on the New York trip because he had his young bride with him and Brian Epstein had impressed upon us all the importance of keeping Cynthia out of media photographs. To my knowledge, Dezo Hoffmann never took any unwanted shots of Cyn, on her own or with John, but once the group had decided he was not to be trusted within the entourage, I knew there was no way I would be able to reverse their negative feelings. If I had tried too hard I would have risked being on the receiving end of a false accusation that I was sharing Hoffmann's profits.

Dezo's extensive library of historic 1962–1964 pictures remains a valuable archive to this day. His minimally posed studio shots of young Beatles are still widely published along with some of his gimmick-laden location material, particularly the set of photographs he made on the beach at Weston-super-Mare with the boys in Victorian bathing costumes. Hoffmann aimed the session specifically at the US market: "I knew I needed something strong. I had the idea of hiring bathing huts, old-fashioned swimming suits and so on. They loved dressing up in silly costumes, John kept his on back at the hotel long after the session was over." Hoffmann also said later that he believed Dick Lester was inspired by these shots when he directed *A Hard Day's Night*. Dezo Hoffmann's picture book *With The Beatles*, which included material he shot in America in 1964, had a quote from Paul on its back cover: "We thought Dezo was the greatest photographer in the world."

Intense rehearsals for their live and pre-recorded Sullivan shows were spread across two days and took place in the auditorium of CBS Television's Studio 50 on Broadway. On the second day, the Sunday when the first of The Beatles' appearances would be transmitted live, Ed Sullivan was not well pleased to find himself one Beatle short at morning rehearsals – George was back at the Plaza nursing a bad throat. Grovelling, which he did well when it was absolutely necessary, Epstein apologised for the lack of a fourth Fab, saying he was sure George would be OK by show time and in the meantime Neil Aspinall would stand in for camera rehearsal purposes. Po-faced and poker-voiced, the humourless Mr Sullivan replied: "He'd better be or I'll put on a wig myself." Apparently this was the closest the ageing Sullivan came to cracking a joke. Later, having seen how well the group went down with his studio audience, Sullivan suddenly became keen to tell as many people as possible about the part he played in spotting the group's potential popularity: "I was at London airport and there were mobs. There must have been 50,000 girls there. I said to Mrs Sullivan: 'Here is something'. It was just like years ago when I was travelling in the South and I used to hear the name Presley at fairs. Of course, he was all wriggling and sex. These boys are good musicians, these boys have something." A report in the *Herald Tribune* broke down that "something" into specifics: "75 per cent publicity, 20 per cent haircut and 5 per cent lilting lament." Meanwhile, Presley himself used a curious turn of phrase in welcoming The Beatles to his land: "If there's nothing but catfish in the market not many come to buy. If there are several kinds of fish it draws a bigger crowd, and that's good for showbusiness."

The boys were delighted by some of the descriptions of themselves that appeared in the US newspapers. One thought Paul shook his head on stage "like a wet puppy stepping out of a shower" and another writer called Ringo "the shaggiest of the bunch". The *New York Journal-American*'s somewhat pompous television critic did not enjoy The Beatles' performance on the 'Ed Sullivan Show': "Sartorially they're silly, tonsorially they're wildly sloppy, musically they're not quite hopeless." A majority of the show's record-splintering 73 million viewers seemed to disagree with this damning appraisal. Most media reviewers overlooked the fact that The Beatles' singing was a bit flat on some notes. In an interview with *Photoplay* magazine, Paul explained this away by saying that there was "something wrong with the microphones and we couldn't hear a thing we were singing". In the wake of the boys' first performance on US network television record sales soared and a total of two million American Beatle People placed advance orders for the next single, 'Can't Buy Me Love'.

Before leaving for Miami, the boys had a final night out on the town, returning to their new favourite clubbing destination, The Peppermint Lounge, where they partied with a gaggle of gorgeous women including the perky dancer Geri Miller and the actresses Tuesday Weld, Stella Stevens and Jill Haworth.

The second of The Beatles' live performances on the Sullivan show was televised from the Deauville Hotel, Miami Beach, on Sunday February 16. The local WFUN radio news director Larry Kane, later to become a top television journalist known as "the dean of Philadelphia television news anchors", attended the evening performance at the Deauville and wrote in his recent book *Ticket To Ride*: "For three Sunday nights, The Beatles owned the American television audience, satisfying their loyal fans beyond all expectation and instantly welcoming millions of new fans. I expected them to sound much different in person. After all, what group could duplicate the intricate sound of a produced recording? What I saw, along with millions of others watching at home, was a brilliant performance, unaccompanied by the embellishments of pre-taped music or the flourishes of extra musicians. It was plain and simple – four band members striking notes of harmony and grace. That twelve-minute segment on Sullivan, combined with the first appearance the week before, drew a television audience of 150 million people. In both performances, The Beatles were electric." Kane acknowledged in his book that Sullivan played a major role in the success of The Beatles' "American gamble" by offering them the platform of primetime television.

Although the Maysles' high-quality production started life as a humble but inventively shot television documentary, it has since taken on special significance as part of The Beatles' history. In the Sixties, relatively few celebrity documentaries were made and a pitifully small amount of visual evidence has survived on tape or on film into the new century to show what went on behind the scenes during the Beatlemania years. The film depicted John, Paul, George, Ringo and Brian Epstein, each doing their diverse jobs in a wide spread of situations. Much of the footage featured the band's impromptu fooling around in hotel suites and on the train between New York and Washington where, for example, George donned a waiter's hat and served drinks while

Ringo threw every available camera round his neck and staggered up and down the carriage making a hilarious spectacle of himself. Such sequences provided an amazingly accurate preview of the slapstick comedy style that would become a hallmark of The Fab Four's first (fictional) feature movie, *A Hard Day's Night*. Personally, I still find the unscripted and unrehearsed visual humour of the documentary, particularly Ringo's antics, funnier than the feature film. The Maysles' effort was eventually modified decades later in 1991 under the auspices of The Beatles' self-management company, Apple Corps, the current keeper of so much priceless and unique archive material on the group. Sequences from the 'Ed Sullivan Show' and the group's Washington concert were edited and the name of the ever-faithful former roadie Neil Aspinall, who had now become the boss of Apple, was added to the credits as Executive Producer.

At the end of their fortnight in America, the showbiz bible *Variety* declared that The Beatles had "shattered the steady day-to-day domination of made-in-America music here and abroad". At home in London a Fleet Street journalist called me: "I hear Paul married Jane Asher in America. She was seen with The Beatles in a wig and dark glasses on several occasions." Not so, I assured him. The mystery girl was Cynthia, John's wife. A publicist at Capitol Records told me that the money they had spent on the launch had done "what was expected of it and a whole load more". There would be no need for Capitol to mount further costly campaigns. The Beatles were now so well-established that the company's main job in future would be to release records at the most advantageous times and to see that adequate stocks were available to meet public demand. Less than a year earlier the Capitol supremo Alan Livingston had suggested to Brian Epstein that The Beatles might tour the United States as a supporting act to another of the label's groups, the Beach Boys.

For our part, we kept up the publicity pressure on US publications and radio stations in the knowledge that within six months The Beatles would be back in the USA for a full-blown concert tour. The size of the venues selected thus far for the month-long tour was awe-inspiring. Many were stadiums that had seating capacities between 10 and 20 times larger than the cinemas and theatres the band was accustomed to playing in Great Britain.

*

Without pausing for a break The Beatles threw themselves into a new round of recording sessions, including some of their freshly written songs that would be heard on the soundtrack of *A Hard Day's Night*. Knowing that they had less than a week to work with George Martin at Abbey Road before the first day's filming, Lennon and McCartney hastily put the finishing touches to the soundtrack songs – although the most urgent requirement was to complete the single 'Can't Buy Me Love' for release on both sides of the Atlantic in March. Work on recording this title had begun way back in January while The Beatles were in Paris, but there remained the all-important task of mixing and finally preparing masters. On the day that shooting began, I was sending out my last press release from the Monmouth Street offices to inform everyone that our much-postponed move to new headquarters in Argyll Street was about to happen. At Brian Epstein's command, the release revealed home telephone numbers for the company's key executives, although not of course Epstein's. This had less effect on me than on some of my colleagues in that Fleet Street was already accustomed to calling me at home outside business hours to discuss breaking news stories or confirm facts about our artists. At the same time Epstein signed a personal letter to each member of staff, stressing that "NEMS Enterprises provides the finest and most efficient management/direction of artists in the world". He added: "This must be without question our principal aim and should be borne in mind by all staff. Our organisation is very much in the public eye, it is most important that we present the best possible 'front'. By this I mean that ALL visitors must be treated with utmost courtesy. I really hope that you will be happy and as comfortable as possible in our new surroundings."

The making of *A Hard Day's Night* was a strange time for me. I was expected by Epstein and the boys to keep a constant eye on what went on in the way of media photography and interviews but I was unable to go on location or be present during any of the actual filming because of prevailing union regulations. I didn't have the right ticket to let me work on site as a unit publicist and in the movie world every slightest union rule had to be obeyed if financially damaging retaliatory action was to be avoided. A strike could cripple an entire shooting schedule and send budgets flying through the roof. For the duration of filming I had to co-ordinate everything from a distance through the officially recognised unit publicist and in turn he would refer special media requests to me for consideration. It was a long-winded business that made our working lives more difficult, but we coped. This coincided with a transition period when I didn't have a dedicated PR person specifically and exclusively looking after The Beatles on our behalf. Brian Sommerville was on his way out and Derek Taylor was not yet installed as his successor. On the first day of filming The Beatles also found themselves without the right union ticket to act in a movie. On location at Paddington station where initial train scenes were to be shot, frantic arrangements were completed for the boys to join the actors' union, Equity, their race-against-time membership being proposed and seconded on-the-spot by two of the supporting cast, the character actors Norman Rossington and Wilfred Brambell. Later that week, George took an immediate fancy to one of the pretty young actresses who were playing schoolgirl passengers on the train, his future wife, Pattie Boyd.

A little less than eight weeks later, the final scenes for *A Hard Day's Night* were filmed with Ringo cavorting for the cameras in a West Ealing street. The cast and crew joined the production team at the Turk's Head pub in St Margaret's, Twickenham, for a traditional wrap party. In professional moviemaking circles eight weeks was considered to be a dangerously short time-frame in which to shoot a full-length film for theatrical release. At the party, someone tried to make serious conversation with John on this topic and got the reply: "Well, it was only black and white, of course." The craziest part of the whole escapade was that The Beatles also managed to keep all manner of other appointments rather than giving their entire attention to filming. John launched his book *John Lennon In His Own Write*, confessing that it was made up largely of stuff he had jotted down on scraps of paper or drawn on the backs of envelopes. "There's nothing deep in it, it's just meant to be funny. If you like it, you like it; if you don't, you don't." The publisher, Jonathan Cape, sold almost a quarter of a million copies of the book, paving the way for a sequel, *A Spaniard In The Works*. In March and April The Beatles also attended the 12th annual Variety Club Awards at London's Dorchester Hotel on Park Lane, to pick up their Showbusiness Personalities of 1963 award, did a bunch of radio and television spots and started to rehearse their own television special, 'Around The Beatles', with the maverick director Jack Good. On the afternoon of Sunday, April 26, they topped the bill at Wembley's Empire Pool (later known as Wembley Arena) in the *New Musical Express* Annual Poll-Winners' concert, receiving their awards from the screen star Roger Moore.

Before the premiere of *A Hard Day's Night* in July the group fitted in a four-week trans-global concert tour that took them through Denmark and the Netherlands, on to Hong Kong and culminated in Australia and New Zealand. The most noteworthy aspect of these gigs was that Ringo was absent from the group's line-up, replaced at George Martin's recommendation by an unknown drummer named Jimmy Nichol until midway through the Australian dates. Ringo was laid low in London with severe tonsillitis and pharyngitis after collapsing during a photo shoot for the *Saturday Evening Post*. We crossed our fingers and hoped that we would not be faced with protests from disappointed Ringo fans. What if The Beatles met with booing at their concerts? But that didn't happen. Derek Taylor called me from most stops along the route of the tour and, to everybody's immense surprise and relief, was able to assure me that the substitution made absolutely no difference to The Beatles' reception at any point during the tour, and there was no apparent deterioration in the music they made on stage. This could only have happened with Ringo – The Beatles would have insisted on cancelling the trip altogether if John, Paul or George had fallen ill.

John and Paul had mixed feelings about their first full-length feature film. Paul said he found it hard to "act like a Beatle but conform to Alun Owen's script". John described Owen as "a professional Scouser (Liverpudlian)", complaining that many of the lines he gave them were based on a superficial acquaintance and a shallow assessment of their four personalities, which pigeon-holed each of them: John as witty, Ringo as dumb and so on. I argued that The Beatles were not supposed to be playing themselves but a quartet of screen characters concocted for them by Alun Owen, who just happened to be called John, Paul, George and Ringo. John said: "Bullshit! We believe it's about us, the fans will know it's us, it's a film about Beatlemania but because it's a musical there's an element of fantasy in it." He added that he felt self-conscious about the film's dialogue "because somebody else tried to write lines they thought we'd say in real life and got it very wrong, at least in parts". The general agreement among the group was that the screen version of the Fab Four made them into thinly-drawn caricatures and their basic fear was that the group itself would follow the example of *A Hard Day's Night* and cast themselves as fools in real life. This was precisely the opposite of the direction in which The Beatles wished to progress but they accepted the unarguable fact that the film would be a box office winner and an international crowd-pleaser. Made in black and white because United Artists wouldn't afford a colour production for a pop group with no track record in the cinema, the 85-minute film, just several minutes longer than the Maysles' piece, was rushed out that summer, premiering in the UK in July, and in the US the following month on the eve of The Beatles' first big concert tour of North America. The press reaction to *A Hard Day's Night* in the US was mainly flattering. The *New York Times* called it "a whale of a comedy", *The New York Daily News* said it was "clean wholesome entertainment not only for the teenagers but for grown-ups as well". Suggesting that the constant screaming that had become a fixture at Fab Four concerts was now finding its way into cinemas too, The *Washington Post* said: "The audience sort of over-participates." The film opened simultaneously at around 500 cinemas across the US, a perfect curtain-raiser for our upcoming tour.

Looking back, if the key role today of *A Hard Day's Night* in the context of The Beatles' history is to depict Beatlemania in a fun way for those who were not around in the Sixties, it does a fair enough job. The danger now, as then, lies in the ease with which one can forget the fictional script-based element altogether and think of *A Hard Day's Night* as a documentary portrayal of what the Fab Four were all about. Miraculously, in view of the little time they had to prepare it, the music on the soundtrack stood up satisfactorily alongside most of what the group had recorded before, although it didn't move them forward in any significant way in terms of their musical development. The only innovations here for those few souls who noticed them were the use by George of a new Rickenbacker 12-string guitar, a radically new and much sought-after instrument at the time, and the earliest influence of Bob Dylan on John Lennon's work. But the Fab Four's musical output stood little chance of making more substantial creative progress when most of their days were spent scampering from country to country, from job to job. Thankfully, the Lennon and McCartney combination often worked well under pressure, when deadlines loomed, and the numbers written for the soundtrack of *A Hard Day's Night* included several that were special even by the dynamic duo's high standards. Even our sternest critics had to admit that John and Paul never turned out soundtrack songs that were as dire as some of those to be encountered in Elvis Presley's screen vehicles.

The Beatles were denied any sort of pre-tour break before flying to the USA in August 1964. Right up to the last minute they were doing Sunday concerts at seaside resorts including Brighton, Bournemouth, Blackpool and Scarborough. Meanwhile, I discussed our media tactics for the US tour with Derek Taylor. I felt much more comfortable with Taylor than I had done with Sommerville, probably because of Derek's journalistic background, which made him sympathetic to the needs of the press on such a tour but also diplomatic and benign in his handling of The Beatles. I outlined the importance of holding daily one-to-one interview sessions for the handful of international journalists and deejays who would be on the road with the show. To avoid these sessions becoming overcrowded it was equally important to fix large press conferences to which local concert promoters could invite a wide range of local media people. Derek was pleased to hear that he would have an assistant press officer with him – Bess Coleman, who worked with us on the launch of The Beatles when she was with EMI Records in London. She had since relocated to New York where she was building her knowledge of the US music scene and its specialist writers.

As we made final tour preparations, August issues of America's teenybopper magazines carried useful editorial coverage of what John, Paul, George and Ringo had been up to in recent weeks together with new pin-up style publicity shots of the boys. Meanwhile, the fans' parents saw an amazing new picture on the cover of the *Saturday Evening Post* showing the boys in slick city-style business suits and bowler hats, each carrying a rolled umbrella. The headline read: "SUMMER MADNESS – THE BEATLES ARE BACK". But the visual message we successfully put across with the picture was that The

Beatles were a clean-cut group of smart youngsters, even if they did have mop-tops hidden beneath those bowlers.

The Beatles flew to San Francisco via Winnipeg and Los Angeles on August 18 for their opening gig at the Bay City's Cow Palace, a 17,000-seater venue where the boys got through their 12-song set in one minute under half an hour. This was almost certainly one of The Beatles' shortest stage performances as bill-toppers during their touring years but no complaints were made because Beatle People were only too pleased to spend 29 minutes in such a heavenly place. Inevitably, however, press reporters picked up on the brevity of the appearances at various places on the tour. In Canada, beneath a banner headline that ran "20,000 BEATLEMANIACS PAY SO MUCH—FOR SO LITTLE", reviewer William Littler wrote that fans at Vancouver's Empire Stadium had been treated to a mere 27 minutes of playing and singing by John, Paul, George and Ringo. He then went on to show the full extent of his dislike for the music of The Beatles: "As a music critic I have had to subject my eardrums to more than a little of the cacophony which currently dominates the hit parade, but the stuff shouted by three Liverpudlian tonsorial horrors left me particularly unimpressed." Ah, but what did he think of the fourth Beatle's singing? Too sickening to put in print or too wonderful for words? Supporting acts included the Righteous Brothers and the country-pop singer/songwriter Jackie DeShannon. With a headline that ran "FANS SWOON FOR THE HAIRY IDOLS", the *San Francisco Examiner* reported that, because of yelling fans, all that was heard was "something like jet engine shrieking through a summer lightning storm".

Contemporary celebrities galore, from Liberace to Pat Boone, turned up to meet the boys at their concerts. The star they were most eager to see for a second time was Bob Dylan, who turned up for the end-of-tour bash held in a top-floor suite of the Riviera Motel close to New York's Kennedy International airport. Brian Epstein met informally with Elvis Presley's mentor/manager Tom Parker and arranged for Paul and Elvis to talk on the phone. Both Paul and George had to deny reports that they were leaving the group, and Paul was repeatedly asked to confirm that he had married Jane Asher. At a lavish party thrown by the Capitol boss Alan Livingston the boys pressed the flesh of an impressive list of screen icons including Edward G

Robinson, Dean Martin, Jack Lemmon and Shelley Winters. John and the Hollywood sex symbol Jayne Mansfield met up and went clubbing together on Sunset Strip. In Kansas City, hotel managers sold the bed linen The Beatles had slept on and a Chicago businessman cut it up into 160,000 pieces and sold them to fans at one dollar each. Controversy surrounded a date in Jacksonville, Florida, when The Beatles refused to play to a racially segregated audience. Paul said: "We don't like it if there's any segregation, because we're not used to it." Hedging his bets a little to reduce the contention factor, he added: "It may seem right to some people, but to us it just seems a bit daft." The local concert promoter promised that the audience would not be segregated.

Departures from venues were being planned with increasing ingenuity. At the end of each concert, decoy Cadillac limousines were allocated to our media entourage while the boys clambered into less conspicuous getaway vehicles such as ambulances and delivery vans that were off and away before the audience realised that the group had left the building. Derek Taylor arranged with the party of travelling press people that they would be ready to leave the moment The Beatles finished their final song. Their signal to move was 'A Hard Day's Night', giving adequate time for everybody to be seated and locked in the decoy limousines which outsiders believed The Beatles would use while John, Paul, George and Ringo were on their last songs. Few promoters along the way understood in advance the full implications of securing their venues – and their stars. Arrogant local town halls and their police forces laughed off suggestions of any need for extra protection for the general safety of all concerned, including thousands of near-hysterical fans. They all thought they knew best and in most cases they were to learn their lessons the hard way. Too many young girls were injured at or near the concerts, too many hurt themselves in attempting to gatecrash the hotels and too many narrowly escaped death when they swarmed around and on top of moving vehicles in The Beatles' motorcades. On Labor Day weekend in Atlantic City, where The Beatles reportedly received a more boisterous reception than President Lyndon B Johnson, 18,000 noisy but orderly fans filled the Convention Hall, but sheer mayhem reigned outside when the police lost control of a mob of thronging fans. According to Derek Taylor, The Beatles' car was surrounded by kids. "They broke into each of our vehicles one by one, attacking Bess Coleman among others. They didn't know who we were. The police rescued us, barely. Atlantic City may have seen some wild conventions in its time but this was the biggest thing that ever happened. They're saying it's not like Sinatra, Presley or the late President Kennedy. It's The Beatles and it's without precedent."

Inadequate crowd control at open-air concert venues led to mass break-outs by fans and uncontrolled invasions of the stage. Concert comperes, usually deejays from local radio stations, joined forces with our own entourage of aides to keep the stage areas secure, but fans were breaking through police lines left, right and centre, causing The Beatles to speed up their performance, abbreviating or dropping the patter they'd prepared to link the songs. On more than one occasion their performance was halted and they left the stage while someone in authority calmed the crowd down and restored some order. In Cleveland, Derek Taylor carried out the task of cooling everyone down and the boys said he was particularly good at it because the American fans liked his smooth English accent and the fact that "he didn't yell at them like the cops did". To the average member of The Beatles' concert-going public who saw little of the tour's security failures and backstage problems, this series of gigs was mightily successful, a feeling shared by The Beatles, who, like the rest of us, set aside the bad memories and set the good ones in stone. The end-of-tour party at the Riviera Motel near JFK International was marred for those of us in the group's inner circle of aides and associates by the news that Derek Taylor had quit, both as PR man and as a personal assistant to Brian Epstein. The resignation, irrevocable this time, followed the latest flare-up in the stormy and contentious relationship between Taylor and Epstein. Taylor put it bluntly: "I'm not taking any more of this man's shit. I love The Beatles but I'm not hanging around to be fired another hundred times, I'm off."

The media tried to persuade Brian Epstein to put an accurate figure on the income earned by the Fab Four from the tour's two dozen or so shows, but he resisted the temptation and any figures published were journalists' guesswork. Norman Weiss of GAC commented that it would be impossible to work out what it cost to put on or precisely how much cash went to The Beatles but he added: "We could easily have charged three times the ticket price and still sold out, but Brian put maximum ticket prices in the promoters' contracts because the boys wanted to be fair to their fans." What Epstein did confess in private afterwards was his strategy for fixing the fees he demanded from concert promoters. The Beatles had never played such large venues and few other concert attractions were comparable in terms of popularity. Epstein told me he tried to find out the biggest fee previously paid to any top star to perform at each place. Then he'd ask for double that amount. I said: "Are we talking about double Presley's fee, Sinatra's or what?" He didn't answer but merely smiled and patted the side of his nose with an index finger. I knew what some promoters paid because I saw copies of their contracts and I think Epstein was grossly exaggerating. I guess he was giving me what he hoped might be the germ of a well-spun, albeit not entirely factual, story for the press, which I decided not to pursue. From the figures I knew, I remember working out at the time that The Beatles were earning an average of £1 for each US concert ticket sold.

In 1964 The Beatles turned their impossible dream into rewarding reality by gate crashing the American music market and holding the door open so that colleagues from London could follow them in. But after such a year of record-breaking international achievement, what was there left for The Beatles to do? What more could they possibly achieve? The answer was that they could give the most memorable stage performance of their career at New York's Shea Stadium, they could party with Elvis Presley at a summit meeting of the King of Rock'n'Roll and the Monarchs of Mersey Beat, and they could collect MBE awards from Buckingham Palace. And they would do all these things and more in 1965.

7 | On The Road Again

BY THE LAST months of 1964, Beatlemania was at boiling point in Britain and there were wild scenes of fan fever in towns and cities around the country as The Beatles took to the road again for their latest series of UK gigs. Now billed as the World's Top Disc Stars, the Fab Four began their latest homeland concert tour on October 9 at the Gaumont cinema in Bradford. With them went "special guest star" Mary Wells, "direct from America", plus no fewer than five new Epstein signings, Tommy Quickly, Michael Haslam, The Remo Four, The Rustiks and Sounds Incorporated. By then, Brian Epstein had realised exactly how much box-office cash from concerts was being allowed to leak away to outside impresarios who put on The Beatles' stage shows and he plugged the hole by co-presenting the new tour with our usual promoter, Arthur Howes. Although he pleased five of his own acts by putting them out with the Fab Four's package, both he and they might have realised that to support such a mighty popular bill-topper was a mixed blessing in that noisy, impatient Beatle People gave most other performers an exceedingly hard time. In this particular show only the marvellous Mary Wells and the sensational Sounds Incorporated managed to take the minds of the audience off John, Paul, George and Ringo.

The boys played over 50 shows in just under five weeks, bringing out mobs of ardent Beatle People who caused streets to be closed adjacent to the theatres and kept the group's fellow hotel guests awake half the night. Such riotous scenes generated front-page stories wherever we went, but the whole affair must have appeared pretty tame to John, Paul, George and Ringo after the much larger places to which they had grown accustomed in North America. With scarcely a pause for breath The Beatles did a string of promotional television and radio spots to coincide with the pre-Christmas release of their latest record, a double A-sided single that coupled 'I Feel Fine' with 'She's A Woman'. More or less simultaneously, the group commandeered the No 1 slot on the album charts with *Beatles For Sale*. Then they saw the old year out and the new year in at Hammersmith's Odeon cinema in 'Another Beatles Christmas Show' with a strong supporting cast headed by The Yardbirds, Elkie Brooks, Sounds Incorporated and Freddie and the Dreamers, compered by the eccentric 'Top Of The Pops' presenter Jimmy Savile. Meanwhile, The Beatles' music publisher, Dick James, who had been a professional singer in his past and had managed to enjoy chart success five years ago with his vocal version of television's 'Robin Hood' signature tune, decided the time was right to hit the market with a comeback single. He chose to record a medley of The Beatles' hits and succeeded only in proving to himself and the world that not all things Lennon and McCartney automatically turned to gold. Personal visits by the Fab Four to television studios for live broadcasts were becoming problematic to programme producers because the crowds of fans disrupted the making of other shows in the same building. The answer was to pre-record the group's spots at unexpected times and at unpublicised places, at short notice so that news of our plans had no time to travel along the fans' extremely efficient grapevine.

Looming largest on our calendar for 1965 was the next concert tour of North America because we realised that The Beatles' popularity in that vast territory would require constant refuelling, not only by regular record releases but also in-person appearances. Serious security failures and problems with stage equipment had to be addressed well in advance to avoid the chaos that had been repeated at numerous stops on the1964 US tour. We were doing well at winning over the minds of average US citizens, represented by those who watched the 'Ed Sullivan Show' the previous summer and approved of those nice-looking boys from Liverpool, England. Included in this category were not only Gloria Stavers' impressionable young readers, but also a vast number of mature middle Americans who generally deplored what they saw as the shoddy and even dangerous influence of rock'n'roll music on their sons and daughters, but who had taken the superficially clean-cut image of The Beatles to their hearts. They felt threatened by the new wave of mainly black American singers who chanted outrageous phrases like "awop-bop-aloobop-awap-bam-boom", which they couldn't pronounce, let alone understand. They failed to realise that rock'n'roll and sex were, are, and always will be one and the same thing. At this point, The Beatles were perceived to be neither sexual predators, nor political subversives but contemporary heroes – and this was the status quo we did our best to foster for the foreseeable future, in America and elsewhere around the world. While Elvis Presley was frowned upon for swivel-ling his pelvis, it was OK for the Fab Four to shake their fringes. The quivering quiffs were allowed even by the solemn, staid Ed Sullivan. Television producers insisted that the cameras should stay focused well above Presley's jiggling hips but The Beatles could be shot in full length from their shaking mop tops to their Cuban-booted-toes! All the fuss about Janet Jackson's briefly exposed right nipple on US network television as recently as 2004 indicates that after 40 years some things haven't changed.

Within several days of 'Another Beatles Christmas Show' closing in Hammersmith, Brian Epstein flew to New York to meet with GAC people. For the 1965 US tour we were keen to work with many of the same local promoters as last time, even if they had made mistakes. It was a case of the devil you know. On the other hand, we had to consider the advantages of going into new territories, places The Beatles had not visited previously, where tickets were likely to be snapped up fast. Before Epstein's trip, we made a list of the 1964 venues and tried to recall the best and the worst of each one, noting how primitive the sound system had been at this place or how comfortable the dressing rooms were at another. Most important, how many seats were there at the places that were OK in all other respects? Epstein made it clear to us in private that the bigger the money-making potential of each concert venue, the more interested he was in negotiating again for 1965, pushing hard to increase the group's fee wherever there was the slightest chance of doing so. If the profit motive had been subdued in the past, it was blatantly revealed now. I had the distinct impression that Epstein saw this as the peak year for Beatlemania – make or break time – and the time to cash in as aggressively and as quickly as possible on what he quite rightly predicted would be The Beatles' biggest-ever concert tour. Relying heavily on the acumen of his freshly appointed chief executive, Geoffrey Ellis, for advice on financial affairs, Epstein also wanted to maximise existing sources of long-term income other than personal appearances. This meant looking into the music publishing side of The Beatles' business and considering the idea of putting shares in Northern Songs on sale to the public. So the publishing company was launched on the London stock exchange in February 1965. At the same time they looked into ways of stashing the Fab Four's income in one or more faraway tax havens to reduce the total amount payable and, while they were at it, renegotiating the terms of the current miserly EMI recording contract to increase the artists' royalties.

At this time The Beatles seemed happier with life than at any other point in their career since the Cavern days. They laughed and smiled a lot, looked forward to their gigs, enjoyed making their music. In 1964 they had looked forward to their first major US concert tour with some awe and a lot of trepidation. America was tough uncharted territory, homeland of their greatest rock'n'roll idols from Chuck Berry to Little Richard, Buddy Holly to Bill Haley. Having proved to themselves that America wanted The Beatles, they could return there in 1965 full of confidence and bursting with high spirits.

The spin-off benefits of gaining fame and having best-selling records were beginning to make sense to the boys. They could quit their flats and buy big houses, whether in St John's Wood or Surrey. John, Cynthia and their son Julian had already moved out of central London in the summer of 1964 and bought a 27-room mock Tudor mansion called Kenwood in Wood Lane on the exclusive St George's Hill estate at Weybridge. A year later, Ringo and Maureen became the Lennon family's neighbours, buying a house called Sunny Heights on South Road, St George's Hill. In February 1965, George and his partner, Pattie Boyd, chose Esher, buying a small but exclusively located bungalow named Kinfauns on Claremont Drive, part of the private Claremont Estate. Paul was the only remaining "townie", staying with Jane Asher's family in Wimpole Street until 1966 and then buying 7 Cavendish Avenue, a three-storey detached house in St John's Wood, NW8 – one of the many homes he still owns today. Having conquered America, the Fab Four could afford just about anything on their wish lists, from luxurious holidays to classy cars.

George lost little time in deciding to switch his E-type Jag for a James Bond model, a white Aston Martin DB5. As soon as possible after their Christmas show they took off on holidays. Paul and Jane chose a villa in the (then) undeveloped Tunisian resort of Hammamet, while John and Cyn went to the Swiss Alps for some (novice) skiing and bob-sleighing with record producer George Martin and his future wife, Judy Lockhart-Smith. I remember asking George to tell me his holiday plans and he replied: "I've got a new nest to feather so I'm holidaying at home." Meanwhile, Ringo married his long-time fiancée and hometown sweetheart from Cavern days, hairdresser Maureen Cox, at very short notice. Brian Epstein took personal charge of making the wedding arrangements, warning us that heads would roll all over the place if details of the secret register office ceremony leaked out. The couple honeymooned for just three days afterwards at the weekend home of Brian Epstein's lawyer, David Jacobs, in secluded Prince's Crescent, Hove, where swarming press reporters and photographers broke up the out-of-season peace of this respectable English south coast resort by besieging the bride and groom until they gave an impromptu press conference in Jacobs' unglamorous back yard. At the Caxton Hall ceremony, a smiling George Harrison commented: "Two down, two to go."

We were not at all surprised by the fact that Ringo and Maureen were marrying. In the privacy of The Beatles' inner circle, they had acted like a pair of love birds, cuddling "ascloseasthis" at clubs and parties for as long as we could remember. (Writers of the *Alley Cat*, the back-page gossip column in the *New Musical Express*, invented the word "ascloseasthis" to describe loving relationships; they also used the self-explanatory word "infanticipating" to describe what often followed.) The only thing that shocked us was how quickly the wedding plans were put together. Paul didn't make it to the ceremony because he was still in Tunisia. In those long-gone days before fax and e-mail the fastest form of international communication other than the phone was the telegram. A local telephone operator read our telegram to Paul saying: "Rich wed early this morning." The boys called Ringo by shortenings of his real name, Richie or Rich. Paul told me later that he had difficulty understanding the Tunisian operator: "I thought she was on about early morning tea and I couldn't see why we were getting a message about that from London. When the original telegram was delivered the following morning I still didn't get it. Eventually, I saw the wedding story when we picked up a newspaper and realised it referred to Richie and Mo getting married. It was just a drag I wasn't there because I would have enjoyed it." The main reason for marrying suddenly in the Sixties was the discovery that one's girlfriend was pregnant, so we all started counting the months from February 11. Maureen gave birth to their first child, Zak, on September 13.

On February 22, less than a fortnight after Ringo's wedding, The Beatles packed their bags again and flew to the Bahamas to begin filming *Help!* at locations on New Providence Island. When asked which he preferred doing, concert tours or films, Paul countered with an obvious question of his own: "If you were lying about in London on a perishing cold February day and some bloke said 'Hey! Let's fly off to the Bahamas to make a film', how do you think you'd feel about it?" Then he answered more seriously: "I like doing a film for a change but the waiting around while they change cameras and all that gets boring. With a film you've got to wait months before you see how the whole thing has turned out. With a concert you get reaction from an audience right away."

In 1965 backstage VIP catering facilities for concert stars were primitive or non-existent. Today the job is done by specialist companies and a band like The Beatles would enjoy five-star gourmet meals between performances. In the Sixties "catering" consisted of sending Neil or Mal to the nearest takeaway, so one thing the boys liked about filming as against touring was the food they could get during their working day. On one occasion I discussed the topic of eats-on-the-job with John, who told me: "Film people know how to eat. They have mobile canteens when you're on location, but getting decent meals is still the most difficult thing about touring. In the early days on the road in Britain when most of our concerts took place in cinemas, we just got Neil to buy us hot dogs from the front foyer of the cinema. Then we got around to sending out to caffs for proper hot meals, but by the time they reached us they were greasy, soggy and lukewarm-to-cold."

There were several reasons for choosing the Bahamas as one of the two main places where *Help!* would be made. The gloriously warm and sunny climate clearly appealed to the boys and they believed they could indulge in their latest pastime of smoking unbranded cigarettes more freely and with less fear of hassle from the authorities or the media in the relaxed environment of the Bahamas. It became common knowledge on the film set that the boys were increasingly and openly smoking pot to relieve their stress and alleviate their irritation with the slow filmmaking process. Lennon put the situation in a nutshell: "We were smoking marijuana for breakfast." There was another good reason for filming in such a paradise. Their presence on a working assignment added credence and substance to the plan hatched by Epstein and Ellis to keep most of the group's movie earnings tucked away in a Nassau-based bank account. It was good to let the dreaded taxman see that the boys were actually spending a little time in the region where their dosh was stashed. They were booked into sumptuously appointed accommodation at the Balmoral Club, whose very name had a ring of high colonial luxury about it.

As had been the case with *A Hard Day's Night*, the producer Walter Shenson and director Dick Lester agreed that it was pointless to give the characters The Beatles were playing any names other than their own. Calling the new production a mad, zany comedy thriller, Shenson confessed that he couldn't see The Beatles improving their acting skills "in a million years, maybe more" but promised that *Help!* would be visually spectacular. Shenson and Lester surrounded the Fab Four with a larger team of well-known professional British actors for *Help!*, including Leo McKern, Eleanor Bron, Roy Kinnear, Warren Mitchell, Alfie Bass, Patrick Cargill and the perennial Victor Spinetti, most of them playing comic-strip heroes or villains. Also hired to play a drama teacher charged with the job of giving elocution lessons to The Beatles was the very camp, often brilliant comedian Frankie Howerd, but unfortunately his entire sequence finished up on the cutting-room floor. The main difference was that *Help!*, a sort of *Carry On James Bond* production with music, would be shot in colour, a must if photogenic locations like Nassau and the Austrian Alps were to be shown off to best advantage on the big screen. While black and white suited the newsreel atmosphere of *A Hard Day's Night*, colour was needed for a fairly limp story that relied upon the appeal of fantasy characters (such as a corny old mad scientist) and a crazy plot set against a series of exotic backdrops.

Shooting in the Bahamas was not without its moments of off-camera fun. One scene that centred upon Ringo jumping into the sea from a yacht caused the cameramen problems and had to be re-shot several times. Eventually, Ringo pleaded: "Please, not again." "Why ever not?" queried Lester. "I can't swim!" "You didn't say!" "I didn't like to!" The Beatles had looked forward to sunshine in Nassau but, as Paul observed, "it started to rain almost every time we finished filming and could have been lying on the sand". George had his own theory: "We're not shooting the film in chronological order so they don't want us to look tanned when we come to do the alpine scenes in Austria. I reckon the producers have organised this wet weather with the rain gods."

If Lennon and McCartney had been given more time, they might have followed the conventional method of writing songs for stage or screen musicals, dropping relevant songs into carefully selected places in the story where the action would be enhanced or actually moved forward in some way via the lyrics. Instead, as Paul admitted at the time, their way of doing it to such a strict deadline consisted simply of writing enough songs for the soundtrack and then finding spots where the action could be halted and held up while the songs were performed. With their popularity at such a high peak, The Beatles did not have to worry about such details. One major responsibility that The Beatles did take on was to think up a good title – around which they would have to write words and music. At the beginning, *Help!* was not at hand and Dick Lester's first idea of calling the film *Beatles 2* met with instant opposition. "How can we write a song called Beatles 2?" asked John. This was ruled out and Ringo suggested *Eight Arms To Hold You*, which even appeared on some early promotional copies of soundtrack recordings. The film's shooting moved from the Bahamas to Austria, on to Salisbury Plain in south-west England and, finally, to Twickenham in west London – still with no title number in the can. Eventually, when *Help!* was chosen, John and Paul did one of their fastest-ever writing jobs to create the title song. Paul left this one to John, who said to me: "I'm glad they ditched Ringo's title, that would have been a real old fucker to write! I'd have passed that one back over to Paul!"

One could never be sure with Lennon whether stuff he said was on the level or tongue-in-cheek. For example, when he told journalists later that his lyrics for *Help!* represented a real-life personal cry from the soul, was he playing around with them or confessing to genuine self-doubt? Doing his drama queen bit, which he was good at when the situation suited and there were reporters around to hear him, John said: "Most people think it's just a fast rock'n'roll song. I didn't realise it at the time, I just wrote the song because I was commissioned to write it for the movie, but later I knew I really was crying out for help. I am singing about when I was so much younger and all the rest, looking back at how easy it was. Now I may be very positive but I also go through deep depressions where I would like to jump out of the window. I was fat and depressed and crying out for help." My own interpretation is that he was feeling jaded, fed up, no worse than that, but his emotions welled up and got the better of him as he wrote *Help!* He had found the filming schedule painfully boring because of all the waiting around between each scene. He had voiced dissatisfaction over his own somewhat uninspiring role, describing it to Dick Lester as a "bit part in a daft film" but a daft film with music by the Fab Four probably ticked all the boxes for the majority of Beatle People. In the event the title number from *Help!* went down as one of the most powerful commercial hits in the John Lennon songbook. Although Paul was generally accepted by the rest of us as the Beatle with the most acting ability, Ringo was the one who had the most right to be totally happy with his contribution to *Help!* His natural flair for silent comedy, seen a year earlier in the documentary footage shot in America by the Maysles brothers, came to the fore, creating a mix of likeable lunacy and comic mime that the cameras loved. He found it easy to pull faces and do silly walks. Moreover, he was pleased to find himself so much closer to the centre of activity on the film sets than he usually was in the recording studios at Abbey Road.

While The Beatles were shooting final sequences for *Help!* at Twickenham Film Studios a right royal drama was unfolding behind the scenes at NEMS Enterprises – and I mean a Royal drama. We had augmented the fan club's staff substantially after the scandalous delays in dealing with incoming letters and membership applications experienced during the autumn of 1963 but it was still common to find a fair number of unopened mail bags in the office awaiting attention. The fan club's Monmouth Street address had been thoroughly publicised at the time of our move to Argyll Street in March 1964 but a number of teenybopper fanzines around the world continued to publish out-of-date information resulting in fan mail arriving at both our addresses. Occasionally, this meant that The Beatles' business mail became mixed up with fan mail. To our horror one day we found four official-looking envelopes in a sack that was waiting to go over to Monmouth Street, each addressed formally to a Beatle. It was obvious from other surrounding mail that these had been lying in our offices for some time. Could they be subpoenas of some sort? It was well known that in the pop music business, writs and hits went hand-in-hand. Or were they tax demands from the Inland Revenue, perhaps? Not a bunch of paternity suits, not four at a time surely?! When we opened the envelopes we found letters to John, Paul, George and Ringo from Downing Street informing them that the Prime Minister Harold Wilson had recommended each of The Beatles for Member Of The Order Of The British Empire (MBE) awards in the forthcoming Queen's Birthday honours list. Such invitations required the written acceptance of potential recipients by a given date and we were relieved to see that we had not missed the deadline – which might well have led to automatic invalidation. Brian Epstein was not available so the documents were shown to Geoffrey Ellis. He decided that they needed to be rushed to The Beatles by hand for signatures of acceptance despite the fact that this risked bursting in on them and interrupting work on *Help!* The four boys were genuinely impressed by the offer of MBE "gongs" and signed their letters amid hugs and broad grins. By curious coincidence the final scenes for the film involved exterior shots of Buckingham Palace which were to be edited with interior shots showing The Beatles in rooms dressed to resemble those at the royal residence but actually done at Cliveden House, the home of Lord and Lady Astor, near Maidenhead. George said: "We'll have to see if this place is as posh as Buck House."

On the morning of Saturday, June 12, the official announcement of the MBE awards broke in all the national papers and a battery of media reporters and photographers – particularly from the Sunday newspapers – invaded Twickenham Studios where The Beatles were being shown the first rough cut version of *Help!* We made an instant decision to round everyone up and hold a proper press conference rather than face a day of disorganised approaches from individual journalists. Coming during a weekend, when Fleet Street was often (and is today) short of news stories, the MBE news received extensive coverage internationally in all media, press, radio and television, a timely burst of publicity to boost box-office ticket sales for our upcoming August concert dates in America, where there was always a healthy appetite for any story associated with British Royalty.

Around this time I prised open a narrow window of opportunity in which to fix a few interviews for the boys before they left London to do a short series of gigs in France, Italy and Spain. I admit that by the summer of 1965 we were becoming as blasé about voluminous press coverage as we were about getting records to the top of the charts. We expected The Beatles' singles to go straight to No 1 and, for my part, I was demanding front cover pictures from magazines that wanted to interview the boys. I had only to notice a forthcoming primetime television appearance in our diary and I was on the phone to the *TV Times* or *Radio Times* to talk about cover shots. Most editors agreed because they knew that putting the faces of John, Paul, George and Ringo on front covers guaranteed extra sales. I used some of this interview time to collect material for some articles I was "ghosting" in their names for pre-tour publication in US magazines. I found out that John's latest hobby harked back to his college days: "I've bought all the gear, brushes, paints and canvases, and I'm doing odd bits of painting but I never get enough free time so I've got a pile of half-done pictures so far." George looked back on filming in the Bahamas: "We had trouble with the spectators in Nassau who didn't wait until the end of each scene but walked straight up to us for autographs while we were standing in front of rolling cameras. My best memory of the Bahamas is the seafood dishes, some of them called the same as they would be in England but with very different tastes so that you never knew what to expect." Paul was taking in the technicalities of filming: "When you see an outdoor scene and the actors are miles away from the camera, they can't use microphones so if there's dialogue they have to put it on the soundtrack afterwards. That's called overdubbing." I asked Ringo to talk about the continental dates: "We don't expect to have any language problems on the tour – we'll just go about not understanding anybody." Paul joined in: "If they ask about our new album in Spain I'll just tell them it's *El Helpo!*"

Nothing weightier than this sort of stuff was needed to satisfy the teenybopper magazines and at least it was one step up from: "What's your favourite dish?" "What colour do you like best?" and "What do you look for in a girl?"

As The Beatles' fame became more widespread so did media interest in their personal lives, including incidents and episodes that they preferred to keep private for one reason or another – not always scandalous stuff but stories that touched sensitive nerves. It was my responsibility to play down or wholly suppress stories we considered to be detrimental, or stories the boys found embarrassing. Showbusiness PR practitioners have always made a big deal of the protective aspect of the job, inferring that this is the area where true professional expertise comes into play. Protecting The Beatles from damaging press grew to be an important concern for me but the solution was not particularly complicated once I had established a good working relationship, not only with journalists but their influential editors. When an inquisitive reporter came across an "awkward" news story about a Beatle that we wanted to keep out of the paper, my answer was to offer the editor an equally interesting but more positive story on an exclusive basis if he dropped the one we disliked. It might not work today, but it did in the more friendly Fleet Street of the Sixties. Give the dog a new bone to get his teeth into and he'll drop the old one at which he's been gnawing away. It was never going to be possible totally to prevent Fleet Street – particularly the popular tabloids – from having a go at the boys from time to time, but this technique worked well as a rule.

It was inevitable that having spent at least 18 months helping to build up The Beatles with positive stories, the press were by now only too ready to take a knock at us on unsold concert tickets. An *Associated Press* report from Rome suggested that on the European mini-tour there had been "no full houses yet for The Beatles". In Genoa "the audience barely reached 5,000, including 1,000 police on hand to keep order." Perhaps, said *PA*, the current heatwave was keeping the crowds down. To be frank, I never thought of the continental European market as being close to the epicentre of Beatlemania. As long as I was getting healthy feedback from our US concert promoters about the brisk business being doing at advance box offices over there I was satisfied that John, Paul, George and

Ringo were not losing their touch in the part of the world where it mattered most.

Strong concert ticket sales in the US were matched by high demand among American editors for fresh material on the Fab Four. In today's fiercely cash-conscious PR climate we would have been negotiating enormous fees for each interview The Beatles gave. Today's typical showbusiness PR person is little more than a trader whose job is to sell his or her famous clients for cash to the highest-bidding publishers with little or no regard for career longevity or image protection. In the Sixties we carefully separated promotion and sales. All but the most exceptional stories were treated as useful publicity rather than additional sources of income. With a band of The Beatles' calibre we were able to demand maximum editorial control over the way feature articles finished up in print. We deemed this power to be vital in controlling the continuity of The Beatles' image. Often we had the final say over the choice of pictures used to illustrate an interview-based article and we would claim the power of veto over copy that we considered to be in any way unflattering or detrimental. With a top-earning group such as The Beatles, this was a much more satis-factory situation than simply selling their words and photographs to whichever editors might have been prepared to pay the most money.

By 1965 we were also making the most of each interview and photo shoot by encouraging syndication at every opportunity. This meant that a single feature article or picture spread would not merely appear once in the original UK publication that commissioned it but would be made available internationally to appear many times in different territories around the world, having been passed on through syndication agencies to editors for local reproduction. What we derived from syndication was wider exposure without the need to do additional interviews. In the period leading up to The Beatles' 1965 series of US concerts, syndicated material originated in the UK played a large part in our pre-tour PR campaign and at the same time simplified my job.

Getting complimentary stories in newspapers and magazines may have been at the core of my job but there were important peripheral tasks to be taken care of when it came to getting The Beatles' show on the road. At Brian Epstein's request I became directly involved with co-ordinating security strategies with local concert promoters in the US. This included devising and producing effective access passes so that the right people could get into restricted areas at concert venues. Apparently, backstage security had broken down on numerous occasions in 1964. I made the new passes as distinctive as possible and shipped off suitable quantities to the US accompanied by detailed pamphlets that included illustrations of specimen badges with different colours designated for performers, concert management and media. In an operation the size of a Beatles' tour there are bound to be inevitable flaws. In the case of my meticulously planned security passes, I have no doubt that concert promoters duly distributed the passes and the accompanying information efficiently to their security people but at ground level a lot of the guys ultimately responsible for controlling points of entry and access chose to ignore our instructions and invent their own set of rules as to who was allowed through and who was turned away. Significantly, most of the venues that had presented The Beatles the previous year were much more efficient at security and other logistics by the time the 1965 concerts came around. It was the newcomers who thought they knew best and didn't need management advice from London that caused us the most headaches. Women among our management team and our travelling media entourage came off worst because there appeared to be a prevailing mentality among American security people that females couldn't possibly have significant professional roles to play and therefore should not be granted any sort of privileged access!

In the month before we flew to America, there was a great flurry of record releases on both sides of the Atlantic. The group's latest Capitol compilation, called *Beatles VI*, went to No 1 in the US album charts. The soundtrack album *Help!* and a single featuring the title song coupled with 'I'm Down' came out to coincide with the UK and US film premieres and were instant best-sellers.

On Friday, August 13, we flew from London to New York and the boys were immediately upset when they saw the first evidence of tightened security after we touched down at Kennedy International Airport. Instead of approaching the terminal buildings and giving hundreds of fans a close-quarters chance of welcoming the group our TWA aircraft taxied some two miles away into a remote corner of the airport to offload The Beatles. Although they had agreed to this move back home in London, the boys now argued that it was unfair to deny frustrated fans the slightest glimpse of them. We shifted the blame onto the airport authorities, muttering stuff about "public safety considerations" but the group remained in disgruntled mood as we swept them off in limousines to the Warwick Hotel. Outside the hotel, located on the corner of Sixth Avenue and 54th Street, it became clear that someone had tipped off New York City's Beatle People to the new precautions in place at the airport because there were more fans outside the Warwick than at JFK. Seeing this mob of waving fans and hearing the rapturous reception they were being given, the boys visibly brightened and George said to me: "So the Americans still like us, after all." It must have crossed their minds that maybe we had avoided the airport terminal building because too few fans were gathered there to greet them.

Often on this and other tours I arranged for press conferences to take place in my own hotel suite. This was very convenient because I could tell journalists in advance where to come to before I even knew my room number. It also ensured that I was allocated a large suite, which annoyed Brian Epstein when his didn't live up to mine. I made an exception at the Warwick, having been warned by Sid Bernstein, the New York-based promoter of the tour's opening show at Shea Stadium, that this would be a particularly large event and we would need to use the hotel's ballroom or most spacious function facility. As usual, I arranged to hold the conference as quickly as possible after our arrival because this reduced the pressure of media questions and requests for the rest of our stay. Also the quicker I held the initial New York conference the more chance I had of rounding up the boys before they found their beds and fell asleep after the tedious transatlantic flight. I took a look at the long banqueting room that Sid Bernstein had booked and guessed it would hold up to 100 people comfortably. "How many people are we expecting?" I asked him. "Around 250," he replied proudly, adding, "That includes the competition winners and such like." So much for my pre-tour briefing that pleaded with all promoters to make press conferences properly businesslike affairs by restricting invitations to accredited professionals! Bernstein was beaming with innocent delight as if he had successfully "sold out" his conference and I left him to wallow in his sense of self-achievement.

The next time I entered that room it was heaving wall to wall with a mixed assortment of noisy, chattering press photographers, television cameramen, journalists, deejays, a lot of technical lighting and sound equipment – and scores of over-excited teenage competition winners! Those towards the sides and back of the room stood on chairs and tables. The Beatles' table was covered with microphones belonging to radio stations. As usual I placed name cards in front of our own four individual microphones where each Beatle would sit. Even at this late stage I felt it necessary to identify the four for the benefit of non-specialist media people and I always made a point of laying out the cards in the same left-to-right sequence: John, Paul, George, Ringo. There was a wild stampede when I invited photographers to come down and position themselves in front of the table at which The Beatles would sit. Politely, but as firmly as possible, I told a couple of dozen teenagers that their competition win did not qualify them as photographers in this particular situation and asked them to move back to their seats. Hiding reddened flight-weary eyes behind sunglasses, Brian Epstein asked if I knew about the planned presentation of a set of gold discs to mark one million sales of the new *Beatles VI* album and I told him it was all in hand. Then I brought in the boys to tumultuous prolonged applause and the first thing they did was to change their seating sequence and make a bit of pantomime business over the name cards, revising the left-to-right to become Ringo, John, George and Paul with me leaning over Paul's shoulder with a fifth microphone of my own to communicate with the assembled crowd. Let the snapping begin.

As always the standard of questioning throughout the press conference was abysmal. From a professional, not a teenybopper prizewinner: "What do you think of girls from Brooklyn?" Other typical samples:

Question: How do you add up success?
Answer: (all four in unison)   Money!

Question: Would you ever accept a girl into the group?
Ringo: How tall is she?

Question: Did you use four-letter words on the tourists when you were filming in the Bahamas?
John: Yes. I said, "Gosh".

Question: George, is the place where you were brought up like
    Greenwich Village?
George: No. More like the Bowery.

For the most part the fans listened intently and clicked away with their cameras. The sheer size of the conference – and the fact that this was New York – meant that I had to let the questioning go on longer than usual. In the circumstances the boys were patient and dealt charmingly with even the least intelligent questions. When time was up we hustled John, Paul, George and Ringo to the closest service lift (how did those six girls get in there?) and took them back to our heavily guarded 33rd floor. "You haven't finished yet," Epstein warned the boys. "We've promised a few deejays a taping session in your suite in half an hour." Four-letter words filled the air and the little girls at the back of the lift giggled. As we left the lift I wrenched the last of the Fab Four from the clamping arms of a weeping, giggling blonde and pressed the Lobby button for her. Throughout our several days at the Warwick The Beatles were almost unnervingly co-operative in every situation from their intensive 'Ed Sullivan' television studio rehearsals to their informal chat with the youthful staff of Beatles (USA) Limited, during which Paul instigated a game of Scrabble with the all-but-overwhelmed girls – John won by including words none of us had ever heard of.

Saturday's 'Sullivan' rehearsals took almost ten hours because of horrendous sound problems that the boys insisted upon sorting to their satisfaction. A year earlier when The Beatles did their first appearance on Sullivan's show I doubt if his people would have let us go into so much expensive studio overtime in the pursuit of better quality sound. Each time we left the Warwick to drive across town to the 'Sullivan' studio located at West 53rd Street and Broadway, NYPD traffic cops rode ahead of us, clearing busy main streets of traffic to allow our convoy a non-stop run through red lights and even at one point down a No Entry side street. West 53rd Street was blocked off at both ends. Although The Beatles were less tense than when we did the 1964 shows for Sullivan, John in particular was ill at ease in the studio, sweating a lot, clasping and unclasping his hands nervously and clearing his throat incessantly. As the time approached for Paul to rehearse his 'Yesterday' he became as visibly agitated as John. Sullivan himself was far more friendly to us than last year, which helped to ease the atmosphere. In the event, Paul did a marvellous 'Yesterday' and John roared through 'Help!', both giving performances that were as near flawless as the television environment allowed.

We got the same VIP traffic treatment from the NYPD on the Sunday when we raced from the Warwick to Manhattan's East Side waterfront heliport en route to Shea Stadium. Hotly pursued by a mob of screaming fans, we ran from our limousines towards the waiting helicopter. Suddenly, above the screams of the teenyboppers, I could hear an urgent shout just behind me. A cop was yelling: "Hey, are you Epstein? Which of you guys is Epstein?" It sounded as if some serious crisis had arisen so I pointed him in Brian's direction and kept running. The cop grabbed a startled Brian Epstein by the shoulder, swung him round and shouted into his face: "You're the guy I need! I want two sets of autographs for my daughters. Here are their books. Get them back to me at the Precinct. They'll love you for it. We'll all love you forever. Have a great show at Shea!"

The helicopter trip was sheer magic. As we flew out over Manhattan and the East River, Paul stared out of the window at the wondrous sight of the New York city lights shimmering and shining below us. For George and John it was a white-knuckle flight. George couldn't see the need for it and swore he'd go alone by road next time – but faced with fear he liked to counter-attack by saying something funny. I told him: "We've asked the pilot to circle a few times so that we can see the sights of Manhattan." George replied: "Well, tell him to forget that and fly straight to Shea Stadium. I don't want to be impaled on the top of the Empire State Building." Ringo tried to capture the sensational views on film but he knew that nothing he shot could capture the breathtaking reality of the Manhattan skyline. When we reached the airspace around Shea Stadium even George forgot to be nervous and smiled broadly. Below us some 56,000 fans realised that The Beatles were circling the stadium and thousands of flashbulbs popped off almost simultaneously to create a momentary display of dazzling light that lit up the evening sky. For the first time as we looked down at this unforgettable sight, it dawned upon four awe-struck Beatles that this might just turn into the greatest gig the group had ever done. Utterly overwhelmed, we descended in stunned silence to the landing site of The World's Fair, a mile or so from the concert venue, and transferred into a waiting Wells Fargo armoured truck. Each Beatle was given a Wells Fargo Agent's badge, the real thing, and we were told: "OK, hold on tight! We'll drive you to the rear of the stadium and take you all the way round the field to second base. That's as close as we can get to your dressing rooms."

While the boys waited backstage the supporting acts took to the stage one by one. Sid Bernstein's protégés, The Young Rascals, The King Curtis Band, Cannibal And The Head Hunters, Brenda Holloway and our own Sounds Incorporated did their stuff. The Beatles lost all their usual pre-show nerves as they heard the resounding welcome being given to the other artists. At the last moment they donned their new khaki military-style stage uniforms and, surrounded by our entire management entourage, they headed at a jog-trot for the makeshift platform erected in the middle of the field. During the following 30 minutes The Beatles gave the most memorable performance of their short-lived concert career – not the finest musically, far from it, because few stage shows offered a suitable environment for anything approaching artistic perfection, but certainly a one-off experience worth remembering for a lifetime. As he watched the whole show from a vantage point on the grass to one side of the stage, Brian Epstein's face glowed with pride. Tears of joy ran down his cheeks long before the boys finished their set. The main reason for this very special performance was that John, Paul, George and Ringo were hugely excited by their surroundings, by the unprecedented size of that stadium audience and the sheer electricity that was sparking away across the field between the stage and the stands. Inspired by the grand setting and the fantastic reception from the fans, their performance was thrice as large as life. They exaggerated every facial expression and bodily gesture in order to reach out to the crowd on the far side of this vast field. Never before had I seen the Fab Four play and sing with greater energy and enthusiasm. Their every slightest wave of a hand was rewarded with a swelling scream of response and the place went totally wild when John ran his elbow down the keys of his electric piano, the nearest he'd ever get to a Jerry Lee Lewis impression. If Shea Stadium had had a roof it would have been well raised by the end of The Beatles' half-hour stint on stage. They ran off with their shirts and hair dripping, big bath towels around their necks, into the Wells Fargo wagon and off into the night. As we drove away, the continuous screaming of the crowd ringing in our ears, the four boys expressed complete satisfaction with the show, something that rarely happened on tour. Even the sound system got a thumbs-up. As we travelled along in the claustrophobic truck I was already re-living highlight moments of an evening that would stand forever as the most vivid memory of my six years with them. Shea Stadium '65 was in a class of its own. This was the ultimate pinnacle of Beatlemania. This was the group's brightly-shining summer solstice, after which all The Beatles' days would insidiously grow a little darker.

Back at the Warwick I threw a celebratory late-night party in my suite. The original idea was to let members of our travelling media group get to know one another – and us! – but it developed into a come-one-come-all event attended by The Beatles, the media people and several surprise visitors including The Supremes and Del Shannon. Brian Epstein glided around the room shaking everybody's hand and still radiating the pride and joy he'd shown as he watched his boys in action at Shea. The boys were in fine fettle, circulating constantly, cracking jokes and welcoming reporters and radio people they recognised from the 1964 tour.

The boys found it hard to believe that they had a free day after Shea. In fact, this was what the Americans called the "rain check" day for Shea Stadium – if the weather had been bad the concert would have been set back 24 hours. After that we took to our chartered Lockheed Electra aircraft for the rest of the tour, beginning with a flight to Canada for a pair of indoor shows at Toronto's Maple Leaf Gardens. The plane carried not only The Beatles and our immediate circle of aides but also the show's supporting cast, plus everyone from the stage crew to the souvenir brochure salespeople. The other artists and the travelling media party expressed surprise that The Beatles did not hide themselves away in some sort of First Class cabin. They didn't even have reserved seats. Instead, all four boys wandered up and down the aisles chatting freely with everyone and finding seats at random, which much impressed the Americans. The British press was represented by Don Short from the *Daily Mirror* and Chris Hutchins from the *New Musical Express*. Among the US contingent we had Marilyn Doerfler, representing the giant Hearst Newspapers chain, and a mixed bag of radio people led by Larry Kane, news director of WFUN in Miami, who had syndicated his tour reports to 45 stations coast to coast across the US in 1964, and including on some or all legs of the trip Paul Drew from Atlanta and Jim Stagg from Chicago. We agreed on one ground rule with the deejays and journalists – no interviewing on the aircraft. As the tour progressed and individual Beatles made particular friends of various reporters this restriction was set aside by mutual consent to allow occasional interviews. The Beatles never complained to me that this facility was abused. When the boys were not mixing with the rest of us in the aircraft's main cabin they were to be found in a small area curtained off at the rear where they set up an elite little card school in which Neil, Mal and several journalists participated on a regular basis throughout the tour. Whenever I poked my head in to see how the game was going, Paul seemed to be winning, clutching a pile of dollar bills and grinning from ear to ear.

After Toronto came Atlanta where a brilliant sound system (by Sixties standards) at a newly built baseball stadium out-did the one at Shea and, for the first and only time on the '65 tour, I remember being able to hear voices and instruments clearly amplified and beautifully balanced. I wondered at the time why one venue could get it so right while most of the others got it so wrong and I came to the conclusion that the sound system was way down the average concert promoter's priorities because it was assumed that the screaming of the audience would drown out whatever the loudspeakers had to offer. I also noticed that in Atlanta and one or two other places where we had OK sound, The Beatles gave a musically superior performance. If a promoter cared, the boys cared too.

Sometimes, instead of staying over in the city we had just played, we flew out again immediately after the gig and headed straight for our next destination. This decision was based upon the availability or otherwise of suitable hotel accommodation at each place and the length of the flight. There were benefits to arriving in the next city during the night and being able to sleep late the next morning. As a rule, the authorities liked the idea of a night arrival because it reduced the number of fans at the airport and made crowd control easier. We did a midnight flight from Atlanta to Houston, Texas, arriving at two o'clock in the morning. Local security forces had decided that few, if any, fans would turn out at such an hour but they were badly mistaken. Hordes of teenagers poured onto the runway as our aircraft taxied towards the terminal buildings. A small section of the crowd consisted of slightly older fans, some perhaps the worse for drink, who were rowdy and shouting obscenities at the few airport officials who tried to hold them back. They climbed up onto the wings and facetiously pulled faces at us through the cabin windows. At first the boys responded amiably by doing the same thing from our side of the glass until we realised the very real danger posed by the whole situation. The aircraft engines were still running and some of the crowd were smoking in the area close to our fuel tanks. An explosion out there could have caused extensive damage and fatal injuries. Happily, a potential disaster was averted by the swift action of our pilot who immediately turned off his engines. A hairy situation came to a safe conclusion as the pilot held us on board while the rest of our party left. Finally, The Beatles and our immediate entourage, including Brian Epstein, disembarked via a hastily summoned forklift truck that carried us high above the heads of the crowd and right to the door of the nearest building.

Problems such as this tended to have knock-on effects. The trouble at Houston caused the police at our next destination, Chicago, to panic and refuse us permission to land as planned at O'Hare Airport. Instead, we came down at Midway Airport and had to drive back to the Sahara O'Hare Motor Inn. At the motel a large crowd of fans awaited our arrival because the Sahara management had released full details of our stay to rival radio stations. We didn't get a lot of sleep that night. The intense competition between radio stations in most US cities was often our downfall. Deejays couldn't wait to reveal our accommodation locations. Even in Los Angeles where we rented a house at a "secret" address for a few days, it took less than 12 hours for the whole area's network of Top 40 stations to be broadcasting the address: "It's Benedict Canyon, it's No 2850, now let's see if you can get there ahead of all your friends because remember you heard the news first right here on ... " One afternoon, four well-heeled young fans, aged 17 and 18, hired a helicopter to fly above our villa so that they could shout greetings to four sunbathing Beatles.

A highlight of this mid-tour break in the Hollywood Hills was The Beatles' get-together with Elvis Presley on the evening of Friday, August 27, although I have to say that the Monarchs of Mersey Beat found the King of Rock'n'Roll boring. Perhaps we expected too much of the intricately planned occasion. Or perhaps Elvis really was boring whenever he wasn't performing for an ecstatic audience. No media reporters were given the opportunity to witness the ultra-private party, which took place in Presley's Bel Air home at 565 Perugia Way. No pictures were taken, no tape recordings were made and there were no gatecrashers. The absolute ban on publicity was one essential stipulation upon which The Beatles, Brian Epstein and Presley's manager, Colonel Tom Parker, had agreed upon beforehand without debate. Other logistics took longer to thrash out. The idea of bringing the five superstars together for an informal evening came from the *New Musical Express* journalist Chris Hutchins who claimed to be close to Parker.

At first the fact that someone from the press was involved put The Beatles off. George put into words what the others were thinking: "If this is going to be another dirty big publicity thing, let's forget it. We want to meet Elvis but not with a gang of photographers and deejays hassling us." The deal with Hutchins was that there would be no photography, even for the *NME*, and no leaking of details in advance. Since Hutchins was staying in the same Hollywood hotel as more than a dozen other media people who made up our official entourage it must have been difficult for him to keep the time and place confidential, but it was in his own interest to do so if he wanted to have the story to himself. Brian Epstein remained nervous and warned me: "The boys will pull out if the rest of the press find out."

The next hurdle was to agree on where and when the five should meet. Such famous folk dared not drop in on one another unannounced. The very formality of discussing venues made The Beatles uncomfortable. Paul asked me: "Has Parker laid down that we have to go to Elvis? Why can't he come over to us at Benedict Canyon?" Some of The Byrds, the Beach Boys and the actress Eleanor Bron had been over to sit by the pool. At one point, when Epstein was out of the room, John told me: "If we do go to Elvis, I'd prefer it to be just the five of us, not even Brian, the Colonel or you. If both sides start lining up teams of supporters it will turn into a contest to see who can field the most players." Inevitably, power politics came into play. Parker would be present, so Epstein had to be. Having acted as a catalyst to get the whole shindig off the ground, of course Chris Hutchins had to be invited. And if even a single journalist was to be involved, The Beatles wanted to bring me along. Presley would have his army of minders, the self-styled Memphis Mafia, on hand, so The Beatles' roadies, Neil and Mal, made it onto the swelling list of guests, along with their driver, Alf Bicknell. John said: "Let's stop there or it'll get out of control." The boys disliked the idea of an outsider such as Hutchins acting as the go-between to any greater extent than was diplomatically necessary. They told Epstein to call the Colonel personally and get things organised on a one-to-one basis. "I don't have his direct number here," admitted Brian limply, but I got hold of it for him from a local journalist. Epstein seemed somewhat subdued, as if the sheer enormity of the proposed meeting had taken the wind out of his sails. Several meetings took place between Epstein and Parker. On one occasion they talked over a poolside lunch at Brian's hotel, the Beverly Hills, and on another the Colonel paid us a visit at Benedict Canyon and spent some time with The Beatles. While the boys wanted to keep arrangements as loose and informal as possible, the Colonel seemed to put a more businesslike edge on things. At one point he said to Epstein something like: "What's your proposition?" It sounded more like the prelude to a tour negotiation than the planning of a private party. Without much of a fight Brian bowed to Parker's emphatic demand that John, Paul, George and Ringo should make the short trip over to Bel Air rather than Presley visiting them in Benedict Canyon. Parker's argument was that Elvis would happily come to The Beatles if they were all in England but here in America on Presley's home turf it should work the other way around. He also showed concern over possible security weaknesses at Benedict Canyon and promised that Presley's Bel Air property was suitably guarded. John said: "You're going to have to give us directions. We don't know Perugia Way." To our surprise, the Colonel confessed that he'd never been to the villa, adding: "We conduct our business in the office, not at home. But when the time comes someone will drive ahead of you and show you the way."

Friday, August 27 was not the first choice of date. Presley was uncertain when he would be at home, The Beatles had their remaining concert commitments and Brian Epstein was planning a quick trip to New York. On one night the boss of Capitol Records was hosting an almighty party in honour of the Fab Four with a guest list that included Jane Fonda, Groucho Marx, James Stewart and

Rock Hudson. Neither I nor The Beatles wanted to miss that bash. The only person among us unaffected by the politics, responsibilities and routine of fragile negotiation was Mal Evans, who was totally infatuated by the mere idea of being in the same room as The King and couldn't hide his immense glee when told that the summit was certainly on. From that moment on he spoke of little else and wore a permanent grin.

I was not surprised to find that news of the Presley – Fab Four party did reach some of our media entourage despite our great efforts to keep all the details to ourselves. The *Daily Mirror*'s Don Short did his best to get Chris Hutchins to tell him what was happening but the *NME* man fobbed him off with false information. Several of the most enterprising guys, including *Daily Express* West Coast correspondent Ivor Davis and the intrepid Larry Kane, joined forces to tail our limousines as we left The Beatles' villa. As we drove, it was clear that the boys still had mixed feelings about the whole affair. John asked: "Do you think the Colonel has bothered to tell Elvis we're coming?" Mal's face dropped: "Do you think they'll let us in?" Most of the tension was the result of genuine last-minute nervousness which I knew would disappear when The Beatles walked into Presley's home, just as it did when they went out on a stage, the adrenalin drowning the butterflies.

The Presley property was large, round and had many windows. In front of it was a spacious garden with lots of palm trees and an impressive little fleet of Cadillacs and Rolls Royces. A bunch of heavies guarded the gate but they had been primed to let our limousine sweep inside without challenge. The journalists were held at bay but they had expected this. Alerted by the gate guards, Elvis was on the doorstep dressed smartly in a colourful, tightly-tailored red shirt, high-collared black jerkin and light grey trousers. There was a flurry of greetings and small talk as we were led into an enormous circular room bathed in red and blue lights. This was where The King entertained – the Presley playground complete with colour television, a jukebox and a deep crescent-shaped couch.

At least 20 people faced us from the far side of this vast room, including burly minders, some with their womenfolk. Suddenly, as our group lined up opposite Presley's a weird silence fell. For seconds that seemed like hours the English team surveyed the scene, waiting for someone to make a move, physical or vocal. Then Lennon launched into babbling conversation with Presley while Parker put a plump arm round Epstein's shoulder and led him away. This must have been the signal Presley's henchmen had waited for. Minders began to move among us, introducing themselves simply by first names, shaking hands, offering drinks and saying how pleased Mr Presley was that we had come over. Apart from Mal, clearly John was enjoying himself the most, blurting out questions and scarcely pausing to hear the answers: "Why do you do all these soft-centred ballads nowadays? What happened to good old rock'n'roll? When are you doing your next film? How long is it since you were in Memphis?" Paul wanted to know how long it took Elvis to make one of his movies and The King told him: "No more than a month if we're lucky." That was even faster than The Beatles! George told Presley how an engine on our chartered aircraft had caught fire on the flight into Portland the previous Monday night: "We were flying through a sort of narrow canyon, rocks on either side, when Paul noticed the flames. I was convinced we were going to crash." Presley replied by recalling a similar mid-air drama when one of his aircraft engines failed over Atlanta: "When we landed the pilot was wringing wet with sweat." George added: "Another time we were flying out of Liverpool when the window next to me blew out. Scary!"

They swapped tales of touring for some time, recalling how fans had invaded the stage during their shows and how bad the sound systems were in some places. Paul said: "One guy ran on stage, pulled the leads out of our amplifiers and threatened to kill me if I made a move. I never found out if he was protesting about bad sound or didn't like my singing!"

As the boys and Elvis chatted, Brian Epstein huddled with Colonel Parker in a far corner of the playroom. I wondered if Brian was trying to discuss the possibility of UK concert dates for Elvis because I knew he hoped to do so. As I moved closer to overhear what they were saying, the Colonel turned away from Brian and announced loudly to the room in general: "Ladies and gentlemen. Elvis's private casino is now open for your pleasure. Brian, let's play roulette." Parker never talked business at home. Throughout the proceedings, Presley's slender and stunningly beautiful partner, his future wife Priscilla, wafted elegantly to and fro looking like a cross between Cleopatra and Dusty Springfield with her towering black hair, sparkling tiara and heavy black make-up. Years later, George and I had a long argument over what she wore. I was sure it was a full-length lime-coloured gown but George swore it was some sort of tight cream top with long flimsy trousers to match. Eventually, I settled for the cream option and we agreed that the coloured lighting that filled the whole room was the cause of our confusion.

Suddenly, all five superstars ran out of conversation at the same time. At once, Elvis called for some guitars, which he handed out to John, Paul and George. Instead of using the remote control that lay on a nearby coffee table Presley prodded the volume button on the telly with the end of his guitar and asked an aide to start up the jukebox. One of his own recordings belted out at full blast and I remember thinking that, if the summit had been held at Benedict Canyon, we wouldn't have played The Beatles' records. Up to this point, the party had been lifeless and unexciting but as soon as Presley and The Beatles began to play along together the atmosphere livened up. Music was their natural meeting point, their best-known means of communication. The boys found they could make much finer conversation with their guitars than with their small talk about tours and films. Chris Hutchins called it *Sergeant Presley's Lonesome Heartbreak Band*. Elvis strummed a few chords for Paul and said: "Not too good, huh? But I'm practising!" Paul moved between guitar and piano and joked that if Presley kept working on his guitar playing they might find him a place in one of Brian Epstein's groups when the bubble burst. Soon, the jukebox was turned off and they moved on to Lennon and McCartney numbers. Elvis knew 'I Feel Fine' and led the group into that. Without a set of drums, Ringo felt left out of this amazing jam session. For a while he joined in by beating out the rhythms with his fingers on the back of a dining chair or the top of an occasional table, but then he left to re-join a bunch of roadies who were playing pool beneath the blue and red lights.

When they tired of singing one another's hit tunes the five musicians abandoned their instruments in front of the silent but still-flickering television set and we all moved on to play games with Ringo and the minders – one or two at the pool table, others at arcade-style amusement machines and some to gamble with chips the Colonel was dishing out. I can't remember what triggered our eventual departure but it was almost certainly Parker's distribution of presents for everyone, mainly sets of his client's albums. By now the key players appeared to have drained one another of worthwhile conversation – musical and verbal – and to stay longer would have pleased nobody apart from Mal Evans. With his face glowing with happiness, Mal told me that Elvis had called him "sir". Yes, Mal, he did that to all of us, it's his way. During our three hours in his company Elvis and I exchanged few words. Soon after we arrived he asked me if the boys were always as shy as this. A bit later he asked: "Will I embarrass your boys if I get out some guitars so that we can play a little rock'n'roll?" Priscilla took me for Brian Epstein and said: "Would The Beatles like us to fix anything special to eat? You've only to ask, you know, Brian."

At the front door Elvis said: "Don't forget to come and see us again in Memphis if you're ever in Tennessee." The Beatles never took up his invitation. John shouted "Long live The King", but not as though he meant it. As we walked to our limousine John said he thought Presley was stoned out of his mind. George grinned and replied: "Aren't we all?" High as a kite or not, Elvis didn't show too many signs of having enjoyed our visit. John said: "It was more fun meeting Engelbert Humperdinck. I can't decide who's more full of shit, me or Elvis Presley."

Maybe Presley was a little afraid that The Beatles were getting too popular with his fans. In The Beatles' eyes Presley had an iconic reputation to live up to and they were somewhat disillusioned by discovering how ordinary their idol was "in real life" as Paul put it. The party might have been a total disaster if the universal language of music had not brought together these five very different people onto one wavelength. Despite their diverse personalities and backgrounds they set aside professional rivalries and mutual suspicions to create half an hour or so of music that was both magical and memorable. For my part I was amazed to observe the contrast between Presley at home and Presley in public performance, the one an uninteresting guy who found it hard to hold much of a conversation, the other a giant of a man, bursting with talent, hypnotically sexy, power-fully entertaining and at the peak of his fame. I tried to remove the image of the inadequate party host from my mind because I prefer to remember The King as I saw him on stage in Las Vegas, looking magnificent in his rhinestone-studded outfits, sounding wonderful as he sang his best-sellers to a capacity crowd. This Las Vegas headliner bore little resemblance to the uncomfortably self-conscious guy we met in Perugia Way.

One directly visible and highly profitable consequence of the 1965 US tour's extraordinary success was that Capitol issued or re-issued a shoal of Beatles' singles soon afterwards, spearheaded by 'Yesterday' coupled with 'Act Naturally'. The others included 'Twist And Shout' and 'There's A Place', 'Love Me Do' and 'PS I Love You', 'Please Please Me' and 'From Me To You', 'Do You Want To Know A Secret' and 'Thank You Girl', 'Roll Over Beethoven' and 'Misery' and 'Boys' coupled with 'Kansas City'.

On October 26 The Beatles drove to Buckingham Palace in John's shiny Rolls Royce Phantom Five ("just like Elvis has got but mine's with smoked windows") to collect their MBE medals from the Queen. In the wake of their visit, rumours were rife that the boys had smoked forbidden substances in one of Her Majesty's lavatories. I saw them very soon after the ceremony because they showed off their medals to the media at a press conference we organised at London's Saville Theatre, Shaftesbury Avenue, and although they were in particularly exuberant mood nothing about their eyes, their voices or their general attitudes suggested to me that they had been at the cannabis. I doubt if the group would have been foolhardy enough to take unlawful drugs with them into the Palace, which was crawling with all levels of security forces. Standing at their side for the press conference Brian Epstein enjoyed The Beatles' quip that MBE stood for Mr Brian Epstein – but there was a dreamy, faraway look in his eyes that confirmed my impression that he felt Harold Wilson might have had the decency to recommend the award of a fifth Beatles medal for Personal Management services.

8 | Terror in Tokyo

THE YEAR 1966 was a disaster-strewn watershed in the history of The Beatles. This was the year in which I saw Brian Epstein's power to control the group dwindle away. To his horror he found that he could no longer dictate what the boys did and he was forced to look on while they took charge of their own destiny. At the same time I saw the band begin to break up, a slow but irrevocable process that would be spread over a period of several years. Until 1966 no important policy decision was taken within the group without unanimous agreement of all four. This year, for the first time, John, George and Ringo acted without Paul's support to end the touring. From this point on, each of the Beatles, or at least the chief protagonists within the four, began to look after their own individual interests, concentrating increasingly on what they thought was best for themselves and caring less about the welfare of the group as a whole. The self-preservation instinct was kicking in and it was going to be every man for himself.

One redeeming feature of 1966 was the release of what I consider to be The Beatles' best-ever album, *Revolver*, in the middle of a year that in many others ways would be best forgotten. Everything started to go wrong for The Beatles when, within the space of two short mid-summer weeks, the group was terrorised by death threats from extremist students in Tokyo and physically roughed up by armed thugs on the payroll of the President in Manila. Only a month later there arose the very real danger that John would be assassinated on stage by religious zealots as we toured America's southern states belonging to the so-called Bible Belt.

In the wake of these bizarre warnings of serious danger and

actual life-threatening attacks, it would not have surprised us if The Beatles had decided to stop touring solely on issues of security and personal safety. But in the eyes of The Beatles, there were also significant artistic reasons why they refused to do further concerts beyond their scheduled series of summer gigs across the US. Poor sound systems that failed to carry their singing and playing above the screams of stadium audiences caused them genuine concern. They felt that by spending most of their time criss-crossing the world to play stage shows their chances of making essential musical progress were reduced to zero. Far from moving forward, the standard of their performances was deteriorating because the whole concert environment lacked the creative ambience and catalytic discipline of the recording studio. Led by George, whose fear of flying was part of his growing dislike of concert tours, the group decided to come off the road permanently and concentrate on writing and recording, which was where all their truest ambitions lay.

The year's downhill trend began on Friday, March 25, when The Beatles took part in an ill-advised photo session with NEMS Enterprises' "official" photographer, Robert Whitaker. Brian Epstein had been impressed by Whitaker and his camerawork while on a trip to Australia in 1964. On their first encounter, 25-year-old Whitaker saw Epstein as "a bit of a peacock and a cavalier" and this was the impression he set out to depict when he took pictures of his future patron that were obviously flattering in their way. When Epstein fetched him back to London he was introduced to us as the company's new staff photographer, but Whitaker argued that he wasn't on a wage but merely under Brian's management.

I was never in favour of hiring an official cameraman to take pictures of our artists. I found it preferable to match up each of our acts with a compatible photographer and let a good working relationship develop between them based not only on the cameraman's professional skill, but also on the interaction of personalities between photographer and subject. I had a pool of excellent freelance photographers at my disposal and it was obvious to me where their differing talents lay. I would select one to create an innovative album cover because of his or her track record of superior work in that field, another when I was doing a simple news picture, perhaps a contract-signing shot for distribution to the trade press, and a third to give me a fresh set of "pin-up" studio poses for general publicity purposes. Although I commissioned photographers for all these jobs, sometimes we passed the invoice to EMI Records for payment, sometimes NEMS Enterprises would pick up the tab and sometimes we would bill the artist with the cost of a session. It all depended on the eventual use to which we put each set of pictures. Whitaker was with us from August 1964, so by the spring of '66 he felt he knew The Beatles well enough to try some truly outrageous ideas. We arranged for the boys to be at his rented studio at No 1, The Vale, just off Chelsea's fashionable King's Road. As often happened on such occasions, I fitted in several media appointments for them so that they would not be hanging around doing nothing while Whitaker set up each of his special shots. I arranged a group interview for a Brazilian reporter and George spoke about sitar music to an Indian journalist from the Canadian Broadcasting Corporation. I brought in the Radio Caroline presenter Tom Lodge to interview all four Beatles for a spoken-word flexi-disc called 'Sound Of The Stars' which I was producing as a promotional give-away for *Disc And Music Echo*, the weekly pop magazine in which Brian Epstein had recently acquired a large stake. The Beatles' total contribution to the finished version of 'Sound Of The Stars' was accurately described some years later by the author Mark Lewisohn as "one minute and 37 seconds of silly answers to silly questions". I was disappointed to discover that Tom Lodge held on to twenty minutes of additional interview material for his own use on Radio Caroline, although most of that was silly too. To add a further element of mayhem to an already chaotic and overcrowded afternoon, the magazine publisher Sean O'Mahony was invited to bring along *The Beatles Book* photographer, Leslie Bryce.

The presence of so many people, all with their own agendas, upset Whitaker, who had hoped to have the studio to himself. He told me in advance that he had some elaborate and adventurous "set pieces" he wanted to do with the boys but he was reluctant to go into greater detail. When I arrived at the studio I found that Whitaker had assembled a pile of weird props for his session, including broken dolls, strings of uncooked pork sausages, soiled sets of false teeth, cuts of raw beef and a bundle of butchers' smocks. He up-ended one box in front of The Beatles, pouring a mass of dismembered dolls' limbs and prosthetic eyeballs onto the floor. Beside this he emptied a second container full of meat that was dripping blood. By mid-afternoon we had hurried through the other appointments and Whitaker had the Fab Four to himself. With the gleeful look of a small child presented with an unexpected pile of new toys, John donned his smock and began to play. He mixed pieces of doll with chunks of meat and smashed dentures, smearing himself liberally in bright red blood as he did so. The other three looked on quizzically, less enthusiastic, more bewildered. But they were prepared to go along with John and see how the pictures turned out.

The end product of the next hour's shoot was a set of controversial photographs that acquired long-term worldwide notoriety as "the butcher session". Whitaker also took pictures of George hammering nails into John's head and, least tasteful of all, the four boys standing in front of a woman to whom they were linked by a string of sausages which represented, according to Whitaker, an umbilical cord. The Beatles had been prepared for some sort of sensational theme to Whitaker's session but this lot was beyond even John's wildest dreams. The photo session had been fixed at Whitaker's request and the ideas were all his but, knowing that Whitaker was Brian Epstein's own photographer, The Beatles said nothing and relied on Brian to veto all but the roll of straightforward publicity shots which were taken before all those strange props appeared on the scene.

At this time, Capitol Records were pestering us to provide new pictures for the cover of *Yesterday ... And Today*, an eleven-track US compilation album of assorted songs from the UK album *Revolver* and elsewhere. Capitol tended to re-package The Beatles' UK albums, offering an average of three or four tracks less than EMI product sold in Britain, a policy which The Beatles thought was stingy. George expressed their unhappiness with the Capitol situation: "When the American company released albums like *Yesterday ... And Today*, we didn't have anything to do with them. They always put out more albums in the States. If we put out two singles and two albums, they'd convert them to three albums by keeping the extra tracks." If this had not been one of the "filler" albums, The Beatles might have become more involved in the choice of cover photo. As it was, John was pushing Brian Epstein to publish the "butcher session" pictures as widely as possible and the other three were content to leave the decision over the Capitol cover to Epstein. Only half-jokingly, George told Whitaker: "We won't come to any more of your sick picture sessions, Bob."

Holding his cigarette lighter close to Whitaker's sheet of transparencies, Epstein told me: "What I'd really like to do is set fire to the whole lot and never let them see the light of day." I agreed wholeheartedly that the "butcher session" might well be disastrous to the career of any lesser band but I had to say that The Beatles were big enough to withstand the bad publicity. A year earlier, Epstein would have stood his ground and destroyed the transparencies. Like the rest of us, he was sickened by some of the stuff Whitaker had taken but he bent under pressure from John, chose one of the less offensive shots where The Beatles were grinning rather than sneering, and sent the transparency to Alan Livingston at Capitol. He released several other similar shots to EMI in London to use in press advertising for the new UK single which coupled 'Paperback Writer' and 'Rain' and he handed one to *Disc And Music Echo*, which published it in colour on the front cover of the June 11 issue.

In Hollywood, Livingston's delayed reaction was that Capitol couldn't use the "butcher session" picture although this meant recalling some *Yesterday ... And Today* sleeves that had already been printed and put into circulation. The Capitol boss told Epstein bluntly that the dealers wouldn't stock it and the sales people wouldn't handle it. Advance copies sent to US media reviewers and deejays were scrapped and Ron Tepper, Capitol's manager of press and information services announced that the artwork "created in England, was intended to be pop art satire". The few copies of *Yesterday ... And Today* with the original "butcher" cover became highly prized souvenirs and are valued at more than a thousand dollars in today's memorabilia marketplace.

Whitaker was instructed to take replacement shots in a great rush. He took the blandest of group photographs in Epstein's office with the four unsmiling boys posing around and inside a huge travel trunk. Called upon to explain the "butcher" idea on various occasions over the years, Whitaker has said that the pictures were used out of context, "a cock-up". They were intended to be one part of an unfinished three-part concept. In a radio interview he claimed quite incorrectly that The Beatles sent the "butcher" print to Capitol as "a little joke". He told the UK's *Mojo* magazine: "The front cover picture was to be of them holding sausages coming out of the nether region of a lady". This was to represent the birth of The Beatles. Whitaker's two-year stint as official photographer at NEMS Enterprises ended a few months after this extraordinary session.

Probably the least troublesome part of 1966 for The Beatles came in the last week of June, immediately before the Tokyo-to-Manila leg of their tour, when they did several concert dates in Germany as the leisurely first leg of what was to be their last world tour. It was a nostalgic trip with the boys travelling between cities in the civilised luxury of a sumptuously furnished charter train – previously used by Royalty – and partying with some of their old friends from the early Hamburg days.

The Beatles played concerts at handsome and historical auditorium venues in several German cities including the Circus-Krone-Bau in Munich, the Grugahalle in Essen and the Ernst Merck Halle in Hamburg. Germany generally, and Hamburg specifically, brought back a flood of good memories of familiar places and old friends because it was in the colourfully sleazy clubland of Hamburg's Reeperbahn and the St Pauli district that The Beatles had matured musically and paid their dues as a working band five or six years previously. On several extended visits, they built up their repertoire of songs, their stamina and showmanship as stage performers during gruelling all-night sets at the Indra Club, the Kaiserkeller, the Top Ten Club and later, in April 1962, at the internationally renowned Star-Club.

At times when business in a club had been slack, it was up to The Beatles to put on such an exciting stage show that punters dawdling in the doorway would be drawn in to buy beer. Alongside the development of their musicianship those early stints in Hamburg also brought the group into contact with intelligent and creative new friends, artistic young folk from Hamburg's college and university circles who helped them to mould their future image by introducing them to new ideas in clothing, even giving them the basic notion that led to The Beatles' best-known trademark, their distinctive mop-top haircuts. Inevitably, on our nostalgic 1966 return to the scenes of their professional adolescence, everyone partied far into the night, heedless of the longest of days that lay ahead. At midnight John and Paul were strolling down the notorious Reeperbahn with a boisterous entourage of old buddies, pals and mates. The night was yet young.

When Bert Kaempfert, the producer of The Beatles' early Hamburg recordings with Tony Sheridan, called in to say "hi", John and the others serenaded him with a raucous version of his song 'Strangers In The Night', an international hit for Frank Sinatra that summer.

But my strongest memory of the visit to Germany is not of the concerts or the reunions, but of hearing my favourite Beatles album for the first time and helping to come up with a title for it. Sitting in a circle with the four boys I first heard the completed album on George's tape recorder in the Bayerischer Hof Hotel, Munich, and immediately decided that this was the Fab Four's most attractive collection to date. Nothing I heard in later years, even *Sgt Pepper*, made me change my mind. In my opinion every one of the 14 tracks was an instant winner, from Paul's haunting 'Eleanor Rigby' and 'Here There And Everywhere' to George's ground-breaking 'Taxman' and 'I Want To Tell You', from John's hypnotic 'Tomorrow Never Knows' and 'Doctor Roberts' to Ringo's totally infectious 'Yellow Submarine', with which we all sang along karaoke-style. As for finding an album title to fit this lot, we went round in circles, from Magic Circle and Four Sides To The Circle to Paul's suggestion, Pendululm, and Ringo's frivolous one, After Geography, his cryptic nod to The Stones' *Aftermath*, before the group agreed unanimously to call it *Revolver*.

Immediately after Germany, with scarcely any time to change our Deutschmarks into yen, we travelled to Tokyo, where the Beatles' summer of terror began. The death threat was undoubted and unambiguous. The Beatles would lose their lives if they dared to play even one of their five scheduled concerts in the sanctified setting of the Tokyo Budokan.

Our journey to Japan had been a particularly long and arduous affair, prolonged by the lively antics of a typhoon called Kit, which was roving around the China Seas and caused our London-Tokyo flight to be re-routed via Anchorage, Alaska. Here we had an unscheduled nine-hour stopover to await a forecast of more favourite weather conditions ahead of us.

On Monday, June 27, the day after the Ernst Merck gig, when all we wanted to do was sleep off the enormous excesses of the previous night, we were flown back to London's Heathrow airport and trans-ferred almost immediately to the Japan Airlines polar flight which would carry us on to the Orient. As we settled down for take-off, Paul tried to calculate the number of miles we would fly before the summer tour wound up at the end of August at Candlestick Park in San Francisco. "I'm sure the total on the American part alone will be something like 20 or 30 thousand miles," he announced, but none of us could be bothered to tot up the true figure. As we taxied onto the runway John was doing his usual clownish patter, aimed at calming his own and George's nerves: "Are you clinging comfortably to the edge of your meats? Then we'll take off."

What to do on long-haul flights always presented us with a problem. As a rule, however tired the boys appeared to be before takeoff, once we were airborne they were far too tense to get much sleep. Often we would find our way to the lounge area up at the front of a 707 jet and roadie Mal Evans would produce a deck of cards. Poker was the favourite game. On the Tokyo flight they opted for Dictionary, a word game the group claimed to have invented, but in reality prob-ably borrowed from something they'd seen on TV – the game seemed to me to resemble a variation on the 'Call My Bluff' format. Manager Brian Epstein, Neil Aspinall and anyone else in our party would be invited to join in. Mal would produce a pocket dictionary and kick off the game by choosing an obscure word. Everybody would write down a made-up definition, the crazier the better and, after they had all been read out, each player would vote for the one he thought was correct. You got a point if your word matched the dictionary definition, or if you fooled another player into believing your spoof definition was true. But the main fun of the game lay in the reading out of all the ingenious guesses – "a partially enslaved worker bee or drone", "a hand-carved shaving mug", "a type of dwarf zebra found in South Australian swamplands". All very childish but, helped along with glasses of Scotch and Coke, it passed the flying time in the days before lap-top DVD players were around.

The captain's announcement about Typhoon Kit wiped the smiles off our faces. All commercial aircraft in the vicinity of Tokyo were grounded and we would need to delay our arrival there by "dropping in" to Anchorage, Alaska. Most of us, our senses numbed by the drink and our stomachs more than satisfied by a filling dinner, took the news well. But Epstein flew into a rage and asked where the airline proposed to put us while we waited for the typhoon to blow itself away. He was not completely reassured by the captain's personally delivered promise that arrangements were in hand to put up our entire party in a down-town Anchorage hotel, probably the Westwood, one of the best in the area and well-known to airline crews. He described the top-floor disco club as a "terrific place to party" and said we would enjoy it. Seeing that Brian was still angry, he returned later to say that he had fixed for John, Paul, George and Ringo to share the hotel's bridal suite and several equally well-appointed adjoining rooms. This caused much amuse-ment among the four boys who instantly began proposing marriage to one another. In the event, the airline did us proud and we took over an entire floor of JAL's chosen downtown hotel where the staff bent over backwards to be as welcoming as possible. They even obeyed my request that staff members should not disturb the four Beatles in their suites to ask for autographs. The deal was that, if the group was not pestered, I would give an allocation of publicity pictures to the hotel manager before we left, all nicely signed well in advance in an excellent likeness of each Beatle's handwriting, by one of the roadies, who had become the secret forgers of almost flawless versions of their signa-tures. At the height of Beatlemania, when the Fab Four were at their busiest and demand for autographs was at its greatest, I would say that at least four of every five signatures were done either by the roadies or by secretaries in our fan club office. Even the autographs reproduced on much of The Beatles' authorised merchandise were written by a road manager, leading to much argument between fans over who had, and who had not, been given the genuine article. Frankly, unless you stood and watched John, Paul, George and Ringo write their names before your very eyes, which was seldom a realistic possibility, it was wise to be highly suspicious!

The Anchorage experience was a memorable one-off. We were transported from the airport to the hotel in an ordinary airline bus. As we stopped at traffic lights on the relatively narrow suburban streets, locals did a double take as they spotted each of the bleary-eyed Beatles staring out at them from the windows of our bus. Our plan to sleep right through the stopover went out of the window when local media people realised that they had the world's most famous pack of pop megastars right under their noses. The Beatles in Alaska? Impossible, but true! One radio station dispatched a news car to our hotel so that their deejay could broadcast the rest of his programme from below our bedroom windows: "Come right on down, folks! The Beatles are waiting to meet you."

Whenever we were surprised by an unplanned encounter with ladies or gentlemen of the media, my policy – if it was at all practical – was to give the journalists a little time to speak with The Beatles, let them take a few pictures and ask a few questions, and then most of them would be on their way without further hassle. Their job was done and so was mine. We made The Beatles far more accessible than any comparable world-class superstar – Elvis Presley, for instance – and this helped to maintain goodwill between the group and the media. Similarly, the Fab Four were very willing to stop and chat briefly to small numbers of fans. To keep the peace in Anchorage, I got the boys to lean out of their windows and wave to the growing crowd. Now that the radio people knew exactly where the boys' rooms were located, they gave their deejay/reporter a roving microphone and sent him straight into the hotel. He came upstairs to the room where we had gathered, broadcasting as he walked, pushing his mike into the faces of each Beatle in turn.

I don't believe any of us managed to get much rest in Anchorage, although I was amazed to hear that a couple of the boys had actually gone on a short nocturnal sightseeing trip around the town with the hotel disco's deejay. My phone rang constantly with calls from news agencies as well as local fans. When we were on the road we blocked incoming phone calls to rooms occupied by the group, but kept my line open so that I could deal with essential matters. Brian Epstein made a habit of stopping calls to his suite and re-routing them to mine without warning, something I found mildly annoying because I had enough to do handling the PR side of things without acting as his unofficial telephonist-secretary. But this was the nature of the job of touring the world with The Beatles. A roadie responsible for the musical instruments might finish up with needle and thread repairing a torn shirt. A PR man would turn his hand to knocking in nails to secure Ringo's drum rostrum if there was nobody else about to tackle the job.

★

I remember nothing of the flight between Anchorage and Tokyo. I think most of us crashed out and deliberately missed out on whatever meals were being served. Our extended day had started on Hamburg's Reeperbahn, taken us through London's Heathrow, on to Alaska and finally landed us safely at Tokyo's Haneda Airport at the unearthly hour of around 03.40 the following morning. The heavy-handed if meticulously organised Japanese security operation went into top gear the moment our aircraft touched down. Normally, on arrival in any new territory, I hoped to grab a few vital words with whoever was in charge of local airport arrangements so that the group's transfer to limousines or whatever would go as smoothly as possible. Before any of us left our cabin I liked to give myself at least a hasty briefing and a fleeting glimpse of what lay ahead – the press situation, the number of waiting fans and where they were located in relation to our route between the aircraft steps and the limousines, the size of the airport's security force and whether everything seemed to be as safe as possible from the fans' point of view as well as the band's. Everybody took it for granted that our only concern was to stop the group being injured by a rioting mob of well-wishers and it's true that usually one or more of the Fab Four would be accidentally hurt by fans in the course of most tours. But the personal injuries were never serious, and we didn't rate this as our top-priority problem. In fact the bigger danger lay in the possibility that fans would hurt themselves by rushing forward recklessly the moment they spotted The Beatles' limousine, and I was always looking for ways of minimising this risk as well as keeping the band safe. On numerous occasions around the world I saw fans on the verge of falling beneath the wheels of our moving vehicles before being plucked away in the nick of time by a parent or a cop.

At Haneda the security forces took total control of the situation, making it clear that there was no need for consultation because our itinerary was organised to the last detail. With military precision we were moved to the top of the aircraft steps where we paused for press photographs, and then down onto the tarmac. Surprisingly, The Beatles did not object when airline staff cloaked them in traditional thigh-length "happi coats" featuring a blatantly large JAL logo on the lapels. One by one we were led smartly towards some sleek white limousines. Insistent guards dictated who went in which vehicle. Two of the boys were shown into the first one and Brian Epstein managed to squeeze past the line of guards to join them. The security people didn't seem too happy about letting anyone else join each pair of Beatles, they kept gesturing wildly that the rest of us should wait for other cars to arrive. But taking my cue from Brian, I brushed past them and into the second limousine. The most remarkable aspect of our airport arrival was that at around 3.40am, a crowd of 1,500 Japanese Beatles' fans were waiting in the darkness to greet the group. Clearly acting on orders that were not to be changed, our drivers ignored our pleas to take us slowly past the fans. Instead, they sped us on our way out of the airport. This was a shame, because the majority of those well-behaved and patient fans had waited an amazingly long time overnight to catch sight of the Fab Four.

The Pacific edition of the *Stars And Stripes* newspaper revelled in the arrival of The Beatles: "If you're not hip to the fact that Wednesday was B-Day in Tokyo then you're either a disgruntled barber or stoutly refuse to admit that there will always be an England – providing The Beatles don't go bankrupt. The four hairy howlers arrived on the skirt-tails of typhoon Kit and there hasn't been such a gathering of Tokyo's finest since last year's policeman's picnic. With Operation Beatles in full swing there are cops on duty 24 hours a day to keep enthusiastic fans at a distance."

On the drive along the metropolitan expressway towards Tokyo we witnessed further examples of the massive security set-up. Roadblocks at intersections diverted all other traffic from our route, clearing our way through the residential suburbs and into the sprawling city. Armed policemen rode alongside us on motorbikes. Later, I took down the statistics from a senior security official. At first, Tokyo police chiefs had taken the decision to ban fans from Haneda but so many turned up anyway that they relented and hastily worked out how to deal with a limited number of carefully supervised observers who might watch The Beatles' arrival from a safe distance. Otherwise, the airport had been closed for most of the night prior to our (considerably delayed) arrival. The 1,500 most persistent fans were vetted by security and approved to become our welcoming committee on the understanding that they behaved themselves. A total of 3,000 police officers were on duty at the airport, two for every fan. I discovered that no less than 35,000 security people took an active part in guarding our every move between the airport and our hotel, to and from the Budokan and inside the actual concert venue. Some were conspicuously armed and wore crash helmets and combat uniforms; others who were members of several elite squads specialising in potential terrorist or riot situations made their presence less obvious. Inside the Tokyo Hilton, 2,000 security people worked in shifts night and day to give us 24-hour protection throughout our stay. Those allocated to rooms on our floor literally slept on the job between shifts.

The Beatles were given the so-called Presidential Suite in the Tokyo Hilton, a spacious and extremely well-appointed set of rooms with which the boys were well pleased. They hated to have separate suites when they were on the road. They happily doubled up to share a couple of bedrooms between the four of them and the pairing off was a random business that took place on the spur of the moment. They were never thrilled at the prospect of spending too much time alone and they liked to have one or both of their most trusted aides, senior roadie Neil Aspinall and his assistant Mal Evans – who were both Liverpudlians – as close as possible at all times. If this left a spare bedroom in a larger suite that might be used to accommodate a female guest or two, so much the better. At the Tokyo Hilton, room-service staff, each shadowed by a watchful security guy, scuttled in and out of the Presidential Suite with bowls of exotic fruits, jugs of iced water laced with slices of lime and a variety of other refreshments – all with the compliments of the hotel management. In many respects, this was one of the best hotels we had stayed in and certainly the most secure.

Meanwhile, the reason for this manic security gradually became apparent. I found out just how serious the situation had become when a small group of tearful Japanese girls collared me in the hotel lobby and pleaded with me not to let the Fab Four endanger their lives by going ahead with the Budokan dates. When I pressed the fans for further information, they told me the full story, stressing that the anger of the zealous student faction was not to be ignored or treated lightly. The girls explained that the threat to murder The Beatles had appeared initially in a semi-underground newsletter circulated mainly among a student readership and had then been given low-key coverage in the popular press. They were convinced that the Japanese authorities had joined forces with the mainstream media to play down the danger of anything nasty being allowed to happen to The Beatles while we were on Japanese soil. I got the impression that the ultimate aim of the authorities would be, not to protect the Beatles from harm necessarily, but to prevent anything disgraceful or scandalous from happening to a group of worldwide celebrities on their patch. Our Japanese hosts would have considered it a great dishonour to themselves if anything had gone wrong and John, Paul, George or Ringo had died violently while in Tokyo.

The would-be killers were a bunch of fanatical right-wing students who cherished the Nippon Budokan as an almost sacred place, a highly respected shrine dedicated to the presentation of traditional martial arts tournaments including high-level championship sumo wrestling matches. They felt that a venue of such special cultural and spiritual importance must not be used to stage rock'n'roll shows, so they came to the Budokan – and to the Tokyo Hilton hotel – and waved their long banners demanding that The Beatles' concerts be cancelled and that the group should leave the country. In the years to come many of the world's most popular recording stars of each era, from Bob Dylan to the Bay City Rollers, would appear at the Budokan on temporary platforms erected in the centre of the judo arena. But for now, in 1966, it remained sacrosanct and in their eyes out of bounds even to the best-known band on the planet. As George remarked later: "In the Budokan only violence and spirituality were approved of, not pop music."

For days after our arrival in Japan, John, Paul, George and Ringo remained blissfully unaware of the full significance of the terrorists' warnings. To this day the surviving former Beatles don't know the full details of the danger they faced. Whenever possible we kept scary news from the band members, particularly when they were abroad and in the middle of a concert tour. We felt that keeping the pressures of Beatlemania at bay and getting the gigs right was quite enough for them to handle. Even if very real threats to their well-being came to our attention, we tried to keep these from The Beatles and deal with them ourselves. In Tokyo the language barrier made it easier for us to do this. In most other territories The Beatles would have seen the stories in the local newspapers and, even without any proper knowledge of the language, they'd have picked up the gist of the assassination threats. Not being able to decipher a single word of what the Tokyo newspapers were publishing, The Beatles noticed only the pictures showing BEATLES GO HOME slogans on bilingual banners being waved around by a crowd of young Japanese boys. These they connected with a controversial story in the communist press ahead of the group's arrival describing the boys as "tools of American imperialism" and they thought it was all a bit of a laugh.

In other countries our local concert promoter took control of routine arrangements and compiled our schedules, discussing late changes with us as they occurred. In Japan our local concert promoter, Tatsuji Nagashima, was a generous host, handing out expensive gifts of the latest Nikon cameras and Canon cine cameras to our entire party, but it was the security team who issued us with our extremely detailed timetables where every minute seemed to count. It was unsettling to realise that our slightest movements were being vetted and controlled with military precision. It was almost like being under house arrest. We were to be ready to leave at, say, 12.07, The Beatles would be escorted from their quarters (Presidential Suite 1005) at 12.10, we would reach the lifts at 12.12 and arrive in the lobby at 12.16. I had never seen such strict and meticulous masterplanning.

When we drove in convoy from the Hilton to the Budokan for the first time, the police and military presence along the urban highway shocked us. Fans were grouped together neatly in orderly bunches on bridges and at intersections. We couldn't hear their delighted screams as we raced by, but we could see their happy smiles and waving flags. Did we really need such intimidating protection from such friendly youngsters? They didn't seem to pose the slightest threat, yet they were held back by an overpowering number of uniformed guards, some brandishing pistols. Of course, our somewhat negative feelings about the tightest security we had ever come across in three years of global touring changed instantly as soon as we became aware that death threats were being made against The Beatles.

Inside the Budokan the backstage hospitality was lavish and continuous. The air-conditioned dressing room area was massive and expensively furnished. There was plenty of space for the boys to tune up their guitars and rehearse and other areas where they could relax comfortably on beds. Pretty Japanese girls in colourful kimonos moved about silently serving an endless supply of tea and Japanese snacks – probably sushi, but we didn't know that word in 1966. The auditorium was extraordinary by any standards. The building itself was almost circular, with seating for almost 10,000 people arranged in two tiers of stands. At ground level there was a large expanse of bare floor without any seating. An imposing makeshift stage, perhaps three metres high and draped in blue, had been constructed towards one side of this empty space. Directly in front of the stage there was a robustly constructed secure area twice the size of the stage with what looked like short lengths of railway track on top of the perimeter barriers. These allowed television cameras to run backwards and forwards at each side of the stage. A small number of photographers were allowed into this advantageous VIP space. In front of all this was a final barrier that included linked metal bars to deter fans from trying to storm the stage. One English-speaking (well, American-speaking) member of the concert promoter's team told me that the metal crush barriers that totally surrounded the stage and encircled the VIP pen were capable of delivering powerful electric current at the flick of a security controller's switch. Surely electrified fencing was an ultimate weapon that might be used against either assassins or out-of-control fans alike if the need arose. But maybe this was my new Japanese friend's idea of a joke.

Tats Nagashima told me that some 209,000 fans had applied for tickets by sending in postcards, but that less than a quarter were successful even after the initial three shows had been extended to five by the addition of matinées. The very beautiful interior architecture and decoration of the Budokan helped to create an unusual atmosphere of calmness for the capacity crowd of happy fans that came to our first concert. One of The Beatles described the ambience of the auditorium as "warm but clinical". The first show was timed to start at 18.30, earlier than usual for an evening when The Beatles would be giving only one performance. I noticed at once the orderly behaviour of the fans. The Beatles used the word "restricted" rather than "orderly". There was a buzz of excitement all around the auditorium, but it was controlled. We had heard that Japanese audiences could be very wild, but this was not the case at the Budokan. Only once before, in Paris at the beginning of 1964, had we come across such a docile concert audience and in that case we had put it down to the preponderance of older boys over younger girls and the reluctance of the boys to let themselves go in front of girlfriends. Maybe the policing of the Nippon Budokan crowd by so many guards, one for every several fans, intimidated the teenagers. In America, they would have been shrieking to one another at the top of their voices even before the band appeared. Here in Tokyo they filed into their seats under the precise instructions of uniformed attendants, chattering eagerly but quietly among themselves, but without a hint of the often scary high-pitched hysteria we encountered in other parts of the world. Both boys and girls were smartly turned out, almost like an enormous party of Sunday School children. Many carried small flags or handkerchiefs which they would wave at their idols once the show was under way. Some had posies of flowers, which I imagine they intended to throw to The Beatles on the stage.

Along with Brian Epstein I found my way into the VIP area shortly before The Beatles were due to come on. Like a lot of other things in Japan our Access All Areas pass differed from any we had come across before. The pass took the form of a cloth armband, printed in Japanese, inevitably destined to become an attractive souvenir item, particularly since so few were manufactured. (Sadly, my own armband was destroyed some years later in a disastrous fire at the west London editorial headquarters of Sean O'Mahony's official monthly fan magazine, *The Beatles Book*, where numerous exclusive photographs of the Fab Four and other irreplaceable items of original one-off memorabilia from the Beatlemania years were lost).

For their 1966 tour of Germany, Japan, the Philippines and North America, The Beatles were fitted out with two completely new stage outfits. In Germany, dark green suits with velvet lapels made their first appearance in Munich. In Tokyo, light grey suits with very thin orange stripes were scheduled for the first show. At the last minute the tight-fitting trousers to this suit needed emergency tailoring, so the boys reverted to the green suits for one concert and wore the lighter jackets with black trousers for another. They had high-collared, open-necked shirts in a deep orange colour that went with either suit. Several years later, brightly coloured shirts with spectacularly high collars were all the rage in London as part of the revolutionary fashion trends introduced by the new Carnaby Street boutiques. I think there was a direct link between those hugely popular shirts of the late Sixties and early Seventies and the ones first worn in public by The Beatles during their final concert tours in the summer of 1966.

When The Beatles came bounding onto the Budokan stage and roared straight into 'Rock'n'Roll Music', the first of their 11 songs, the fans let themselves go, cheering and screaming their hearts out, their tiny bunches of flowers cascading down from the stands in the general direction of the stage. But they soon calmed down again and sat politely, hands on their laps, occasionally whooping with glee, but saving their loudest screams for the end of each number. The Beatles found it difficult to establish contact with their audience because it meant bridging the vast gap between where they were singing and playing in the empty ground-floor arena and the two layers of seating on the far side of what amounted to a big dry moat surrounding their stage. The group also experienced microphone trouble from the outset. Each of the front-line mikes kept dropping into their stands and spinning around so that the volume of singing heard by the crowd rose and fell spasmodically. Time and again, Paul, George and John had to lift the mikes and tighten the rings that supported them. This particularly annoyed John who cursed loudly and yelled for Mal Evans to come and help. Luckily, even the little Japanese girls who knew a smattering of English did not recognise John's expletives. As always, Mal was standing by, but could do nothing to sort out the problems because the language barrier prevented him from requesting replacement mike stands from Japanese stage hands.

Behind the boys a huge sign spelt out the group's name with the words THE BEATLES outlined in lights, a simple but breath-taking backdrop. But, despite the fabulous staging and the all-pervading ambience of the venue itself, The Beatles gave a show that was disappointing. Between 1963 and 1966 I must have watched scores of concerts by the boys but I have to say that this first one in the Budokan was among the least inspiring of them all. The singing lacked emotion or passion, the playing was careless and indifferent. Above all, the group seemed to be limping through their act as though they couldn't wait for it to finish. No band is ever at its best in a stage show but few of The Beatles' live performances were as unsatisfactory as this. Maybe the moat around the stage together with the unusually quiet crowd put them off their stride. The fans were totally oblivious to the fact that they were seeing a well-below-par set. They enjoyed every moment and, although their response was a little less noisy and physically less demonstrative than we saw in other places, it was clearly sincere and heart-felt. The English-language section of the media, represented by the Tokyo-based *Japan Times*, gave The Beatles the benefit of the doubt, not commenting too much on the artistic quality of the musical performance but concentrating on giving a very exaggerated and over-excited account of the audience's reaction. Much of their story could have been written in advance. They thought that our first show was "a howling, screaming success", adding that the only time in the whole half hour that the crowd calmed down enough to hear anything was when Paul sang 'Yesterday': "Overseen by policemen wearing white hats the kiddies screamed and waved their hankies, many with tears streaming down their faces." The same reporter coined the phrase "bushy-haired heroes", which I liked. Maybe I should have hired the guy to join my PR team.

Racing off after their first show, The Beatles knew they had not been on top form. As they towelled away the sweat from their faces in the privacy of the dressing room, George was the first to admit the truth: "That was the worst performance of 'If I Needed Someone' I've ever done!" Ringo shrugged his shoulders and replied with something like: "There are good nights and bad nights on all tours." The others put it down to jet lag, particularly the nine hours added on to our journey by the Anchorage stopover. George was the most candid: "Let's face it, this is as good as it gets for us nowadays on tour. We're burning ourselves out on these pointless stage shows when there are better things we could be doing in the recording studios." They were putting into words what we had all been thinking for some time. The Beatles needed to cut down on concerts and spend much more time at EMI's Abbey Road complex in St John's Wood. In a matter of weeks the others would admit that they agreed with George and the touring era would come to an end.

Back at the Tokyo Hilton the security people kept up the pressure. If any one of us set foot in the corridor outside the Presidential Suite, heads would pop out from the security rooms and we'd be questioned (ever so politely) about where we were going. If we wanted to visit other rooms on the same floor, there was no problem, but if we headed for the lifts we were stopped in our tracks and guided back with a firm persuasion, which we came to recognise as a hallmark of our hosts. At one point, Paul borrowed a shabby raincoat and said to me: "Come on, Tony, let's be the first to break out of

Alcatraz!" Pulling the raincoat collar high around his neck to hide his hairy fringe under a hat that Neil Aspinall lent him, Paul led me from the Presidential Suite to the lifts. Nobody challenged us. By the time we reached the lobby, however, those walkie-talkies must have been hot with the news of our bold escape. We were surrounded by agitated, chattering Japanese officials who herded us back into the lift and made sure we returned to our floor. On another occasion, Ringo and Paul made it all the way to a taxi parked on a rank outside the hotel, before being re-captured. Eventually, John and Neil were successful in evading all our guards and took a taxi down to the local market and went on to look around a nearby gallery. The next day, determined to get in at least a little sightseeing before our brief visit ended, Paul and Mal managed to slip out and visit the Imperial Plaza where, under cover of disguise, Paul took photographs and bought a few souvenirs.

Our thoughtful concert promoter decided that, if we were unable to go shopping, the up-market merchants of Tokyo should come to us. This cheered everyone up because buying Japanese souvenirs was high on our list of must-do things. We were also offered the services of a group of attractive geisha girls, but as John said at the time: "We can get crumpet anywhere. Let's stick to shopping today!" In no time the main lounge within the Presidential Suite resembled an Aladdin's cave. Traders brought in a treasure trove of ivory ornaments, a wonderful array of jewellery, photographic equipment, beautifully carved bowls, traditional silk kimonos in a rainbow of bright colours and variations on the airline "happi coats" the boys had been given at the airport. One tradesman offered sets of square-, round- and diamond-shaped sunshades which we couldn't resist. The boys were also fascinated by traditional Japanese brush-painting sets and bought several complete boxes of brushes, tubes of oil paint, a range of watercolours and all manner of artists' accessories.

Since we were unable to understand anything on the TV, painting became the new hobby of preference. We sent out for large sheets of paper – fine handmade Japanese art paper – and the four boys spread one of these out under the light of a table lamp. Each Beatle claimed a corner of the paper and set to work, busily dipping brushes into jars of water and experimenting with different colours. I seem to remember that John worked in oils, using dark colours to dramatic effect, while the other three went for lighter and brighter watercolours. Never before or after did I ever see John, who was notorious for his short attention span, concentrating with such contented determination on such a non-essential project. On the second and third days we had an afternoon show in addition to the evening one, so the communal painting was not completed at a single session but during various tranquil moments when nothing else was happening. Such moments were not easy to find but gradually the four designs reached the centre of the sheet and this extraordinary multi-coloured work of art was complete. The painting spree was a wonderful therapy for four tour-weary Beatles, relaxing them totally and holding their interest to an unusual extent. A communal painting by all four Beatles would now be worth a fortune, but the finished product was presented to the Japanese fan club branch manager. I told him that The Beatles wanted the painting to be auctioned among club members with the proceeds going to charity. Alternatively, he might organise a competition, perhaps a painting competition, and present The Beatles' work to the winner. I believe this unique trophy has changed hands several times in recent years but to my knowledge it has stayed in Japan.

Having little knowledge of the Japanese media I had not become as involved as usual in advance arrangements for our Tokyo press conference beyond giving Tats Nagashima a short list of priority publications such as *Music Life* for the invitation list. Rumi Hoshika, the editor of *Music Life*, an excellent Japanese magazine that reflected both local and global trends in rock and pop in the mid-Sixties, had been to London to interview The Beatles prior to our Tokyo concerts. We had seen the results in print and the boys were impressed by the volume of the coverage and the quality of the accompanying photographs, although we were unable to read a word of the Japanese text. I also stipulated that for our convenience the press conference must take place in our hotel on June 30, our first day in Tokyo, before we went to the Budokan for the first concert. In my experience hotels or concert venues were the best places to hold these events when we were on tour, because it saved me having to haul John, Paul, George and Ringo out of their rooms and transport them somewhere else. By 1966 the group was spinning well out of Brian Epstein's management control and it was increasingly my difficult, albeit self-appointed, job to get them to media appointments on time. Like everything else in Tokyo, the press conference arrangements were immaculately organised. The venue was the Tokyo Hilton's hugely impressive and sumptuously appointed Pearl Ballroom. When I went there for a sneak preview of the set-up, a long table with four chairs, four microphones, several jugs of water and ashtrays had already been put in position on one of the widest stages I had ever seen in a hotel function room. I was asked to make sure that the four Beatles sat in order from left to right, John, Paul, George, Ringo, to avoid any confusion among photographers or reporters. As a rule I would stand just behind the four Beatles, perhaps a little to one side of them, with a hand-held microphone of my own to do the introductions and then direct the questioning. I had a standard format for on-tour press gatherings, giving photographers the first ten minutes to snap away directly in front of The Beatles before asking them to move to the back while reporters started their questioning. Even the more greedy lens-people usually co-operated by clearing the area in front of the journalists' seats when I asked them to do so because they were surprised and grateful at having been given their own time ahead of the general conference. I had a couple of people with roving microphones out among the journalists so that the person who was asking a question could be heard by everybody when I indicated that it was his or her turn. The Tokyo Hilton staff had put a separate mike for me at one side of the stage which complicated things in that being so far from their table I could not communicate as easily as usual with individual Beatles during the conference, or warn them that I was about to wind it up with one or two final questions. Often, if he was around and inclined to attend, Brian Epstein would stand close to me. I wasn't always happy about this because if a question made him nervous, which many did, he would whisper into my ear asking me to pass on to the next question as quickly as possible. I was confident enough about The Beatles' ability to deal with awkward questions and I could have done without Epstein's asides.

One other thing irritated me, but there was nothing I could do to alter things at this point. I liked to keep conferences informal and would have preferred to place The Beatles' table and chairs at floor level in front of the stage rather than on it. They would have been on the same level as the media guests which would have been much better than being perched up on high. But I understood the Japanese devotion to formality and felt it would be unwise to suggest such a fundamental change at the eleventh hour.

I have no idea why but The Beatles were in much better mood for their press conference than for the first concert. They laughed and joked among themselves for the photographers and then settled down to an amiable Q&A session. Most of the questions were as banal as ever, but several showed a little more ingenuity.

> Q: *How do you feel performing under such elaborate and pretentious security measures?*
> **Ringo**: Very safe!
> **Paul**: The best situation is when the security is strict enough to avoid anyone getting hurt.
> Q: *You have attained sufficient honour and wealth. What next?*
> **John**: Peace.
> **Paul**: Ban the bomb.
>
> Q: *Some say that your performances will violate the Budokan. What do you think?*
> **Paul**: If a dance troupe from Japan goes to Britain nobody tries to say they are violating tradition. All we're doing is coming here to sing because we've been asked to.
> **John**: Better to watch singing than wrestling!
>
> Q: *There was a big typhoon here yesterday and you arrived in Japan. Can you connect the two?*
> **John**: There's probably more wind from the press than from us. (Laughter)

"The conference wasn't a humdinger," said one press report. Well, these things never were. In a place packed with media colleagues, would any sensible journalist give away a really good question to all his competitors?

Realising how poorly they had performed at the first Budokan concert seemed to shock John, Paul, George and Ringo into making a greater effort at each of the remaining four sell-out shows. On the second and final days they were back on form on and off the stage, singing and playing well and generally in much better spirits. A television special made by Japan's NTV carefully picked out the less awful bits of the opening show and edited them in with excerpts from one of the much improved second day's performances.

I can't say precisely when, how, or even if The Beatles heard about the threats of assassination but, whatever snatches of information reached them, I don't believe they took the whole affair very seriously. In any case they played us at our own game by not discussing the matter. From stuff they said much later I don't think Paul and George ever did realise just how close the group came to death by defying the zealous student faction. In the mid-Nineties when the group was putting together *The Beatles' Anthology* book and videos, George's version of what the security people got up to in the Budokan was blissfully naïve, to say the least. According to George, official police photographers with strong telephoto lenses took shots of fans that misbehaved by standing up in their seats or yelling too wildly during the shows. Wrong, George! Those guys were hoping to spot potential snipers in the audience and if they had done so the cameras could have been exchanged for firearms in a split second. At the same time Paul told the *Anthology* how efficiently the guards along our two-mile route from the Tokyo Hilton to the Budokan collected up the fans and grouped them neatly at street corners and on bridges rather than letting them wander around haphazardly. The truth is that the authorities feared the students might have placed terrorist gunmen along the route and by herding the fans into well-contained little groups they were clearing their own field of fire and reducing the risk of stray bullets hitting fans.

What the tearful young teenyboppers told me in the lobby of the Tokyo Hilton about the authorities and the mainstream media conspiring to suppress the assassination threats proved to be so. The closest anybody in authority came to recognising the real dangers The Beatles faced was when a Tokyo-based British Embassy spokesman named Dudley Cheke eventually confessed that "fanatical opponents of the group and of all they were supposed to stand for" had threatened to have John, Paul, George and Ringo assassinated. He also said, that "in a country where crowds can easily become rioting mobs, they had to be protected from fans and foes alike." I think it's always worth remembering that "fan" is an abbreviation of the word "fanatic".

When we packed our bags in Tokyo and headed for Manila we

had no way of knowing that our problems with hostile minorities and would-be killers was about to escalate alarmingly both in Manila and the USA on the final legs of The Beatles' 1966 summer tour. The terror in Tokyo was the tip of an ugly iceberg.

9 | Out Of Control

TRAVELLING DIRECTLY TO Manila from Tokyo was a classic case of flying out of the frying pan and straight into the fire. The main difference was that in Japan the authorities were on our side and meticulously disciplined security forces fell over one another in their hundreds to ensure our safety at all costs, if only to preserve their national reputation for reliability. In the Philippines by contrast the all-powerful presidential government was our obvious enemy and heavy-handed henchmen of the dictator Ferdinand Marcos were our attackers. When we left Manila The Beatles and most of our touring party felt lucky to have escaped with our lives in the wake of horrendous scenes of carefully orchestrated violence and bitter hostility directed against us at the airport.

The Beatles were accused of snubbing the First Lady of the Philippines, Imelda Marcos, by failing to show up for an eleven o'clock appointment at which she and her three children were to have hosted a party at the presidential palace on the morning of the group's two concerts in Manila. A local newspaper reported that "four hundred children (of the aristocracy, high-ranking army officers and government officials) and their mothers waited for more than half an hour in the palace grounds". For the rest of our short but eventful two-night stay in Manila, Marcos sought revenge by arranging for us to be inconvenienced, humiliated and intimidated in a number of very frightening ways. In private, Brian Epstein tried hard to shift the blame for the Philippines fiasco on to the veteran London bandleader-turned-agent Vic Lewis, a recent newcomer to the executive staff of NEMS Enterprises and the person responsible for dealing with The Beatles' local concert promoters in the Far East that summer. In his heyday, Lewis and his orchestra backed some legendary American singing stars on their UK tours. As teenagers in the Fifties, The Beatles and I had seen him on stage at the Liverpool Empire theatre with contemporary bill-toppers such as Johnnie Ray, Guy Mitchell, Billy Daniels and Mel Tormé.

In Manila our local concert promoter, Ramon Ramos Jr., boss of an outfit named Cavalcade International Productions, told me that one quarter of the entire police force was detailed for Beatles duty between the Sunday afternoon of our arrival and the Tuesday of our departure. Ramos expected a crowd of 35,000 to attend The Beatles' Monday afternoon performance at the massive Rizal National Memorial Football Stadium and he thought another 45,000 fans would pack the place for the day's second concert at 8.30pm. In the event, a few less came to the early show and a few more to the one in the evening, giving a combined audience of 80,000, the largest number of people to have watched The Beatles in action on any one day throughout their life as a working band. This was a statistic that was lost forever in the welter of hard news stories generated by the more sensational aspects of our visit to Manila.

An enormous crowd of very young Filipino fans invaded the international airport to greet the group on arrival. Radio and TV reports broadcast an endless flow of information about the progress of our Cathay Pacific flight from Tokyo. To reduce the likelihood of poorly controlled fans mobbing the boys, Vic Lewis fixed with the chief immigration officer and customs, police and health authorities for routine formalities to be waived. Instead of coming in close to the crowds at the terminal buildings, our plane taxied to the outskirts of the airstrip. Here, hidden behind bushes, Lewis had our limousine at the ready and a long metal ladder to let The Beatles climb down from the aircraft before it turned round and took the rest of our party plus the flight's regular passengers to the terminal in the usual way. Before getting into the waiting limousine The Beatles had to let Filipino officials carry out the essential formalities of stamping passports, checking health certificates and clearing hand baggage. At the last minute The Beatles insisted that I should get off with them to cope with any press who might show up along the way. I raced after the boys and was waved through to our waiting convoy of cars to be driven off with an escort of six military-style police motorcyclists.

As we sped through quiet suburban side streets the boys showed concern that Neil Aspinall had been left behind at the airport along with a load of baggage that included their supply of grass. I said: "I'm sure he won't be far behind us." The penny hadn't dropped. I hadn't realised that their real fear was not for the wellbeing of Aspinall but that their baggage would be searched and illegal substances found. Then the boys asked: "Why aren't we heading to our hotel?" Without being able to check with Vic Lewis I couldn't answer but our driver said that his destination was the Philippine Navy Headquarters near the quayside. Apparently this was where the group's formal press conference would take place, but I had no idea why Vic had not insisted that it be held at the Manila Hotel where we were due to stay.

The deal worked out between Vic Lewis and Ramon Ramos was to use our party's hotel reservations as a decoy while The Beatles and immediate aides stayed on a luxuriously appointed yacht named *Marina*, which was moored out in the bay until the following day. As soon as we finished the press session the four boys were led through a rear door and across a roadway to their waiting launch. I went with them, accompanied by Brian Epstein, Neil Aspinall and Mal Evans. Without delay we were ferried from the quay to the yacht, which turned out to be the property of a local newspaper owner, a guy named Don Manolo Elizalde, who was friendly with Ramon Ramos Jr. and was keen to use The Beatles' presence as a status symbol. With the co-operation of the naval authorities, ship-to-shore telephone facilities had been rigged up so that those at the Manila Hotel could remain in round-the-clock touch with the rest of us. Initially, the boys were content with this arrangement and, having verified with Neil that, although the luggage had yet to be delivered, their stash had not been discovered or confiscated, they were enjoying the thought of being cut off from the world for 24 hours. They were sweating profusely in the heavy heat of the afternoon and were not entirely happy to see gun-toting cops marching to and fro on the deck, but they felt that these were inconveniences rather than causes for complaint. Then we were told that we would be landing at a secluded point along the coast the next afternoon shortly before The Beatles' first show, which wiped the smiles off their faces. Our Filipino hosts may have been well-intentioned in their elaborate planning but they had no idea of the group's lengthy pre-show routine, including the preparation of stage suits and instruments.

Nor had our hosts allowed for Brian Epstein throwing a tantrum. Flinging every one of his toys out of the pram he screamed down the phone to Vic Lewis at the hotel: "We're not staying one minute longer on this bloody boat, it's going up and down! The boys are fed up. There's absolutely nothing to do and we don't want to spend any more time on this ghastly little yacht. Tony Barrow tells me there's a launch coming out for him in an hour. It can bring us all ashore. Get everything ready for us at the hotel!" It emerged gradually that only Epstein found the idea of staying on the yacht overnight intolerable. When I spoke to Paul and John they confirmed that they would have been happy to stay out in the bay and go ashore in the morning. The only real concern among the group was the delay in getting their bags and a couple of them were dying for a smoke. Meanwhile, Vic Lewis was faced with another blow. The Manila Hotel had no spare suites and Epstein was demanding one for himself and two more for The Beatles to share between them. Lewis worked a miracle and had other VIP guests moved to accommodate our requirements.

Partly because of the pandemonium over the yacht, the tour itinerary prepared by Ramon Ramos Jr was never discussed properly that evening between Epstein and the rest of us. I doubt if he even read it thoroughly or even noticed the crucial bit suggesting that The Beatles might "call in on" the First Lady, the president's wife, Imelda Marcos, at three o'clock on Monday afternoon "before proceeding on from the Malacanang Palace directly to the stadium for the first concert". The wording Ramos used made this sound like a casual proposal rather than a command from the President's office – not a fixed and formal appointment so much as something to be talked about as a possibility. According to Epstein's own jealously guarded rules, only he himself would have discussed such a matter with John, Paul, George and Ringo. If Ramos had raised the invitation with him directly, Epstein would have turned it down on the boys' behalf, knowing that with an afternoon show to do they would want to be safely installed in their dressing room at the stadium by three o'clock. In any case, The Beatles hated meeting dignitaries of all types from small-town mayors up to heads of state and would have been only too pleased to use their matinee commitment as a get-out.

If Epstein had read that weekend's issue of the *Manila Sunday Times*, which none of us saw until afterwards, he might have viewed the palace invitation in a more serious light. The newspaper made it clear that The Beatles were expected at the palace in the morning, not at three in the afternoon: "President Marcos, the First Lady and the three young Beatles fans in the family have been invited as guests of honour at the concerts. The Beatles plan to personally follow up the invitation during a courtesy call on Mrs Imelda Marcos at Malacanang Palace tomorrow (Monday) morning at eleven o'clock." None of this, neither the formality nor the timing, was in the itinerary our promoter presented us with. Ramon Ramos found himself in a tricky position, forced to promise the Palace that he would deliver four Beatles but afraid to risk a face-to-face confrontation with Epstein, knowing that this might result in a point blank refusal that he dare not relay back to the presidential staff.

Quite early on Monday morning a pair of high-ranking military officers came to the Manila Hotel, a general and an admiral, according to Vic Lewis. They announced that they were the reception committee who would escort The Beatles to the palace. They also spoke of the luncheon laid on by Imelda Marcos "in the group's honour" and attended by hundreds of "children of the aristocracy". Still in his pyjamas, Lewis said he knew nothing of a morning appointment or a lunch party but he would inform Brian of the request. The officers spoke coldly: "This is not a request. We have our orders. The children who wish to meet The Beatles will assemble at eleven." Vic threw on a shirt and trousers, phoned me and we went to see Brian Epstein, who was having a late breakfast. Vic told me: "I have to warn him that these people are hot-blooded. A snub would be unwise." Unsurprisingly, Epstein refused to compromise: "I'm not even going to ask The Beatles about this. Go back, Vic, and tell these people we're not coming." If everyone had acted quickly and positively at this point, the boys could have made it to the palace and avoided a disaster. Our convoy from the hotel to the football ground could have been re-routed via the palace and our stay reduced to a diplomatic minimum. Instead, Epstein left his breakfast to inform the general personally and very pompously that he knew of no formal invitation and he would not wake up the boys until it was time to prepare for their afternoon concert. The officers left without another word but within minutes Epstein took a phone call from the British ambassador's office advising him that we would be playing a highly dangerous game if The Beatles failed to comply with the wishes of the First Lady and reminding him that the "help and protection" that The Beatles were receiving in Manila was courtesy of the President. Epstein remained stubbornly adamant and washed his hands of the matter. The Beatles slept on in their suites unaware of all this mayhem and the rest of us went about the day's business according to our various responsibilities on the day of a concert.

At the first show the fans sweated under the blazing 100-degree heat of the afternoon sun, crowds of teenagers screaming as they were crushed uncomfortably against high metal fencing. Gangs of uniformed security guards carrying hefty wooden batons patrolled the fencing, beating the kids' knuckles at random for no apparent reason. Stuck there behind the fence these youngsters presented absolutely no safety threat to The Beatles. Summing up the concert, one newspaper reported: "The sound was terrible, The Beatles were terrific."

Back at the Manila Hotel between shows I watched the early evening television news with Brian Epstein. As part of an extended report on the visit of The Beatles, which I taped in sound only and kept on my cassette recorder, there were scenes from the Malacanang Palace showing intimate friends of the First Family and their children lining up with a crowd of Manila's upper crust in a sumptuous reception room. "The children began to arrive at ten," the news reader began. "They waited until after two. At first we were told that a mob at the yacht basin was delaying the scheduled arrival of The Beatles. Then we learned that the group was not even aboard. At noon the First Lady decided properly and wisely not to wait any longer. 'The children have all the time in the world, but we are busy people,' she said. The place cards for The Beatles at the lunch table were removed. This was the most noteworthy East-West mix-up in Manila for many years."

Public hostility towards The Beatles escalated with alarming speed after the television broadcast. Staff at the British Embassy warned me that they were receiving death threats directed at The Beatles. In an urgent damage-limitation exercise I wrote a statement for Epstein to read to the media and I persuaded Channel 5 television to send a news crew to film an interview with him in his hotel suite for their later bulletin. Epstein diligently explained to camera that neither he nor the group had been handed any invitation: "The first we knew of the hundreds of children waiting to meet The Beatles at the palace was when we watched television earlier this evening." When his statement was transmitted a few hours later by Channel 5, almost everything Epstein said was blotted out by unexplained interference so that nobody heard his explanation. The sound quality was fine for the rest of the programme.

At the end of the second concert, our police escort back to the hotel was withdrawn and gates were locked against our convoy. This left our stationary limousines at the mercy of organised trouble-makers, scores I would say rather than dozens, pressing menacingly against our windows, rocking the vehicles to and fro and yelling insults at The Beatles which none of us could understand. George said later: "It was a very negative vibe. We were being bullied." Eventually, the gates were opened and we sped away. Back at the hotel we warned the boys to lock their doors and we did the same. An hour later a police deputation took Vic Lewis away for questioning. He told us that at police HQ he had heard the same question repeated over and over again: "You represent The Beatles. Why did you not bring them to the palace?" It was almost dawn when Lewis was driven back to the hotel.

Just after eight that morning a man in a shiny suit carrying a brown briefcase came to deliver an envelope for Brian Epstein: "Here is your bill for the income tax due on The Beatles' fee." Our contract with Cavalcade, as with most concert promoters outside the UK, was very precise on the matter of local taxes. The responsibility for payment belonged with the promoter. Ramon Ramos Jr was contractually liable for the settlement of any tax bills. But the taxman insisted that the full fee was taxed as earnings regardless of any other contracts. His words were confirmed by the *Manila Daily Mirror* headline: BEATLES TOLD: PAY NOW, LEAVE LATER. The newspapers carried hostile headlines such as FURORE OVER BEATLES SNUB DAMPENS SHOW and IMELDA STOOD UP: FIRST FAMILY WAITS IN VAIN FOR MOPHEADS. According to a palace spokesperson, The Beatles had "spit in the eye of the First Family". It was also reported quite erroneously that The Beatles had requested an audience with Imelda

Marcos in the first place, the one press story that brought forth hollow laughter from the boys.

The carefully orchestrated hate campaign, stirred up by the authorities and turned into reality by palace goons, manifested itself in various forms. Hotel staff failed to provide room service, porters refused to handle baggage. We were made to feel increasingly isolated. Loading up for the airport trip, the driver of our baggage truck seemed to be the last adult in Manila loyal to our cause. In the absence of other assistance, I joined the roadies and humped our suitcases and equipment out into the street. Vic Lewis told Brian Epstein that he and I were going ahead to the airport to check our party in with KLM and reminded him that Ramos could only hand over our fee when the tax situation was sorted. As we left, Epstein was pondering how long it would take to get hold of £6,000 to buy his way out of the tax problem by filing a bond.

At Manila airport a cop moved us on as we drew up to off-load all our gear. The concourse was deserted, as if a terrorist alert had caused complete public evacuation. The atmosphere was scary. The airport management was under instructions to let The Beatles fend for themselves. Even the escalators were shut down as we approached them. KLM agreed to delay our flight as long as possible but, when The Beatles joined us, Filipino thugs, some in military uniform, closed in on our party from all sides. Guns were brandished and fired into the air, makeshift cudgels and coshes were waved in our faces. Someone shouted in English that The Beatles were not special and deserved to be treated just like ordinary passengers. John said: "Ordinary passengers? They don't get kicked and thumped, do they?" There was no alternative but to run the gauntlet of the menacing mob. Brian Epstein was punched in the face and kicked in the groin. The roadies got the worst of it. Mal Evans was kicked in the ribs and tripped up but he staggered on across the tarmac towards the aircraft with blood streaming down one leg. We did our best to shield John, Paul, George and Ringo from direct blows. Vic Lewis and I were the last to go. He held an open hand across his back saying it might protect his spine from a sniper's bullet.

The jeering and jostling continued until we were at the foot of the KLM aircraft's steps. Even when we had made it into the cabin our ordeal was not over. A command crackled through the loudspeaker

It was normal not to sell the seats directly behind the band. But at this particular show, on August 21, 1966, at the Twin Cities Metropolitan Stadium in Minneapolis to 22,000 people, demand was so great they sold some of the seats offering a view of the backs of the boys' heads. (PHOTO COURTESY OF BILL CARLSON.)

In the Summer of 1966 The Beatles made a promotional film for 'Paperback Writer' in the grounds of Chiswick House in West London. Pictured are director Michael Lindsay-Hogg (left) who went on to direct the movie *Let It Be*, John, chauffeur Alf Bicknell, Ringo, Neil Aspinall, Sue Mautner of *The Beatles Book*, Paul, a cameraman in the background, Brian Epstein, and behind him, George, Mal Evans ... and Me.
(THE SEAN O'MAHONY COLLECTION.)

The Beatles give a press conference before their show at the Twin Cities Metropolitan Stadium in Minneapolis, 1966. The WDGY on the makeshift poster behind the boys refers to the local radio station for the area. And the shadow next to it … the ghost of Sgt. Pepper?
(PHOTO COURTESY OF BILL CARLSON.)

> The Beatles make their way to the stage in Germany on the first leg of their last tour in 1966. This was a typical backstage scene in Germany where the military-style security outnumbered almost everyone.
(THE SEAN O'MAHONY COLLECTION.)

The infamous US deejay Murray The K, the self-styled fifth Beatle, interviews John during an inter-city flight across America.
(THE SEAN O'MAHONY COLLECTION.)

Yet another overcrowded press conference that clearly went out of control when the Q&A was coming to an end. I am standing with a couple of microphones thinking, "How can I wind this up?" Far left behind George is Neil Aspinall, thinking, "How can Tony wind this up?"
(THE TONY BARROW COLLECTION.)

< Ringo, John … and Me, and the familiar globe-balloons, at the press call on the morning before the recording of *All You Need Is Love*, June 25, 1967, for the BBC's *Our World* – the first worldwide satellite television link-up, live from Studio 1, Abbey Road. Over 100 journalists and photographers attended the event.
(THE SEAN O'MAHONY COLLECTION.)

More balloons … and Me, this time addressing the 1999 Beatlefest in New York that attracted some 7000 fans.
(THE TONY BARROW COLLECTION.)

At the 1999 Beatlefest in New York with Sid Bernstein, promoter of The Beatles' 1965 Shea Stadium concert. On several occasions Bernstein offered the boys a (then) massive one million dollars to re-form for a comeback concert. The Beatles turned him down.
(THE TONY BARROW COLLECTION.)

At the Fest For Beatles Fans in Chicago, 2004, I signed hundreds of books and pieces of memorabilia brought to the event by Beatles fans. I also posed for hundreds of photographs, here with one of Paul's fans.
(THE TONY BARROW COLLECTION.)

At the Fest For Beatles Fans in Chicago I also did an unrehearsed chat-show style session on stage with fellow author Larry Kane, the former US TV news anchorman who was part of The Beatles' media entourage in 1964 and 1965. The event also served as the US launch for my book *Paul McCartney: Now & Then*.
(THE TONY BARROW COLLECTION.)

My wife Corinne ... and Me, at a signing of my book *Paul McCartney: Now & Then*, during the Fest For Beatles Fans in Chicago.
(THE TONY BARROW COLLECTION.)

... Me with the Vox Continental organ that John played at The Beatles' Shea Stadium concert in August 1965. The organ went on show at The Beatles Story museum in Liverpool for a limited time in April 2005. I was invited by exhibition founder and director Mike Byrne to mark the instrument's arrival, along with an array of jackets worn by John and the others in the Sixties. I posed for photographers at a press reception as I recalled how John ran his elbows up and down the keys of the organ in a wild Jerry Lee Lewis impression during a rendition of "I'm Down" at Shea Stadium.
(THE TONY BARROW COLLECTION.)

system. "Mr Tony Barrow and Mr Malcolm Evans must return to the departure building." I muttered: "They're going to take it out on us two." Mal asked someone to contact his wife. Inside the building Mal and I were told that we could not leave the Philippines because there was no documentary evidence that we had arrived! Our papers had not been processed with the rest when our incoming flight taxied to the far end of the airfield. I suppose we could have been arrested. Instead, we handed over our passports, they were duly stamped and we were free to leave. Mal and I smiled at one another, tremendously relieved that we were not to be made scapegoats and kept behind. While the authorities were sorting out our formalities, Vic Lewis walked up the aisle to where Brian Epstein was sitting and asked him quietly if he had resolved the tax problem and received the concert money. Epstein flew into a rage. His face turned purple with undiluted fury as he shouted: "Is that all you can think of, Vic? Bloody money at a time like this?" Lewis told me later: "This was sheer hypocrisy on Epstein's part, of course." The two men had always disliked one another but this incident placed them further apart than ever and in future Epstein avoided Lewis's company whenever he could. The bottom line was that, although a record-breaking 80,000 saw The Beatles in concert in Manila, NEMS Enterprises lost money on this leg of the tour.

It was now well past the flight's scheduled departure time, but in separate pleas to the captain Vic Lewis and Brian Epstein persuaded him to hang on for us. As soon as KLM flight 862 aircraft rose up from the runway at 4.45pm that afternoon our entire party broke into spontaneous applause. George leant across the aisle between his seat and mine and said to me: "The only way I'd ever go back to that place would be to drop a dirty big bomb on it." Paul asked me if I had recorded Brian's television statement and if so could he hear it. I told him: "I have it on a cassette. You can hear the newsreader's introduction but the rest is a blur. They blotted out the whole of Brian's explanation." Before Paul left the Manila Hotel in a typical gesture of PR goodwill on behalf of the group, he did a radio interview apologising for The Beatles' failure to meet Imelda Marcos and saying that they knew nothing of her lunch party. At all times, even in adverse conditions, Paul carried an ample supply of oil for pouring onto troubled waters. Back home in London he gave the press a graphic account of our departure: "We were being pushed and banged around from one corner to another. With the escalators switched off we couldn't go anywhere very fast. When they started knocking over our road managers everyone was falling all over the place. I swear there were at least 30 of them surrounding us." George had the final word. Asked on his arrival in London what was next on the group's agenda he replied with only the merest a hint of a smile: "We're going to have a couple of weeks to recuperate before we go and get beaten up by the Americans." Neil Aspinall said philosophically: "The Philippine experience became one of the last nails on The Beatles' touring coffin." A whole bag o' nails, I'd say, Neil!

In retrospect, I find it ironic that The Beatles were accused of snubbing the President's wife when in truth they didn't know anything about her invitation "to drop in". I readily admit that on other occasions Brian Epstein or I used to tell white lies to get The Beatles out of civic functions or state ceremonies that would have embarrassed and bored them; we usually made their excuses without even consulting them. But in the case of the Manila palace lunch we were seriously under-informed by our own local promoter and had no idea that The Beatles would be letting down hundreds of invited guests by not attending.

The year continued chaotic and with an undercurrent of danger. For John Lennon, the most disastrous episode of his entire time with The Beatles had begun earlier in the year, on Friday March 4, 1966, when London's *Evening Standard* published an interview-based feature article by Maureen Cleave on John's lifestyle.

John's "crime" had been to claim in an interview with the London *Evening Standard* journalist Maureen Cleave that The Beatles were now more popular than Jesus. The re-quoting of his statement emblazoned on the cover of America's *Datebook* fanzine led to public album-burning ceremonies orchestrated by radio deejays who did it more for the publicity than because they were offended by John's remark. This was one of her series of in-depth profile pieces entitled "How Does A Beatle Live?" Buried away in the eighth paragraph was a quote from John that was to bring down the wrath of religious zealots on his head and haunt him for the rest of his career with the Fab Four: "Christianity will go, it will vanish and shrink. I needn't argue about that, I'm right and I'll be proved right. We're more popular than Jesus now. I don't know which will go first – rock'n'roll or Christianity. Jesus was all right but his disciples were thick and ordinary. It's them twisting it that ruins it for me." John was heavily into books about the world's philosophers and religions at the time and was making what he considered to be a valid comment on the contemporary decline in church attendance among Christians. This was not merely Lennon's view, it was a matter of fact. In other words, while fans of The Beatles were packing out Britain's Odeon and ABC theatres to see the group's concerts, fewer Christians were going to church on Sundays. Elsewhere in the same article, Maureen Cleave drew attention to precious possessions John had shown her on her visit to his 27-room mock Tudor residence at Weybridge: " … a huge altar crucifix of a Roman Catholic nature with IHS on it" and "an enormous bible he bought in Chester".

Initially, John's observation did not raise any eyebrows or cause the slightest indignation among *Evening Standard* readers, whether believers or non-believers. Then, in the last days of July, the September edition of America's *Datebook* magazine was published, well-timed to reach news-stands in the run-up to The Beatles' US tour and including a version of Maureen Cleave's article reproduced as part of the monthly's "Shout-out" issue. *Datebook* had a reputation for being ever-so-slightly more serious in its approach to the teenybopper scene than, say, the bigger-selling *16*. On its front cover the latest *Datebook* ran a massive pin-up picture of Paul and beside it a column of celebrity quotes from Paul, John, Scott Walker, Dylan, Tim Leary and others. John's quote was: "I don't know which will go first – rock'n'roll or Christianity." This and the remainder of John's comments were presented inside in a more sensational context than that of the original *Evening Standard* article. They caused uproar among various religious organisations, many of whose members must have half-read John's words or not seen them at all. Some Christian believers mistakenly assumed that John's reference to "thick and ordinary" disciples was intended to disparage them, not Christ's contemporaries of 2000 years ago.

Presenters and deejays at radio stations in the South, across the so-called Bible Belt of America, jumped on the bandwagon and urged young fans to rally round and build ceremonial bonfires on which The Beatles' records were burnt. Some of these stations had never played the group's records in the past but were now moved to ban them anyway. In Mississippi an Imperial Wizard of the Ku Klux Klan announced that he believed The Beatles had been "brainwashed by the Communists". Joining in the holy war with enthusiasm, the Grand Dragon of the KKK in South Carolina tied a bundle of The Beatles' albums to a cross, which he then set alight in front of a cheering crowd. To all but the most biased and prejudiced observers, the fires were publicity stunts to raise the public profiles of the organising broadcasters. Without the snowballing media attention which these ceremonies generated, I doubt if the *Datebook* material would have been seen as so outrageous, but America's press, radio and television outlets took up the cause of the bible bashers and turned the full strength of their venom on John Lennon. Radio station WAQY in Birmingham, Alabama, announced that The Beatles had been banned because "we consider them unacceptable to many lovers of good music". WTUF in Mobile denounced Lennon's statement as "an outright sacrilegious affront to Almighty God". The gospel-orientated Texan station KZEE decided to ban The Beatles "eternally".

Elsewhere in the world, the South African Broadcasting Corporation banned the playing of Beatles' records, a Spanish station followed suit and there were attempts by sections of the Dutch population to ban the group's records and refuse permission for The Beatles to appear again in Holland. From London we countered as hard as we could, claiming that John's remarks had been perspicacious and perfectly reasonable social comment, not blasphemy at all. Maureen Cleave, an outstanding feature writer of her day, had gained the respect of The Beatles and developed a particularly close relationship with John. She would not have done anything deliberately to harm John or damage the group's image. She said her article had been misinterpreted and John had not intended to be flippant or irreverent. He was deploring rather than approving of the present state of affairs where Christianity was so weak that many young people were more aware of The Beatles in their lives than of Jesus Christ. She said: "Sectors of the American public were given the wrong impression, and it was totally absurd."

In London at the beginning of August, Brian Epstein cut short his pre-tour break at the Italian-style North Wales resort of Portmeirion

– where he was recovering from a dose of glandular fever – to attend an emergency meeting of NEMS executives. At the meeting, those of us in The Beatles' inner circle debated the seriousness of the US reaction and whether we dared go ahead with a concert tour when such an escalation of public hatred was under way there ahead of our arrival. Press headlines described the uproar as a "US holy war against The Beatles". One radio station that had not previously played The Beatles' records now decided to do so at 30-minute intervals, each play preceded by an announcement saying that to ban the group's music was contemptible "hypocrisy personified", adding: "Some of the stations which have banned The Beatles play other songs that are the most pornographic since Elizabethan times. Perhaps The Beatles could be more popular than Jesus, perhaps that is what is wrong with society, and you, dear friend, made them so, not Jesus, not John Lennon and not The Beatles". You might say that this was another way of leaping aboard the same bandwagon! Unexpected support for The Beatles also came from Salt Lake City, Utah, where the programme director of station KCPX said: "I don't believe in religious bigots any more than I believe in Beatles bigots. I'm playing their records, not their religious ideals."

At the end of the first week in August, Epstein flew to New York with the intention of quelling further anger. He told the US media that the whole affair was a typical Beatles furore: "Lennon is deeply interested in religion and was talking seriously with Maureen Cleave, a good friend of The Beatles. He did not mean to boast." Murray (The K) Kaufman got in on the act too, saying: "I think the statement did provoke and inspire churchmen who believed that what John was saying was the truth." Arguments rattled on in all sectors of the US and international media, leaving us with the ongoing dilemma as to whether we would risk John's life by going ahead with our US concert schedule in the face of assassination threats, particularly surrounding the Memphis gig. It was decided that nothing more could be done in advance to sway public opinion and we would have to devote our first press conference in Chicago to the Lennon situation. I flew ahead of the boys to Chicago and set up camp at the Astor Towers Hotel from where I began to assess media and public feelings.

As soon as The Beatles arrived John asked for a meeting with Brian Epstein and myself. We sat down together, just the three of us, and I briefed him as far as possible on what to expect from the international assembly of journalists, including people from all three American television networks, ABC, CBS and NBC, who were about to cram into my suite on the 27th floor. Never before or afterwards did I see John in such a distraught state, not because he believed he owed anyone an apology, but because he knew that the tour could be cancelled unless he swung the media over and gained their support at the imminent conference. After hearing what we had to say, John leant forward in his chair and fell silent, his head in his hands. We realised that he was sobbing and Brian put a comforting arm around his shoulders. John raised his head: "I'm willing to apologise if you tell me that's what I must do. I'll do anything, whatever you say. How on earth am I to face the others if this whole tour is called off just because of something I've said? I didn't mean to cause all of this." I suggested to John that he should concentrate on trying to explain rather than telling the press he was sorry. Brian Epstein broke his own rule by warning John directly that there was a very real fear of an attempt on his life if the mood of America's bible bashers did not improve. He said: "I would sooner cancel the concerts than take such a risk, John, and I'll take the responsibility for telling George, Paul and Ringo."

When it was time to face the press conference we collected the other three and went to my suite. We found it heaving with people, cameras, lighting rigs and other press paraphernalia. In my absence the table behind which The Beatles were to sit had been moved back towards the wall to accommodate the crush and there was only just enough space for the four boys to squeeze into position. From the outset this conference was unlike any other the boys gave during the six years I was with them. Looking pale and frightened, John almost flinched in front of the first barrage of photographers' flash bulbs. Then he began his long meandering explanation, faltering at every sentence, sometimes staring straight at the television cameras but mostly casting his eyes down at the table: "Look, I wasn't saying The Beatles are better than God or Jesus. I said Beatles because it's easy for me to talk about Beatles, I could have said TV or the cinema, motor cars, or anything popular and I would have got away with it. My views on Christianity are directly influenced by *The Passover Plot* by Hugh J Schofield. The premise is that Jesus' message has been garbled by his disciples and twisted for a variety of self-serving reasons by those who followed."

So far, so good. Then came the questions. "What was your own formal religious background, John?" "Just what were you trying to get across with your comments, sir?" "Mr Lennon, do you believe in God?" "Are you sorry about your statement concerning Christ?" John was never good with words when it came to formal speeches. Somewhere between his brain and his tongue what he wanted to say got scrambled and when the words finally came tumbling out of his mouth they made less sense than he intended. If he had been able to turn his Chicago statement into the lyrics of a songs it would have been different. John made much more sense and had greater impact in the lyrics he wrote rather than the words that he spoke. In Chicago he stumbled on, occasionally losing his way, but lacked the impact he needed to convince this roomful of hard-nosed news people. "I'm not anti-God, anti-Christ or anti-religion. I was not saying we are greater or better. I believe that what people call God is something in all of us. I believe that what Jesus, Mohammed, Buddha and all the rest said was right, it's just that the translations have gone wrong. From what I've read, or observed, Christianity just seems to me to be shrinking, to be losing contact."

The questioning became painfully repetitive and John tried to re-phrase his one answer in ways he hoped the journalists would find more satisfactory. Paul came to his rescue from time to time, adding additional weight and a second voice to John's responses. One guy asked: "Do you really think Christianity is shrinking?" Paul chimed in: "And we deplore the fact that it is, you know, that's the point." John was becoming desperate: "I'm sorry I said it, really. I never meant it to be a lousy anti-religious thing." One reporter asked: "To what do you ascribe your immense popularity?" Ringo brought a moment's levity to the unusually serious conference by replying: "Ask Tony Barrow that one." Told that a deejay in Alabama demanded a straightforward apology, John replied: "He can have it. If he's upset and he really means it, then I'm sorry. I apologise to him." An "I'm sorry" addressed to one individual wasn't good enough for some of the media inquisitors and John never did come out with the over-all apology that he and I had agreed would be necessary at John's unprecedented pre-conference briefing. Several ceremonial bonfires in

Alabama and elsewhere across the bible belt took place while others were cancelled in the wake of John's explanatory speech, which lasted something like 20 minutes.

At a short-notice meeting with representatives of our US booking agents and the Chicago show promoter, it was agreed that we should go ahead with the series of 15 concerts as planned. John told the press: "We are still looking forward to our tour. We could have hidden in England and said we wouldn't come." In private, John quickly bounced back, the old Lennonesque resilience replaced the brief show of remorse and he described the bonfire protesters as "middle-aged deejays burning a pile of LP covers for an audience of 12-year-olds". After watching one of the album-burning ceremonies on television, Paul said: "They were zealots. It was horrible to see the hatred on their faces."

Three days into the tour, we encountered a tiny group of Ku Klux Klan goons demonstrating at Washington's District of Columbia Stadium and, four days after that, half-a-dozen Klansmen outside the Mid South Coliseum in Memphis encouraged a mob of fanatics to yell obscenities at our vehicle-of-the-day, a Wells Fargo truck, as we arrived at the venue for the first of two shows. This was the most stressful date on the tour, all of us aware that, if John was to come to any harm at the hands of protestors, here was the place it was most likely to happen. At the second show someone in the crowd threw a fire cracker – a "cherry bomb", the Americans called it – which exploded with a loud bang close to the stage. Our heads swung round instinctively to face John, as did those of the other three boys on stage. Our fear was that a sniper had fired a fatal shot at John and we would see him sink to the floor in a heap. Thankfully, that fear was unfounded – or, more accurately, it was premature by a matter of some 14 years.

10 | The End Of The Road

THERE WAS A stiff Pacific breeze blowing in off the bay on the prematurely autumnal evening when The Beatles played the last concert of their 1966 US tour at San Francisco's Candlestick Park. I stood in the middle of this large and slightly dilapidated baseball field shortly before the last 25,000 fans ever to see the Fab Four in a full-length concert began to file into the two-tiered stands. I was making a mental note of where the towers of loudspeakers were positioned on the grass on either side of the temporary stage. I was planning to record the show and needed to decide where I should position myself to get the best sound quality on my pitifully lo-fi recording equipment. It was going to be a matter of simply holding a microphone up in the air and hoping I could capture a reasonably balanced sound from the stage on my primitive little Philips cassette recorder. All I needed the machine for as a rule was to make spoken-word recordings of interviews between The Beatles and various journalists while we were on the road and in terms of sound quality that was a far cry from attempting to record a whole concert in a baseball park. I had no idea how bad the balance might turn out to be between voices and instruments, or if the boys' "patter" between each song would be heard clearly enough to record at all. If the wind blew stronger during the evening I also ran the risk of picking up the sound of each gust as well as The Beatles' music. However, the finished recording was not intended for any commercial purpose but was purely for Paul to keep as his personal souvenir of the show.

There was no official suggestion that this would be The Beatles' last-ever stage appearance for a crowd of paying customers but there was a cheerful, "end-of-term" atmosphere among the boys because this was the end of a particularly arduous, traumatic and stressful round-the-world tour and all of us looked forward to getting home to be with family and friends. Candlestick Park was what the American tour manager, Ira, liked to call one of our "in and out" jobs – a flight in from the previous gig in Los Angeles and a flight out again right after the concert, with no overnight stay in San Francisco. For security reasons, our journey from the airport to the venue was by privately hired bus. Everyone, including the main supporting acts, The Cyrkle and The Ronettes, plus our travelling entourage of press people, piled into this less-than-luxurious vehicle and heard Ira warn us that a particularly large crowd of fans had gathered at the Park. Probably the last form of transport they'd expect to find The Beatles using would be this well-worn bus. During the drive Paul asked me if I had my tape recorder with me. On tour I carried it everywhere so that I could play back interview and press conference material to journalists back home who hadn't made the trip. I also used it to keep my own record of what went on. "Make me a recording of tonight's final concert, will you?" asked Paul. I remember wondering what I should read into this unusual request. None of the boys had ever asked me to record souvenir tapes of previous concerts. Had Paul already made up his mind that he was going to be outvoted by the others on the issue of future concert tours? Was he resigned to the fact that San Francisco was the end of the road? Or did he merely want a tape to remind himself of this particular tour, something to play for his girlfriend Jane Asher once he and she were reunited in his new London home at St John's Wood? As we approached Candlestick Park we listened to a deejay on the local KYA Radio relaying details of our progress over the air. No wonder there was a big turn-out of fans awaiting our arrival!

The bus idea backfired when it reached the Park. We drove through a vast and, as yet, empty car parking area to a specified entrance without attracting any attention from little groups of chattering fans who scarcely gave us a glance. Unfortunately, the guy who was supposed to unlock the entrance gates was nowhere to be seen. Gradually, small clusters of girls surrounded our bus as we waited with the engine running. Finally, someone caught sight of a Beatle: "It's Paul! It's Paul!" We had two choices: to remain stationary and let the crowd of fans swell by the second or to drive off and circle the

Park. Bess Coleman told me afterwards that she and several of the other journalists on the bus were genuinely afraid that the growing mob of fans would turn the bus over. Ira took a quick decision: "We can't stay here. If those kids start climbing over the bus somebody's going to get hurt." As we moved off a few fans got into their battered old convertibles and others followed our bus on foot as we circled the parking lot, weaving our way between the pursuing cars and swerving to avoid clusters of excited fans on foot. Nobody was controlling this increasing flow of human and vehicular traffic and our driver had to brake violently on several occasions to prevent a collision. Eventually, we spotted a man waving at us frantically from the gate through which we were supposed to enter the Park and the dangerous white-knuckle ride of real-life dodgem cars came to an end. This incident lived on in Paul's mind to become his inspiration for the crazy coach-and-car race in *Magical Mystery Tour*, which we filmed the following year at an airfield in West Malling, Kent.

At eight o'clock, with night falling quite suddenly upon Candlestick Park, The Beatles' show got underway. Although I didn't fancy my chances of making a brilliant recording of the concert, one thing in my favour was the great distance between the stage and the stands at this particular venue. Because of this, I guessed I might be able to capture sound from the stage without picking up too much of the non-stop screams and shouts of the fans coming from the stands. The fact that it was an open-air gig also helped. In an enclosed auditorium it would have been impossible to pick up the sound of the music without picking up too much crowd noise. When the last of the supporting acts came off stage I went out on the field ahead of the boys. When John, Paul, George and Ringo ran out across the grass a roar of approval went up from the stands and, as they did a quickie tune-up on stage, each chord they played caused a further roar. One of the US deejays in our travelling party, who I had prevented from recording an earlier concert on the tour, saw me holding my mike up in the air and mimicked my words of warning back to me: "On Brian Epstein's orders there must be no recording of the performances. Please turn off." With a finger to my lips, I indicated to him to shut up, I didn't want extraneous voices on my "official" concert recording. Up on stage one of the boys yelled "Hello" to test his voice mike and in another moment the group tore into Chuck Berry's 'Rock'n'Roll Music'.

Not to be outdone by Paul's idea of making a souvenir recording of the concert, John had taken his camera on stage and clicked away in the faces of the other three between songs. He also held the camera at arm's length and took several shots of himself. At one point Paul mentioned the cool wind blowing across the Park, remarking that it was "a bit chilly". For the most part, other than a few remarks added in simply because this was the end of the tour, The Beatles introduced their songs just the way they had done throughout the past three years. I have compared recordings of their first US concerts in Washington and New York with the one I made in San Francisco and been fascinated to note that the boys used almost identical wording to address the audience between songs. While the patter worked, why change it? In those days portable cassette recorders used standard tapes that were 60 minutes in length, 30 minutes either side. My tape ran out at the end of side one soon after Paul had started to sing 'Long Tall Sally', the last number in the set. Interestingly, on this night he almost forgot the golden rule of never saying "Good Night" to an audience because if everybody knew this was the end of the performance they'd leave their seats and rush to block our getaway route! Paul cut himself short after saying "Goo … " and jumped into the song. As usual 'Long Tall Sally' was the cue for our party, including the press, to make its way back to the waiting bus so that we could drive away the moment the four sweat-soaked boys climbed on board to join us, as always accompanied by tumultuous applause from all of us! Apart from the nonsense in the parking lot beforehand it was a very average evening, although a local newspaper called it BEDLAM AT THE BALL PARK.

When we boarded our charter aircraft for the final flight of the tour, down the Californian coast from San Francisco back to Los Angeles, George sank down into the seat next to me and said: "That's it then. I'm not a Beatle any more." He didn't intend to imply that he was leaving the group, just that he and the other three could now turn their backs on all the hassles of Beatlemania and concentrate on some serious music-making in the recording studios. George admitted to me that the threats by American religious fanatics to kill John were the last straw. When I asked him what he really thought of the ceremonial bonfires built along the Bible Belt to destroy The Beatles' albums he grinned and said: "Well, they had to buy the albums before they could burn them!"

John shouted across the aisle to me: "Where's Eppy? Was he there tonight?" I said that I hadn't seen Brian at the show and I didn't think he was in San Francisco, but that he would surely link up with us again in Los Angeles. The truth was that Epstein's briefcase – containing a substantial stash of cash, some 20,000 US dollars I was told, a pile of very private papers including contracts for The Beatles' concerts and a bottle of unlawfully acquired Seconal barbiturates – had been stolen from him while he was out to dinner at the Beverly Hills Hotel. With the help of his New York friend and business partner, Nat Weiss, who had stuff stolen by the same guy at the same time, Epstein was making final desperate efforts to track down his property before we left America. He had confided in me that some highly sensitive personal documents were among the items that had gone missing and his greatest fear was that they might have been stolen by – or passed on to – a potential blackmailer. Epstein told me: "If you discover that any of the press have wind of this, for God's sake tell me at once and don't say a word to anybody else." In the event, the two men did receive blackmail demands with the threat that Brian's unauthorised possession of drugs would be made known to the authorities, or the media, or both. The fear of scandal was of much greater concern to Epstein than the loss of cash because some of the muck raked up in the papers might damage the image of The Beatles. Epstein was forever concealing his own mistakes and misdemeanours because he believed that if he generated bad publicity some of it would wash off on his artists. In due course, the thief, a former boyfriend, was arrested and Brian's briefcase was returned to him in London. The Seconal bottle had been emptied.

At San Francisco airport, as our plane prepared to take off, Paul's head came over the top of my seat from the row behind: "Did you get anything on tape?" I passed the cassette recorder back to him: "I got the lot, except that the tape ran out in the middle of 'Long Tall Sally'." He asked if I had left the machine running between numbers to get all the announcements and the boys' ad lib remarks. I said: "It's all there from the guitar feedback before the first number." Paul was clearly chuffed to have such a unique souvenir of what would prove to be an historic evening – the farewell stage show from the Fab Four. Back in London I kept the concert cassette under lock and key in a drawer of my office desk, making a single copy for my personal collection and passing the original to Paul for him to keep. Years later, my Candlestick Park recording re-appeared in public as a bootleg album. If you hear a bootleg version of the final concert that finishes during 'Long Tall Sally' it must have come either from Paul's copy or mine, but we never did identify the music thief!

The 1966 world tour is remembered by those of us who travelled with The Beatles mainly for the shocking events in Tokyo and Manila, plus the whole "more popular than Jesus" hullabaloo. These horrendous episodes tended to overshadow all other happenings, but within hours of John's embarrassing press conference at Chicago's Astor Towers Hotel, the group bounced on stage in "show-must-go-on" mode at the International Amphitheatre in Chicago for the first of two resoundingly successful performances. The totally positive reaction of the audience cheered up the boys who feared that John's much-resented remark might have changed the attitude of American Beatle People, not just Bible Belt religious groups. Wearing the striking new stage outfits of bottle-green suits and light green shirts that had made their debut in Tokyo, the boys were greeted by thunderous screaming and yelling from Chicago fans. During the early show someone accidentally disconnected the plug from George's amplifier so that he was left standing there to strum a silent guitar. While the roadies tracked down the fault, John, wearing his orange-tinted Granny glasses, entertained with an impromptu soft-shoe shuffle while Ringo vamped away on drums in accompaniment. John connected the unplugging with the "more popular than Jesus" episode, insisting that none of the stage crew could have done this by accident. We tried to convince him otherwise but obviously the nightmare was going to live on in his mind whatever we said. The group kept up their new 1966 trend for brighter stage gear by wearing their recently introduced, light-grey-and-pink pin-striped suits with perfectly fitted pink shirts at their next gigs in Detroit. Adventurous Detroit fans cottoned on to the fact that we were travelling from there to Cleveland by road immediately after the second concert. A convoy of open-topped cars sped after our bus and stayed with us well into the four-hour late-night drive.

One of the wildest shows took place at the Municipal Stadium in Cleveland – where the crowd broke loose, crashed through a four-foot security fence and invaded the field during 'Day Tripper'. Hopelessly outnumbered and overwhelmed, the local police simply gave up and stood back while hordes of fans took control of the stage and the "secure" grassy area around it. The boys rushed off to their makeshift dressing room – a caravan/trailer parked behind the stage – and the concert was stopped for 30 minutes while private guards and police reinforcements restored order. At the end of that show roadie Mal Evans had to stop fans from stealing the boys' instruments from the stage as souvenirs. In Cincinnati on August 20, torrential rain caused the cancellation of the show at Crosley Field Stadium, the first and only time this happened during The Beatles' touring years. The decision to put off the boys' appearance was taken when Mal was thrown several feet across the stage while plugging into a wet amplifier. We were advised that touching any of the stage's rain-soaked electrical equipment could be lethal so Epstein had no option but to call off the concert. The group's commitment to Cincinnati fans was honoured by the hasty scheduling of a replacement show for lunchtime the following day by which time the place had dried out sufficiently for the electrical systems to be relatively safe.

One noteworthy innovation I introduced during this tour was a separate "junior" press conference in my suite on the 28th floor of the Warwick Hotel in New York on August 22, the eve of our Shea Stadium date. My motive was two-fold: this would reduce the number of non-professionals and youthful competition winners at the main press conference and at the same time the additional event would be seen by fans as a kindly goodwill gesture on the part of John, Paul, George and Ringo. Nobody over the age of 18 years was admitted and instead The Beatles faced questioning from 150 youngsters including listeners to WMCA Radio and local members of The Beatles Fan Club. I would love to report that the teenagers came up with more intelligent questions than their elders but they didn't. Most of the younger girls wanted to probe Paul about his continuing and much-publicised relationship with the English actress Jane Asher. One was interested in John's hair:

Q: John, when did you last go to a barber's shop?
A: I haven't been to a proper barber for years. George often cuts my hair when we're on the road and Cyn does it when I'm at home.

In Seattle, Paul was questioned by journalists over a rumour that he was about to get married. Gossip had spread through the city suggesting that Jane was due to fly in to join Paul. The word was that a wedding cake had been ordered and a bridal suite reserved at a local hotel. A reporter said: "Mr McCartney, would you please confirm or deny reports that you plan to marry Jane Asher here in Seattle this evening." Playing along at first, Paul grinned broadly and said: "It's tonight, yeah!" Then he added more seriously: "No, she's not coming in tonight, as far as I know. I do hope it's not true. I'm going back to Los Angeles tonight so if Jane flies in I'm not even going to see her, let alone marry her!"

In relatively serious mood for an in-depth interview with the New York-based English journalist Bess Coleman, who was reporting on the tour for America's *Teen Life* magazine and a string of radio stations, Paul talked about the way The Beatles had changed in the two years since their first visit to the US. Having worked in the London press office of EMI Records at the time of The Beatles' launch in 1962 and later having accompanied the group's 1964 US concert tour as assistant press officer, Bess was treated as an old friend. Paul reminded her that The Beatles had gone almost directly from their schools and colleges to their early professional gigs: "In 1964 we were still young mentally and were unable to cope with being Beatles. We were all fresh from Liverpool and felt that we constantly had to prove that we were as good as anybody else. People laughed and sneered at us because we had long hair, and any chance we had to have a dig back we did. Now we realise that that was silly." According to Paul, even if press conference questioning remained banal and vacuous, the general level of one-to-one interviews rose substantially during the touring years: "We were asked so many stupid questions in 1964 that we just gave back stupid answers. Now people realise that we're not just an idiotic lot of mop-heads. They ask us serious questions about our music and our views on other subjects. We feel now that we have been accepted as reasonably intelligent human beings. The main change has come about because we have all matured. We realise now that we are not the greatest thing that ever happened. We were so new to the business in 1964 that when people kept telling us (we were the greatest) we believed them."

The next bit of Paul's interview with Bess Coleman hinted at things to come. Paul said: "We've quietened down now and know that we're just normal human beings like anyone else. And that's how we want to be accepted." This was the first time that Paul aired his "I'm just an ordinary human being" attitude that was to become a cornerstone of his self-tailored PR strategy in years to come. I heard him take a similar line in several other interviews during the tour. Over the years since then Paul has liked everyone to believe that he is no different from the rest of us, that he leads a normal, simple everyday lifestyle that borders on the frugal. Here, as early as 1966, he was sowing the seeds of a personal image that he would develop with some dedication over the following 40 years. The sincerity of this attitude has often been questioned by journalists and commentators. I hoped his second marriage, this time to the feisty, anti-minefield fund-raiser and former model Heather Mills, might help Paul to reassess his outlook and properly appreciate the sweet comforts of life that are available to a multi-millionaire megastar. I think that he's always been a material boy at heart.

When Paul talked to *Teen Life* about the higher standard of media questioning The Beatles were facing during their 1966 US tour, he was thinking of the personal interviews he and the others had with selected journalists – those in our travelling entourage – who were starting to touch on grand political issues, like war and peace, with The Beatles and getting some strongly-phrased reactions by way of response, particularly from John and George. I saw no such raised standards in press conference situations. Before the tour's penultimate concert at Dodger Stadium, Los Angeles, The Beatles gave their very last press conference as a touring band in a spacious first-floor suite at Capitol Tower, the impressive Hollywood headquarters of their US record company, which was built to look like a tall stack of records. This 23-minute event attended by some 250 people, including distinguished international journalists, was also the last Beatles' conference that I would organise and introduce and it culminated with the presentation of an award to the boys by the company president Alan Livingston for record-breaking initial sales of *Revolver*. Over one million copies went over the counters at US record stores in the first fortnight after release and *Revolver* remained at the top of Billboard's US album charts for six weeks.

Compared with similar conferences in previous years, this one was almost wholly devoid of The Beatles' hallmark wisecracks and quick-fire, one-line gags. This time they were flippant without being funny, although some over-enthusiastic members of the crowd applauded and laughed so heartily that the conference sounded more like a hilarious vaudeville variety show in full swing than the meaningless exchange it turned out to be. Only McCartney made any meaningful attempt at more than monosyllabic answers. Otherwise, The Beatles' replies to conference questions showed a lack of respect for the prestigious media people they were addressing, a careless indifference that came close to contempt. In their defence I have to admit that The Beatles had taken a mental and physical battering on this extraordinarily eventful and dangerous tour, but I was surprised and disappointed to see them abandoning their usual professionalism so blatantly for this last press conference.

Once or twice, when the boys did show short glimpses of their flair for spontaneous comedy, they drew huge applause from a supportive crowd that was obviously hoping for the best.

Q: A recent article in *Time* magazine put down pop music and referred to 'Day Tripper' as being about a prostitute and 'Norwegian Wood' as about a lesbian. What was your intent when you wrote them?

A: We were just trying to write songs about prostitutes and lesbians.

Q: What was the inspiration for 'Eleanor Rigby'?

A: Two queers.

Next to nothing new was said. It was no great revelation to hear that contemporary US groups favoured by John and Paul included the Beach Boys, The Byrds, The Lovin' Spoonful, The Miracles and The Mamas And The Papas. Nor was I surprised when the "Jesus" thing cropped up again.

Q: John, would you clarify and repeat the answer you gave in Chicago?

A: I can't repeat it because I don't know what I said.

The movie director Dick Lester must have felt let down by John not using a golden opportunity to publicise his forthcoming appearance in the anti-war film *How I Won The War*. One reporter gave John a superb opening to talk about his debut as a straight screen actor and the film's message when he asked how the Beatle had made up his mind to take part in Lester's production. John threw away the chance with a lacklustre one-line reply: "He asked me and I just said yes." John was due to fly to Germany a week later to begin shooting his quirky role as Private Gripweed on a NATO tank-training base at Bergen-Hohne outside Hanover.

John also missed an ideal opportunity to publicise his book *In His Own Write*:

Q: John, under what conditions did you write *In His Own Write*? Those wild, kinky words, how did you piece them together?
A: I don't know.

The Capitol conference as a whole showed that between 1965 and 1966 The Beatles had largely lost the will to work very hard at pleasing a media crowd. They made it clear that they were not feeling at all Fab any more. They were too tired, low-spirited and fed up to fight their fatigue. Threatened with multiple assassinations less than two months ago in Tokyo, mobbed and mugged by hired thugs from the presidential palace in Manila and stalked by the very real fear that Klansmen might attempt to murder John in Memphis, I suppose it was no wonder that The Beatles lacked their usual vivaciousness and sparkle during the tour's final exchange with the press. Perhaps the natural reaction in the circumstances was to call a halt to this risky job of touring the world. Certainly, performing in public had lost its artistic appeal because The Beatles knew they couldn't be heard above the constant screaming of the fans. Bum notes went unheard. Off-key vocals were not noticed. John said to me: "We might as well send out cardboard cut-outs of the Fab Four and a tape of pre-recorded farts. The fans would still turn up."

The tour's penultimate concert at Dodger Stadium, Los Angeles, on August 28, found 45,000 fans virtually out of control due to poorly constructed crowd barriers and inadequate policing. We were driven to the stadium in an armoured car that was parked immediately behind the stage. At this late point in the tour I suspect that the fans' grapevine had circulated full details of the boys' act, giving everyone prior warning of the songs that would end the set. Even before the group started Little Richard's 'Long Tall Sally', hundreds of fans invaded the field and surrounded our getaway car. By the time The Beatles left the stage and we were ready to pull away, many hundreds if not thousands more had positioned themselves across our path. Our driver yelled: "Hold very tight, folks!" Then he slammed his gears into reverse and we sped backwards across the field at breakneck speed. Panic-stricken fans flung themselves out of our way. I was amazed that we didn't smash into anyone. The trick failed to clear a path for our escape and the driver gave up. At high speed he headed for a dugout at the far side of the field and we hurriedly raced underground out of sight of the noisy hordes of fans. For two hours we were imprisoned in a team dressing room for our own safety while extra cops came in to start clearing the hysterically boisterous crowd. The getaway car we hoped to use was severely damaged and put out of action. Two girls even ran off with the ignition key as a souvenir! All four boys were on the point of despair and we were discussing the possibility that our party might have to stay cooped up at the stadium overnight. Ringo broke the ensuing silence by saying in a small voice: "Can I please go home to my mummy now, please can I?" Two further unsuccessful attempts were made to get us out using decoy limousines and the third try was equally disastrous. We were put into an ambulance that managed to crash into a heap of broken fencing, after which it couldn't be driven any further. Extra squads of police from the sheriff's department eventually escorted us away to safety in an armoured car. Silently to ourselves we repeated Ringo's heartfelt plea. We wanted to go home now. Please could we?

In the first week of September, while John went to work on his solo movie project, the other three Beatles took a short break. George took Pattie to India where he received sitar lessons from his idol Ravi Shankar in Bombay. Ringo and Maureen went to Spain. Apart from a weekend in Paris, Paul spent much of September settling into his new home in Cavendish Avenue, St John's Wood. Around this time I suddenly found myself taking an alarming number of phone calls from Fleet Street news desks enquiring about Paul's whereabouts and state of health. Some reporters veiled their questions: "Have you talked to Paul today? How is he doing? Is he OK?" Others were more direct: "The rumour we're hearing is that Paul is dead. Can you confirm or deny this?" It was not unusual for me to deal with bogus reports that a Beatle was seriously ill, had been badly hurt in a road traffic accident or even killed in some macabre way. At least one such call came in to my office each week. Sometimes the source of the rumour would be an ingenious fan, keen to find out where her favourite Beatle was today and sure that the news desks of Fleet Street could track him down for her. I didn't always check out these stories with the boys because, to be frank, they – and I – had better things to do. The sudden spate of calls about Paul, a dozen or so in a single afternoon, had me worried. To be on the safe side I thought I'd better ring Paul in St John's Wood. He had just given me his new number at the Cavendish Avenue house and I had it handy. I'm not sure who picked up his phone, not a voice I recognised, probably somebody who was working there. But, for all I knew, it might have been a doctor or a paramedic. As you do, I feared the worst. Then Paul came on the line sounding as fit as a fiddle and I felt very foolish. I stopped myself saying something like: "So you're alive then!" Instead, I babbled on like an idiot about something and nothing for a good ten minutes, just chattering away in the hope that I'd think of something sensible to ask the guy or some suitable way of rounding off the call without embarrassing myself. At length I paused for breath and there was a moment's silence. Then Paul said blankly: "Tony, what the fuck have you called me for?" I had blabbered on and said absolutely nothing! So now I thought up a trivial question and pretended that a teenybopper magazine reporter had asked it. Paul sounded less than convinced that this was the real reason for my call but I left it like that. I never discovered why there had been this unusually large flurry of calls from Fleet Street or why it was Paul rather than one of the others who was thought to be dead. I returned all the calls, telling everyone that I'd just spoken to the Macca man himself who was very much alive and rocking. Naturally enough, nobody bothered to print the story because of its weak ending.

On a couple of other occasions, Paul was involved in minor road accidents and each time I heard about them from the press before I heard from him. Three years later in 1969, Paul was also the subject of a much more widespread Beatles hoax suggesting that he had been dead for some time and that we had been covering up the truth by sending out carefully tutored lookalikes whenever The Beatles had to appear in public. The rumour circulated around the world. George Martin was questioned about suspicious "clues" that he was accused of planting on album covers – on *Sgt Pepper* Paul was pictured with his back to the camera; on one *Magical Mystery Tour* shot he was wearing a black carnation while the others wore red; and he was barefoot in a photograph taken for the Abbey Road cover. The rumours came from so many different places at the same time that on this occasion the papers did print the story and for a while Paul joined in the joke. With a straight face and in a voice to match he told acquaintances that he was a stand-in, not the real McCartney at all. Peter Blake, designer of the *Sgt Pepper* album cover, was told when he visited Paul at home: "You know I'm not Paul McCartney. You met Paul when you were working on *Sgt Pepper* and he didn't have a scar on his mouth. Look, I've got a scar."

Sgt Pepper's Lonely Hearts Club Band

The writing, arranging and recording of the spectacular *Sgt Pepper* album filled the hyperactive minds of some of The Beatles almost from the moment they finished touring. John and Paul recognised the project as a make-or-break point in the band's career. They had taken themselves off the road to concentrate on progressing their writing abilities and recording techniques and it seemed as if the world was watching to see what rock'n'roll miracles they could pull off. For John and Paul the greatest challenge was to prove themselves to one another. The era of silly love songs was long gone. They'd proved that with the marvellously innovative writing in the *Revolver* collection. No more wanting to hold hands and I love you and please please me. Now McCartney and Lennon needed to confirm that *Revolver* was no one-off flash-in-the-pan. They had become grown-up songwriters and the group as a whole wanted to show rivals ranging from the Beach Boys to The Rolling Stones that they were still top of the heap and best of the bunch. In my view *Sgt Pepper*, five months in the making, became a monumental showcase of musical self-indulgence. George

Martin confessed to me that this was the most indulgent thing he and The Beatles ever did, adding: "We were only able to do this kind of stuff because the group was so uniquely successful that nobody among the EMI hierarchy dared to challenge what we were doing." Everything George Martin had taught them about orchestral music and recording studio facilities since the autumn of 1962 was brought into play. To augment their own guitars, keyboards and drums they hired in brass and string sections and drew on George Harrison's new-found knowledge of Indian instruments and rhythms. One evening when I called in at Abbey Road, the two Georges were briefing a band of Indian musicians who were seated on a big colourful carpet in the middle of the studio floor. Although individual egos were so obviously at work and internal rivalry within the Fabs had reached an all-time high, hugely inventive and greatly entertaining music was being made with or without the help of mind-enhancing substances. Abbey Road became a hive of intense industry with open-ended day and night sessions. It also became clear to me, as *Sgt Pepper* took shape, that each one of the boys was working in his own interests. Their work was increasingly self-centred, rather than group orientated.

John, Paul, George and Ringo made it clear to the rest of us that they were to be disturbed as little as possible until the album was finished. We were not to bring non-essential problems to them and we should not visit them at Abbey Road while they were recording unless on the most urgent of business. This suited me because I had never been happy to spend long hours at recording sessions. If I went at all it was either to get urgent answers to something important or, in the case of our various rising stars, to show support for the artists. In my view recording sessions were boring affairs for anyone not directly involved in the music-making or the provision of technical services. In the case of The Beatles during the creation of *Sgt Pepper* I shelved routine media enquiries to be dealt with later. But inevitably there came a time when an outstanding editorial opportunity presented itself, something I had been working on for some time involving a cover photo and in-depth article for one of the prestigious Sunday newspaper colour supplements. Brian Epstein was extremely difficult to pin down at this stage but I caught him in one of his increasingly rare clear-headed moments. I asked him: "What do I do? Break The Beatles' rule and put this to them, or postpone and maybe lose it?"

He told me to leave it with him, that he would find a suitable time to relay the request to the boys. I must have reminded Epstein at least three or four times and been fobbed off on each occasion with stuff like: "Don't rush it, I'll get back to you." Inevitably, the magazine's editor handed me an ultimatum: "It's a great idea, we want to work with you on this, but give me a firm reply, yes or no, by the weekend or we'll have to forget the whole thing." Even when The Beatles were at their peak I always believed that they needed a certain amount of regular high-class editorial exposure in the right publications. I put the position to Brian one more time. His response surprised me: "Tony, for God's sake realise that I've done all I can on this. There are many ways in which The Beatles are no longer co-operating with me and this is not even one of the more important examples. I've made it clear that I want this front cover story to go ahead and they've refused point blank. There's a limit to the grovelling and pleading I can do." There were tears in his eyes as he spoke and obviously it was painful for him to admit his inability to force the issue with the four boys and get a positive result for me.

Via this one heartfelt speech Epstein had put in a nutshell the serious deterioration in his relationship with John, Paul, George and Ringo. At one time neither a grovel nor a plea would have come into it and there would have been no question of the Nemperor having to humiliate himself in front of his boys or his PR man. "Eppy" would have asked his boys firmly to do something and they would have complied, cursing and grumbling perhaps, but they'd have done what was requested of them. Until that moment I blamed Epstein for not dealing with the Sunday supplement matter more effectively and urgently. Now, all of a sudden, I appreciated his true position and recognised the extent of his loss of power. The boys were now beyond his control, a situation that must have sent shivers up and down Epstein's spine.

For the last month of 1966 The Beatles were so deeply involved in their work on *Sgt Pepper* that they scarcely noticed the increasing absence of Brian Epstein from his Mayfair offices. They were embroiled in 12-hour recording sessions from four in the afternoon until four the following morning. Each of the boys had sprouted moustaches, George's accompanied by a ferocious-looking Captain Birdseye beard. George Martin turned a blind eye to the heavy drug-taking that hallmarked the new series of Abbey Road sessions, happy, he told me, to let them get stoned off their heads if they felt it added an extra dimension to the amazing music they were creating. Taking their heads away into a make-believe world of tangerine trees, marmalade skies and marshmallow pies, the boys convinced themselves that hallucinatory substances improved and accelerated their creative thought processes. Friends who joined them in their chemically-induced paradise actively encouraged the boys in this belief, while some of us looked on – and, like George Martin, silently gave them the benefit of the doubt. We will never know to what extent drugs assisted The Beatles in the production of *Sgt Pepper* or whether they simply acted as confidence boosters.

By this time Brian Epstein had his own quite different reasons for resorting to cocktails of alcohol mixed with forbidden chemicals. Gloom was descending upon the Nemperor and he was turning to excessive doses of strong drink and abusive drugs to soothe his troubled mind. He was greatly upset by the boys' recent rebellious behaviour towards him and was increasingly worried that they might give him a hard time when their management contract was up for renewal in 1967. The biggest blow of all for him was their refusal to even sit down to discuss future concerts. Three out of four told him bluntly: "We're not going on the road again, Brian, get that into your head." And the fourth, Paul, simply shrugged his shoulders and walked away. Even then, Epstein refused to agree to any formal announcement that there would be no further touring. In Britain, apart from the roof-top performance they put on in their final days together for the documentary film *Let It Be*, The Beatles' final stage appearance had consisted of a 15-minute set in the *New Musical Express Annual Pollwinners Concert* at the Empire Pool, Wembley, on Sunday May 1, 1966. In November of that year, Epstein was obliged to deny a newspaper story claiming that The Beatles had been in discussion with the powerful and reputedly ruthless American entrepreneur Allen Klein over their future business management. In private, Epstein prayed they had not been looking elsewhere for the career guidance they were no longer seeking from him.

Despite his failure to keep daytime business appointments Epstein continued to demonstrate his flair for hosting starry nocturnal gatherings at his Chapel Street house and one party he threw for

The Four Tops was hailed by celebrity guests as one of the year's best pre-Christmas shindigs. Epstein's New Year's Eve was a less salubrious affair. When he took George, Pattie and their close pal Cream guitarist Eric Clapton to the famous Annabel's night club in Mayfair's Berkeley Square, his party was refused admission because George was not wearing a tie and would not put on the one offered by the management. They all moved off to dine at the decidedly downmarket Lyons Corner House restaurant and saw in the New Year there. For the remaining months of his life we found it very hard to communicate with Brian Epstein during business hours or beyond. His faithful secretaries, assistants and household staff made every possible excuse for him but we knew they were shielding a boss who was no longer reliable. He showed every sign of having lost the plot. He had emigrated to Planet Epstein, a weird and wondrous domain somewhere on the far side of the universe or beyond where responsibilities disappeared from view, where nothing was real, there was nothing to get hung up about and it was playtime 24/7.

Paul and John decided that their 1967 album should be a concept job with some sort of running theme to link all the songs. They had a vague idea of getting back to basics by writing a set of songs about their own past, The Beatles' beginnings and their hometown haunts. The music would be progressive but the lyrics could be nostalgically retrospective. Both Lennon and McCartney went off and wrote a pair of songs about Liverpool locations. Paul's idea of a nostalgic hometown song was the busy, sunny 'Penny Lane', John's was the darker, mysterious and hypnotic 'Strawberry Fields Forever', both based on parts of Liverpool they had known and loved in childhood. Paul and the others knew Penny Lane very well; it was in their ears and eyes – on the destination blinds of Liverpool Corporation buses. Paul and the others had enjoyed pre-adolescent snogs and fumbles with giggly young girlfriends in the shelter on the roundabout where, if they were lucky, the lads might get a little fish and finger pie to round off a date on a summer's evening. Last time I was there, the shelter and adjoining toilet block had been replaced with a restaurant although the shell of the original buildings remain. In childhood times John had used the thickly-wooded grounds of the orphanage called Strawberry Field (sic) as a natural adventure playground, ideal for games of cowboys-and-indians or hide-and-seek. One area also served as a very secluded secret garden when John wanted to be alone to sort through his confusion of personal problems. In its musical style John saw the new song, written while he was filming *How I Won The War*, as a more commercial sequel to 'Tomorrow Never Knows'. He never explained to me why his song added an "s" to the end of "Field" although he spoke of the orphanage's sprawling gardens as "fields".

All four Beatles were considerably angered when these first two album tracks were snatched from under their noses to be released as a single. Lennon and McCartney considered these to be particularly powerful numbers, which they saw as sturdy cornerstones of their yet-to-be-named album. On EMI's behalf George Martin had to push The Beatles for a new single. He argued that the record company was already most upset that a fresh album had not been delivered in time for Christmas, forcing the issue of a compilation entitled *A Collection Of Beatles Oldies*, including 'She Loves You', 'From Me To You', 'A Hard Day's Night' and 'I Want To Hold Your Hand'. The Beatles disliked the timing of this oldies-but-goldies bundle. They would have preferred to get *Sgt Pepper* out first to show off their latest stuff before re-warming these early tracks. Martin and Epstein joined forces to press home the commercial good sense of getting a new single out into the marketplace without further delay. Reluctantly, the group agreed and 'Penny Lane' and 'Strawberry Fields Forever' made it into the shops on both sides of the Atlantic around Valentine's Day, February 1967. In advertising the single, I stressed the real-life Liverpool connection, by using a map of the city as the centrepiece of the ad artwork with the two song titles shown as actual loca-tions. We used the same simple but powerful artwork in the British music papers and the international trade press including America's *Billboard*.

Having put out these two tracks The Beatles lost interest in a hometown retro theme for their album and switched to Plan B, Paul's 'Billy Shears' Show' concept. This developed from a "simple, infectious little ditty" (Paul's own description) called *Sergeant Pepper's Lonely Hearts Club Band* into the full-blown album that bore the same name. At the other end of the musical spectrum was the meticulously crafted 'A Day In The Life', a mind-blower if ever there was one, truly a ballad of epic proportions and one of the only real Lennon and McCartney collaborations in the *Sgt Pepper* set. John brought the first verse of 'A Day In The Life' around to Cavendish Avenue for Paul's approval and embellishment. They sat together in Paul's music room and constructed the rest of it, eventually making a full-blown production number out of it in the recording studio. "Look what we can do, isn't it awesome?" John and Paul seemed to be screaming. The trick was that once Billy Shears' band had been introduced on the album, it could perform in any number of various styles and guises, giving John and Paul unlimited scope to include whatever songs they liked. The plan was as loose as that; no firm promises or parameters. The final product was perfectly timed to coincide with the so-called "Summer Of Love" and it was musically spectacular, lyrically progressive and bravely experimental. The cost of preparing the elaborate album cover with its photo-montage and inserted souvenir "kit" was 50 times higher than that of the average EMI album for that year. *Sgt Pepper* was released on June 1, less than three months before Brian Epstein died. The almost unanimously favourable reviews included high praise not only for The Beatles' music but also for George Martin's high production standards.

Two of the last parties Brian Epstein threw were in honour of *Sgt Pepper*. The first took place in his Chapel Street town house on Friday May 19 when we gave a small and élite bunch of journalists and deejays an opportunity to hear a preview copy of the album accompanied by a typically lavish Epstein menu of fine champagne and expensive snacks. Strictly from the PR point of view, the gesture was superfluous – *Sgt Pepper* would have got a good press with or without the party. The second event, held on Sunday May 28, was an equally lavish, but far more private affair. This happened at Kingsley Hill, at Warbleton, near Heathfield in Sussex, and was a combined house-warming party for Brian's new, remote country house and a celebration for *Sgt Pepper*. For guests unfamiliar with that part of England, Epstein arranged for clusters of balloons to be hung from trees and wooden gates along the lanes in the final mile or so to his house. John, George and Ringo attended with their womenfolk, John causing quite a stir by driving up in his new Rolls Royce, which was elaborately painted with gypsy caravan designs and colourful psychedelic scrolls against a vivid yellow background. In between *Sgt Pepper* tracks, guests were treated to frequent plays of Procol Harum's sensational new single, 'A Whiter Shade Of Pale', which The Beatles had watched the group perform live at London's fashionable Speakeasy Club four nights earlier. I wasn't at Kingsley Hill for this wild weekend but Kenny Everett, who stayed overnight like a number of others, told me afterwards that a particularly potent batch of LSD, fresh in from California, had circulated in generous doses. He also related in exceedingly graphic detail the vomiting and worse that went on: "There was widespread puking and bedwetting and one famous guest lost the contents of his intestine involuntarily at the height of the orgy." It was all a source of merriment and mirth to Cuddly Ken, the flagship presenter on the soon-to-be-closed-down pirate station Radio London.

Although Paul did not turn up to this particular party, he was about to admit in public that he had taken LSD four times: first in an interview with *Life* magazine and later on the UK's Independent Television News. Paul defended himself simply but usefully. To the suggestion that he should have kept his drug-taking to himself, Paul told the television news reporter: "I was asked the question by a newspaper and the decision was whether to tell a lie or to tell the truth. I'm not trying to spread the word about this but the man from the newspaper is the man from the mass medium. I'll keep it a personal thing if he does too, if he keeps it quiet. It's his responsibility, not mine." Paul dismissed the idea that fans might take drugs just because he did. I had a lot of professional respect for the cool and suave way in which Paul handled this episode with only a minimal amount of help from me. I couldn't help comparing it with John's amateurish effort at the previous summer's Chicago press conference when he tackled the "more popular than Jesus" affair.

How do you cap such a universally well-received achievement as the *Sgt Pepper* album, which is still regarded today by many as the pinnacle of the Fab Four's career? The BBC gave us the answer by inviting the boys to take part in a global television broadcast called *Our World*, which was eventually seen by a reported 400 million viewers. The group's contribution to this historic programme, done "live" from Abbey Road studios on June 25 in front of an invited audience of celebrity friends, was a party-style performance of 'All You Need Is Love' in a studio festooned with balloons. We nicknamed this song "the hippy hymn" and it was the ideal international flower-power anthem for the summer of '67. A wary and wise George Martin took the precaution of pre-recording parts of the song which could have been called into play if anything had gone wrong artistically or technically with the 'live' studio performance.

Meanwhile, unlike The Beatles, Brian Epstein's dependence on drugs had developed into total addiction. In the very week of his Kingsley Hill bash for *Sgt Pepper*, The Beatles had quietly and without publicity registered a new company called Apple Music Limited, the first of a wide-ranging group of Apple companies to be launched by John, Paul, George and Ringo. Knowing about this can only have deepened Epstein's despondency, despite the fact that they made the token gesture of naming him as a director.

Drink and drugs killed Brian Epstein as surely as if he had deliberately overdosed on the Saturday night of his death during August Bank Holiday weekend. He had hoped to fix up a last-minute party at Kingsley Hill over the holiday but he left the arrangements too late to round up the names he wanted. Dissatisfied with the company of merely the couple of close friends who were to weekend with him in Surrey, Brian drove himself back to London and his Chapel Street house where he watched Saturday evening's broadcast of *Juke Box Jury* alone. He carelessly threw sleeping pills and other stuff down his throat on top of his customary tumbler of vodka and other assorted shots of booze. Apparently he forgot that he'd taken his prescribed sleeping pills and took a second large dose. I don't believe he had suicide in mind that evening but together the mixture he had swallowed represented a lethally toxic cocktail. Brian put himself to bed and did not wake up. Failing to arouse his employer on Sunday, the butler, Antonio, eventually broke down the sturdy oak doors to Brian's bedroom and found him dead.

The first call I had on the tragedy was from the *Daily Express* newsdesk. In the ensuing hours half the world's press were onto the story and for once neither my promotional nor protective PR strengths were of the slightest use. All I could do was act as an information source, assemble statistics, read out biographical details and give my honest opinion that Brian Epstein had not intended to kill himself. Several of us split the job of ringing round all our artists to relay the terrible news – it was far too big a job for any one person.

The Beatles had to be informed in Bangor, north Wales, where they were on a Transcendental Meditation course with Maharishi Mahesh Yogi. John was the hardest hit; I could almost hear the lump in his throat as he spoke to reporters. Gerry Marsden had to be reached at his holiday home on the isle of Anglesey and Cilla Black had to be contacted on holiday in Portugal, but communications were problematic and she couldn't be reached at the nightspot where she and her husband, Bobby, were dining with Tom Jones. At length, a waiter broke the news to her and she was inconsolable. She told me later: "I felt isolated and desolate. Anyone who was really close to him loved Brian. He was so much more than a manager to me, he was my friend and adviser." Close to his deathbed Brian had left a handwritten but unsigned note for his personal assistant, Joanne Newfield, that read: "Please send suitable cable to Cilla requesting she calls me where I am (Sussex or here) S.A.P. Say I've tried to contact her but impossible. Urgent matter." Had Cilla reached him in time, his news would have been that he had secured a BBC Television series for her and the contract was ready for signature. Cilla had never lost anyone so close or attended a funeral before. Ironically, she had very recently told Brian that she was seeking new management and he had implored her to stay with him, saying that he loved only five people in the world – John, Paul, George, Ringo and Cilla. Having established that Brian was dead, the media then wanted tributes from the principal stars he had represented. I had to contact in turn not only The Beatles and Cilla Black but also Gerry Marsden, Billy J Kramer and other key names on the NEMS roster to agree their personal quotes with them. All the artists were appalled and saddened by the news and gave some beautiful comments that I relayed to Fleet Street.

I have to say that I was so exceptionally busy with this work that my own grieving over Epstein's senseless and dreadfully premature demise took the form of a delayed reaction. It was only after the press had run their first wave of news stories and we returned to the NEMS offices after the Bank Holiday weekend that the full impact of Brian's death hit me. But for Brian's initial contact with me at Decca Records in December 1961 and my subsequent first meeting with John, Paul, George and Ringo eleven months later in the Devonshire Arms, I would not have lived through the totally amazing experience of working with the world's top band for the last five years and would not have crammed the thrills and shocks and one-off adventures of a lifetime into this short but memorable period. Epstein's mass of personal and professional flaws, faults and weaknesses paled into insignificance as I took stock of what the mid-Sixties had meant to me and I wondered how my working lifestyle might change now that this extraordinary man was gone. I had already discussed with Epstein my wish to quit NEMS in order to set up my own independent press and public relations consultancy. In principle he had given the move his blessing. He agreed that it made good business sense for me to broaden my client base and what I was proposing amounted to a major expansion strategy. Epstein promised that I would continue to represent his companies and the acts he was managing. The more diverse showbusiness celebrities I had on my books the more powerful my business would become, which could only be good for Epstein and NEMS. I considered my immediate situation carefully at the time of his death and decided that the company and its famous clients would need the strongest possible integral PR division during the coming months. I made up my mind to shelve my departure from the firm by up to a year.

After the inevitable post mortem, the Westminster coroner described Brian's passing as an accidental death, ascribing this to an incautious self-overdose. Nat Weiss had arranged for Brian to fly to New York on September 2 and then on to Toronto to host a pilot music programme for CBC television, one of several new projects that pleased and excited him to such an extent that he might well have fought hard to come off his drugs to ensure his fitness for the jobs. By mutual agreement with the Epstein family, The Beatles stayed away from Brian's funeral. *Time* magazine disparagingly misinterpreted the group's absence and I contacted them to complain. I expected vague excuses and maybe a verbal apology but they went further and agreed to publish a formal letter from me correcting the earlier misinformation.

John was on the point of going to India with the giggling little Maharishi, who had promised to ease The Beatles' grieving by meditation. John said he was sickened by the speed with which people expected him to get back to Beatle business in the immediate wake of Brian's death. On the one hand there was wind of an approach by the American showbusiness accountant and wheeler-dealer Allen Klein, who flew to London and contacted Brian's younger brother, Clive Epstein, to fix "an urgent meeting". On the other hand, the freshly installed Robert Stigwood was showing an interest in the Fab Four.

I handled the PR for the launch and early recording career of Stigwood's instantly successful young group The Bee Gees. Although I disliked many aspects of Stigwood's brash business methods I got on very well with the good humoured Gibb brothers, a generously talented trio of lads with whom it was a pleasure to work. Like The Beatles, they wrote their own material and the best of their early singles stood up well alongside the latest Lennon & McCartney compositions, at least in terms of chart potential. Considering their youthfulness they were writing extraordinarily powerful stuff. At this time Stigwood wanted me to initiate a PR campaign to publicise the imminent deportation of the fourth and fifth members of The Bee Gees, lead guitarist Vince Melouney and drummer Colin Petersen. Deportation may be too strong a word. These two Australians were to return home because their visas were running out and the immigration authorities saw no good reason to let them stay in Britain indefinitely. The inference was that the Gibbs, Barry, Maurice, and Robin, could easily hire local musicians in London to replace Petersen and Melouney but Stigwood insisted that this was a very fine opportunity for a bizarre series of publicity stunts (appearing to be) carried out by The Bee Gees Fan Club office personnel. At Stigwood's instigation I hired the services of a benign elephant from Billy Smart's Circus for £200 and we had the poster-draped beast lumber along Whitehall in the direction of the Prime Minister's residence with two fan club girls perched attractively on its back. The unfortunate animal was diverted by police down a side road towards the Embankment, which robbed any of the hoped-for press photographs of a distinctive Downing Street backdrop. We made it onto an inside page of the midday edition of a London evening newspaper and a few provincials picked up the story. Undaunted, I bought the necessary equipment to chain Deidre Meehan, a good-looking girl from the office, to the railings outside Buckingham Palace. This time, on a slow news day, we gained extensive coverage in the *Daily Express* and a number of Fleet Street's other mass-circulation nationals. To place the obliging and publicity conscious Deidre in conspicuous bondage had cost me seven shillings and sixpence (less than 40 pence) for a padlock and chain, as against the one-day elephant rental charge of £200. I feel this says something about the quirky and fickle world of showbusiness PR.

The Fan Club's rather nervous Julie Barrett, a timid 19-year-old, felt intimidated by the daily assignments we gave her as part of the ongoing Keep The Bee Gees In Britain campaign. She took me quite seriously and nearly passed out one day when I said: "Tomorrow, Julie, I want you out on the window ledge of your office protesting with a placard and threatening to jump." Our offices in Argyll Street were on the fifth floor of Sutherland House next to the London Palladium, a perfect spot from the point of view of the press. Of course, I had no intention of endangering the poor girl by letting her anywhere near a fifth-floor office window ledge but she didn't realise I was joking, took the whole situation very seriously and burst into tears. Re-told here all this might sound like good fun (at Julie's expense!) but at the time I disliked Stigwood's definition of a good publicity stunt and felt that his totally fictional stories wouldn't fool Fleet Street for long and debased the PR coinage. The Bee Gees were too talented to need such circus-style trickery to get themselves good publicity in the papers and I remember hoping at the time that Barry, Maurice and Robin realised that the fan-club stunts came from their manager's fertile mind, not mine.

Soon afterwards, Stigwood left NEMS and took both his people and his acts with him. His departure was precipitated by an embarrassing and quite extraordinary meeting of The Beatles plus all the relevant NEMS executives at Brian Epstein's last hideaway office at Hille House on the corner of Mayfair's Stafford Street and Albemarle Street. Stigwood attempted to take centre stage and tried very hard to "sell" his suitability as the new manager of Beatles by pointing out how well he was doing with The Bee Gees and Cream. Paul told him quite firmly that the position was not available to Stigwood or anyone else because The Beatles had every intention of providing their own self-management under the auspices of their new Apple organisation. Stigwood made it clear at once that without The Beatles he was not interested in being Chairman of NEMS Enterprises. This left 90% of the ownership of the firm in the hands of Brian's mother, Queenie Epstein, and his younger brother, Clive, while The Beatles held the remaining 10% stake. According to what I was told at the time, a number of other likely and unlikely individuals had high hopes of replacing Brian and The Beatles.

I was as nauseated as John to witness the bickering and bitching, the grasping and manoeuvring that went on among some of my colleagues at NEMS who seemed to feel that The Beatles' management was their rightful legacy. Several of us, including the office manager Alistair Taylor, booking agent Bernie Lee and business executive Geoffrey Ellis, looked on in horror at the antics that were going on around us. The battle to take over Epstein's artists proved yet again that the poor man had lots of fair-weather acquaintances, but few truly faithful business associates. For his industry track record, Klein looked to me like the most appropriate candidate to handle The Beatles' future affairs. His route to John and the others relied on their mutual relationships with Mick Jagger and The Rolling Stones with whom Klein had been working. The showbiz story about Klein that appealed to me most was the tale of his negotiations with Capitol Records on behalf of Bobby Darin. When the record company grudgingly agreed to an advance of one million dollars, a massive fee in those days, to seal Darin's new deal, Klein was reputed to have answered: "That's fine by me. Now how much for my boy?"

Magical Mystery Tour

In the midst of this surreal scenario, Paul came forward with his own very feasible solution to John's indecision. He proposed that The Beatles should embark immediately upon the making of *Magical Mystery Tour*. My colleagues condemned him for acting callously but Paul explained his motives to me very convincingly: "If most of The Beatles clear off to India now with the Maharishi I doubt if we'll come together again as a working band. The last thing we need now is time on our hands to brood about Brian's death." He felt that throwing themselves into filming would keep the four guys together until they could plan their long-term future with clearer minds. On Friday September 1, Paul convened a meeting at 7 Cavendish Avenue, inviting only the tightest circle of trusted associates. I was asked to arrive an hour before John, George and Ringo so that he could go into greater details about his ideas. I had the impression that he was keen to show off his new home, which after a year of occupation was now looking the way he and Jane wanted it. We spoke in his spacious, light and airy living room at the back of the house. At one point he deliberately walked me out through French windows onto the terrace so that I could look over the large tree-stocked garden.

Paul produced his now-legendary drawing of a *Magical Mystery Tour* cake sliced up into segments to represent eight essential sequences for inclusion in the film. He had written key words that would prompt him when describing the proposed production to others: Commercial, Introduce Tour, Get On Coach, Courier Introduces, Recruiting, Marathon, Laboratory Sequence, Stripper & Band, End Song? In his initial planning, 'Fool On The Hill' was to feature quite early in the film. He specified some of the key passengers, characters such as Busty Hostess, Fat Woman and Small Man. The only actual name he showed beside the "cake" was the clownish Nat Jackley, a contemporary slapstick comic known for his bodily contortions. All the ideas Paul proposed were used in the final production although poor old Nat Jackley's work finished up on the cutting-room floor, as did a one-number contribution from Stevie Winwood's Traffic. Paul made it clear to me that his aim was to make a feature-length film for full-scale theatrical release and he felt that a successful screen "tour" would go a long way towards plugging the gaping hole left by the axing of the Fab Four's concert trips. Indeed, if Paul had managed to produce one successful theatrically released feature film with The Beatles each year, a far bigger potential audience would have seen the group than did in the touring years, and the profit margin for the boys would have been enormous.

When the rest arrived he delegated different Beatles to take care of each segment, encouraging them to come up with their own musical and/or comedy content for specific sequences that would last 10 or 15 minutes. He said his concept was based on the old idea of seaside coach trips, mystery tours, "but this one will have an additional touch of fantasy because four magicians will be at work to make wonderful things happen". Paul insisted that filming must begin the following week, by which time we'd need to have a big yellow bus organised and decorated, a supporting cast of professional actors and variety artists, the necessary cameramen and technical crew and a route for the bus to take us down to Cornwall, our West Country destination.

It was no coincidence that Paul asked us all to meet up with him, to begin our journey in Allsop Place, a tiny side street next to the waxworks museum Madame Tussaud's and the London Planetarium. This had been the traditional meeting point used by the prolific pop package tour promoter Arthur Howes to assemble the stars and supporting casts of his one-night-stand shows in the early Sixties. I stated the obvious: "There's no way I'm going to be able to stop Fleet Street finding out about this. As soon as we make hotel reservations and drive off in a bus emblazoned with *Magical Mystery Tour* posters the press will be after us in droves." "And why not?" replied Paul breezily. "You'll be with us to look after all the journalists."

There was no earthly reason why such a hastily concocted project should work but trivialities such as a professional production team, a proper script rather than a "cake" and the lack of detailed locations did not deter the ever-optimistic McCartney. It was as if the whole crazy shindig has been cooked up under the influence of dodgy drugs – but how far would they replace orthodox filming strategies and procedures once we were on the road and shooting? Most of the professional supporting cast must have wondered what their agents had let them in for. Sitting with them on this mad bus journey were four Beatles dressed in strange outfits, roadies who looked like panto-mime characters and "extras" who were actually area secretaries of The Official Beatles Fan Club. Even I found it hard to tell where reality ended and filming began, when we were and were not supposed to be acting. We'd stop at a chip shop and pile in to buy lunch – but was this for real, a genuine lunch break, or were the cameras still turning? The press drove right behind us in a processional convoy of assorted cars. Some journalists, including Chris Reed from *The Sun* and free-lancer Miranda Ward, booked into the Atlantic Hotel at Newquay a day ahead of us. Sitting on the grass in the weak September sunshine outside the hotel drinking tea and signing autographs, George told Miranda: "We want everyone who watches to be able to freak out, but we don't want to frighten them. Some people get a little fright-ened when the music suddenly goes strange as in 'A Day In The Life' because they don't know what's happening. In this film we don't want them to be puzzled or scared."

That anything worth using finished up on film in such casual and disorganised circumstances was little short of miraculous. The boys simply expected their every last-minute production requirement to be satisfied in full and on time. To shoot the stripper scene we hired Paul Raymond's Soho Revuebar, including his star turn, Jan Carson, and booked the zany Bonzo Dog Doo Dah Band to sing 'Death Cab For Cutie' while she did a toned-down version of her usual act for our cameras. The boys couldn't understand why we were unable to rent a proper film studio stage at Shepperton, Elstree, Pinewood or wherever, to shoot the big finale, an all-singing all-dancing production number, 'Your Mother Should Know'. We had to explain that film people fix their shooting schedules many months in advance and we'd have to make do with a disused hangar at a former USAAF base at West Malling airfield in Kent. At this makeshift location with its assortment of vast indoor and outdoor spaces we shot not only the big ballroom sequence but also the Magicians' Laboratory scenes, George's mist-enshrouded song 'Blue Jay Way', Major McCartney's Recruitment Office and the wacky marathon races. For the spectacular ballroom setting rigged up in West Malling's Hangar 3 we used two dozen youthful cadets from a local squadron of the Women's Royal Air Force and 160 dancers from the Peggy Spencer formation troupe.

In the post-production period Paul asked me to put together and write a picture story booklet that formed part of the elaborate packaging for the *Magical Mystery Tour* soundtrack songs and instrumental music. We illustrated some of the film's key scenes with a series of photographs taken during filming by John Kelly and caricature-style strip cartoons done by *The Beatles' Book* artist Bob Gibson. I wrote a "once upon a time"-style story to caption the pictures. In the event the story we told via the strip cartoon differed in various small ways from what was contained in the finished film. This was an indication of the hair-raising speed at which everyone worked to complete all the various elements of the project – to meet EMI Records' sleeve printing deadline we had to provide our words and pictures before the film editing had finished.

Some said *Magical Mystery Tour* was a brilliant comedy ahead of its time. Most fans of the Fab Four loved it, but the majority of media critics disliked the film. *Daily Variety*, the daily version of America's entertainment industry bible, said: "Beatles Produce First Flop With Yule Film". In London, the *Evening Standard* ran on its front page Paul's quote to friendly Ray Connolly: "We Goofed, Says Beatle". *Time* magazine said simply and somewhat cryptically: "Paul directed, Ringo mugged, John did imitations, George danced a bit." Ludicrously, the finished 52-minute film was aired first of all in black and white on BBC 1 television at Christmas. A major part of the production's appeal lay its colourful costumes and scenery. The BBC anticipated pulling in an audience of 20 million but the final viewing figure was 13 million, one million less than *David Frost's Christmas Special*, which preceded it. A substantially smaller audience was able to see the film in colour on BBC 2 a fortnight or so later.

Behind the scenes, Paul was bitterly upset that the production was relegated to television instead of meriting theatrical release in Britain and America. He had secret hopes that *Magical Mystery Tour* would give him fast-track entry to the epicentre of the world's feature film industry so that he could produce future cinema best-sellers with the Fab Four, an ambition that never even came close to fulfilment.

In my opinion the most entertaining of The Beatles' films – but not the most satisfactory from the musical point of view – was the one with which they were least involved, the innovative animation production, *Yellow Submarine*. This was made towards the end of the group's career to satisfy contractual obligations to which Brian Epstein had committed the boys long before his death. Initially unhappy about even lending their name to this film, the group's eventual half-hearted contribution consisted of providing some less-than-sensational songs and doing a brief "epilogue" appearance at the end of the film.

WHEN THE BEATLES set up their own Apple group of companies, starting with Apple Music and eventually centred around Apple Corps Limited, my job as their PR man looked as if it was coming to a natural end. Since the release of The Beatles' first single, 'Love Me Do', in the autumn of 1962, I had set out to create, develop and sustain an evolving image for the Fab Four throughout the Beatlemania years and beyond. By 1968 John, Paul, George and Ringo were anxious to make a fresh start. In doing so they were putting behind them the era of their greatest worldwide successes as a working band, the era in which I had played my part. As individuals, all four Beatles were bursting with talent and couldn't wait to get started on separate projects, which had been impossible for them to pursue during their days as part of a touring group. John and Ringo had already made solo film appearances in "straight" acting roles; John as Private Gripweed in *How I Won The War* and Ringo as a sex-mad Mexican gardener in *Candy*. Paul McCartney had composed the soundtrack music for the feature film *The Family Way*, a venture in no way associated with his regular writing partner. In 1968 Paul also custom-tailored a new song, 'Step Inside Love', for his Liverpudlian friend Cilla Black to use as the theme song for her first BBC television series. Although the label credit read Lennon – McCartney as usual, everyone knew that this was a solo effort on Macca's part. It was a simple song but, according to Cilla, difficult to arrange: "On the first recording we did Paul played on guitar but the key didn't fit me and I had to have it taken up. The second version was disappointing; I just couldn't get my teeth into it. But we did a great recording in the end." Having spent much time studying the music and culture of India and learning to play Indian instruments, primarily the sitar, George had recorded his *Wonderwall* album and was ambitious to extend his songwriting activities. He also wanted to discover new talent and produce records for The Beatles' own Apple Records label with a range of other artists.

The making of *Magical Mystery Tour* in September 1967 was the last major venture I watched The Beatles tackle together as a co-operative, friendly and enthusiastic unit. Despite – or perhaps because of – the lack of professional supervision during filming, I believe they enjoyed the business of putting together this unscripted production. Once this had been done I didn't see the four act unanimously again as a group. The subsequent panning of *Magical Mystery Tour* by the press did not upset the boys unduly or have the slightest adverse effect upon their future record sales, but I believe it deeply dented Paul's ego and put paid to his ambition as a film producer. It also damaged his credibility within the foursome, spoiling his chances of leading them in any other new directions. After this, whether for songwriting purposes or recording, they worked increasingly on individual initiatives, whatever suited them best at the moment, whether or not it was in the general interest of The Beatles. They had a number of reasons for setting up Apple. They wanted to use the facilities of the new organisation to look after their own artistic and business management. They saw this as a way of severing unwanted connections with the past, which to them was NEMS Enterprises. If Brian Epstein had not died it is debatable whether or not they would have offered him any sort of executive role in Apple. At best I expect they would have fobbed him off with some non-executive job as a "sleeping partner", which he would have found hurtful, boring and probably unacceptable.

Although Epstein was still very much a best friend of The Beatles until the end of his life – and they could not forget the integrity and dedication with which he had guided and handled their career in earlier times – the boys had lost their professional respect for the man and did not want him or any of his key people at NEMS to remain involved with the management of their affairs. They saw Apple as a protective umbrella beneath which they could nurture and bring on new musical talent and invest in a wide spread of exciting business opportunities, both inside and outside the entertainment industry. The demands of the taxman also loomed large at this time and The

Beatles' financial advisers were insisting that a lot of investment in fresh ventures would avoid some of the problems they faced with the Inland Revenue. Basically they were told to do whatever they fancied with their money or be ready to hand almost all of it over to the Government in taxes. "We decided to play businessmen for a bit," was the way John put it.

In October 1967, on instruction from Clive Epstein, I issued a press release that read: "NEMS continues to handle the management, agency and other business interests of The Beatles." This was intended to quell the widespread and well-founded rumours that the group was already beginning to go its own way. The first companies to be set up by The Beatles included Apple Films, Apple Publishing Company, Apple Electronics, Apple Retail and Apple Records. The first public appearance of an Apple logo was on the packaging for the pair of seven-inch EP (extended play) records featuring the soundtrack music from *Magical Mystery Tour*. The former roadie Neil Aspinall became managing director of Apple. Several NEMS people from the office manager Alistair Taylor to telephonist Liverpudlian Laurie McCaffrey defected. Apple's shortest-lived and least-successful ventures were the Electronics firm run by "Magic" Alex Mardas, a boffin who promised to invent all manner of wonderful gadgets and toys including a futuristic recording studio complex, and the boutiques in Baker Street and Chelsea's Kings Road, run by Apple Retail and Apple Tailoring respectively. The Baker Street store was stocked with gear designed by Simon Posthuma, Marijke Koger, Josje Leeger and Barry Finch, collectively known as The Fool. This outlet opened in December 1967 and closed in July 1968 when whatever clothing had not been previously stolen by shoplifters was given away. A proposed chain of tailoring shops and a school never even opened. At the other end of the spectrum, the most successful operation was (obviously) Apple Records, run at first by the American Ron Kass, former supremo at Liberty Records, with Peter Asher, Jane's brother, hired as head of A & R. The Beatles' old friend Derek Taylor came home from California to run Apple's press office.

I don't want to be rotten to the Corps but it did not surprise me, or my colleagues at NEMS, that only those parts of Apple directly concerned with the music business proved to be viable in the long run. Apart from attempting to develop unprofitable schemes,

The Beatles carelessly made unwise executive appointments, hiring buddies, pals and mates on a sort of "do you want to be in our gang?" basis. Several boasted openly about the scams they were able to get away with right under the noses of their benevolent bosses. One senior Apple employee took great pleasure in giving me details about how he was living and entertaining in luxury solely on money claimed as expenses, while his full salary lay intact in the bank earning interest. The Beatles enjoyed playing at being businessmen, clocking in for a day's work at the office when it suited them and distributing internal office memos on a prodigious scale. But the boys were only in love with the idea of being office workers, not with the practicalities of desk-bound, ten-till-six labour, day after day. They did not bother to learn much about business plans and strategies before throwing themselves in at the deep end. They were at the mercy of both insiders and outsiders who found it easy to rip them off. Masses of money went on schmoozing, first-class airfares, five-star hotels and getting stoned. Hordes of visitors, the majority of no commercial value to Apple Corps, were lavishly entertained and given hand-outs in cash or kind. The place was open house to all sorts of people from the gregarious Hell's Angels to a bunch of international groupies who called themselves the Apple Scruffs.

Working as The Beatles' Press & Publicity Officer had been not only a genuine pleasure but also a great professional asset to me in the past, but now it was becoming a drag and a liability. Once Apple was up and running, if a journalist tried to fix an interview appointment with one of the boys through my office, it was likely to be turned down. The Beatle concerned would tell me he didn't want to do it because he was too busy with Apple affairs. The same journalist would put his request to Derek Taylor or one of his PR staff at Apple and an interview appointment would be set up on the understanding that the Beatle's pet Apple project of the moment was discussed. In the late summer of 1968 Paul was keen to talk to the press about his Welsh singing discovery Mary Hopkin with whom he produced the No 1 single 'Those Were The Days'. George was only too happy to be interviewed about his old pal from Liverpool, Jackie Lomax, whose single was one of the first four releases to be issued on the Apple Records label in August 1968. In all probability the journalist would ask all the questions he'd had in mind from the start and get the same answers so his article would be more or less the same whether Derek or I arranged it. But one of us would appear to be efficient and the other substantially less so!

I decided it was time to resign The Beatles' PR account before their reluctance to do any press work outside the confines of Apple activities caused harm to my existing credibility in the business. It was also time for me to leave NEMS and set up my own independent PR consultancy. I formed two companies, Tony Barrow International and, later, Tony Barrow Management, and rented prestigious offices in Mayfair. In due course, Bess Coleman came home from America to join me as a director of the new companies. I minimised the risk of falling flat on my face by acquiring several major clients, including MCA Records, before telling Clive Epstein and Vic Lewis that I was leaving. They kept Brian's promise to me that I would have NEMS Enterprises as one of my initial clients but I was surprised to be told that I would also be retained to continue representing The Beatles. The reason for this turned out to be more complicated than I realised. While NEMS Enterprises went on providing any management services for The Beatles, the company felt it could continue to claim commission from the group's vast earnings. To this end the firm would pick up my bills for PR services just as they had in the past as part of Brian Epstein's deal with John, Paul, George and Ringo. On the other hand, Apple wanted to cut off all slightest connections with NEMS so naturally their policy would be to prevent me from actually setting up any PR work for The Beatles. I was trapped between a rock and a hard place. I am happy to say that I saw to it that this arrangement was short-lived and with mixed relief and personal sadness I deleted The Beatles from the client list of Tony Barrow International. My move to independence had nothing to do with the Apple vs NEMS struggle, nor with The Beatles' departure from NEMS. It was the realisation of expansion plans I had outlined to Brian Epstein during the last year of his life. For a while afterwards I still got calls from the media asking about the downfall of this or that Apple venture but I refused to dig the dirt (and have continued to do so ever since) and simply gave them Derek Taylor's contact number.

I don't believe it was a coincidence that John and Paul chose this time to revamp their personal lives by changing partners. During the final recording years the evolution of The Beatles, in all aspects of their working lives, was accelerated at an alarming pace. I thought it was inevitable that their general re-assessment of career priorities, the revision of their ambitions and the musical and creative changes within the group, would lead at least Lennon and McCartney if not the others to also re-think the state of their private lives. Paul wasn't bored with Jane and John had no fresh reason to feel discontented with Cynthia, but both Beatles had matured considerably during the course of their present relationships and each one had his reasons for deciding to move on. There were new women in their sights and on their minds.

Throughout the Beatlemania years The Beatles' womenfolk had a tough time. Cynthia Powell, Jane Asher, Pattie Boyd and Maureen Cox were all strong independent individuals in their quite different ways, but they were all overwhelmed by the unwieldy wealth and unprecedented popularity of their fortunate and ever-so-famous menfolk. The Beatles were so very much in love with The Beatles that there was little passion going spare to spread around first wives and partners. The exceptional tensions and traumas, stresses and pressures of Beatlemania left little room in their heads or their hearts for story-book romance – and if we're talking about raw sex, well, that was something so readily available to a Beatle at every turn that the act itself must have meant little beyond being a briefly satisfying bodily function that brought fleeting physical relief. In those days the fundamental rule of old-fashioned courtship was that if a boy got his girl pregnant all roads led directly to the altar. No buts, no maybes. Unless one was rich enough or sufficiently aristocratic to flout convention, the options for the girl who "got herself into trouble" were strictly limited. Unmarried motherhood involved the ignominy of social stigma. Few women fancied a single-parent future and just as few were willing to face the life-threatening butchery associated with illegal back-street abortion. Contemplating the imminent but unplanned pitter-patter of tiny feet had the motivating force of a pointed shotgun and the only real option open to the average father-to-be was marriage. The corny joke that went round was that, when a girl told you she was getting married, you would reply: "Really? I didn't even know you were pregnant." And so it was with Ms Cynthia Powell and Mr John Winston Lennon and, later, Ms Maureen Cox and Mr Richard Starkey (aka Ringo Starr). On different occasions both

John and Cyn indicated to me that they married because the baby
Julian was on the way and without this binding factor both might well
have gone their separate ways as soon as The Beatles took off, rather
than six years later. To have kept the baby but not married would have
taken a more courageous soul than John, who was bold but not brave
beneath his leathery mask of bravado.

Cyn was the first to marry a Beatle and, like Ringo's Maureen, was
a Liverpool girl although she was brought up in one of Merseyside's
swankier suburbs "across the water" at Hoylake. Cyn had a silky-
smooth temperament. She was more cut out to be a teacher, a painter
or perhaps a nurse than a pop megastar's wife. She subjugated her
career ambitions to be Mrs John Lennon. She knew John before
The Beatles hit the heights. In student days she found him frighten-
ingly rough and arrogant but she saw great strength in his rebellious
attitude to life and was attracted by his refusal to conform. They
had short-sightedness and a love of art in common. Theirs was an
archetypal case of opposites attracting. After Julian was born in April
1963 Cynthia was content to be a happy homemaker, a devoted wife
and a dutiful mother. She was startled at first by the bright lights of
celebrity but blinked hard and smiled charmingly for the cameras.
She handled herself well as John's partner when the pair appeared
together in public. In February 1964 Cyn went on the road with
The Beatles to America for the first and last time, choosing to be at
John's side for what turned out to be the most chaotic if not the most
hazardous of the group's four US trips during the touring years. One
observer said she "looked like a little child lost in a forest of giant
ogres". She rang her mum in Hoylake most nights to ask after Julian.
At that time she was telling friends that she and John would not be
staying in the south of England for good: "It's back to Hoylake for me
as soon as we can make it, and John feels the same. We can breathe
up north but not in London." But the Lennons continued to live in
the south. Cyn seemed determined to make her marriage work but I
for one was not surprised when it did not. One of her most profound
statements when the couple split up was that she did not feel she had
lost John because she had never felt she had him in the first place:
"Yoko didn't take John from me because he's never been mine."

According to the veteran singer and television entertainer Cilla
Black, who was friendly with John and the others on hometown terri-

tory in the Cavern days before The Beatles found fame beyond the boundaries of Merseyside, John was never very comfortable in the company of females: "John was gorgeous and I fancied him for his wicked wit, but he was very shy of women." From things he said to me over the years and from speaking to girls he'd been with when we were on the road, I would say that nothing excited John as much as the company of females who had plenty of fighting spirit about them and were in control, strong and dominant. This was very different from the image of himself that John projected when I first met him. In those early days he was asking us to believe that his favourite fantasy was to make love to the fluffy French cinema sex kitten Brigitte Bardot. He even encouraged Cyn to alter her hair and make-up and what she wore in order to appear a bit more like Bardot.

John was openly unfaithful and admitted his adultery but Cyn was not stupid and had seen for herself the closeness of John's new relationship with Yoko Ono. She didn't need to have the sordid details spelt out for her. The fantasy may have been Bardot but the reality was Yoko Ono. Arriving home earlier than planned from a holiday in Greece, she found John locked in close conversation with Yoko in her kitchen. They were both wearing bathrobes in the middle of the afternoon. John and Cyn divorced in November 1969.

The length and depth of Paul's very public romance with Jane Asher justified her place within an elite little group of women I called The Beatle Biddies Club – BBC for short. Less well-mannered colleagues substituted words such as "Bitching" and "Bickering" for "Biddies". In all but the paperwork the McCartney-Asher relationship had the infrastructure of a full-blown marriage. To a world that loves a good love story, the doting lovers made a fine-looking couple that looked just great together. The press used phrases such as "fairytale romance" and "made in Heaven". Behind his outward show of closeness Paul had nagging doubts that centred on Jane's high-profile career. Unlike Cynthia, Jane had no intention of setting aside her own ambitions and, although at first Paul enjoyed having a famous lady on his arm, he wasn't sure how successful he wanted her to be. Jane wasn't too keen on the idea of joining the Beatle Biddies Club or of letting herself be thought of as an attachment to The Beatles. She said that Paul acted differently towards her when he was with the boys: "I don't want to be part of a gang. I want to feel that it's the two of us going through life together." I only saw glimpses of angry moments between them but I heard about many stormy exchanges that ended with one or other partner walking out in a huff. This sort of stuff was particularly embarrassing to both while Paul was living under the same roof as his "in-laws" at the Asher family house in Wimpole Street.

Linda Eastman came into Paul's life a couple of years before Jane left him. I remember checking her accreditation as a freelance photographer when she came to The Beatles' New York press conference in 1966. There were many rumours of both impending nuptials and of unilateral dumpings before Paul confounded observers by finally proposing to Jane at Christmas 1967. After that I believe he found it hard to call off a relationship that had lasted almost five years and he used someone I nicknamed "the in-between girl" as a way of easing himself out with minimum unpleasantness. She was a 23-year-old American named Francie Schwartz who sent Paul a message c/o Apple saying that she had written a movie and wanted him to do the soundtrack music. She followed up the unanswered telegram by landing in London and turning up at the Apple offices. Here, her physical charm attracted Paul's attention where her screenplay had not and he told Derek Taylor to hire her to work as a publicity assistant in his press office. She was seen at a few Abbey Road recording sessions and, although she was the height of discretion, news spread around the group's inner circle that Francie had moved from her temporary Notting Hill accommodation into Paul's St John's Wood house. As late as June 1968, when Paul and Jane went to his brother Mike's wedding, the pair gave every outward impression of still being very close. At the McCartney family home, Rembrandt, which had wonderful views overlooking the estuary of the River Dee at Heswall in Cheshire, I remember posing the two McCartney brothers together with their womenfolk in the garden for press photographs. Throughout that evening's wedding reception – a relatively small family knees-up attended by Merseyside members of the extended Clan McCartney – Paul and Jane acted like two love birds and I was prompted to ask them: "Will it be you two next?" Hours later, Jane went back to her latest acting job and Paul went home to Francie at St John's Wood. Most of us couldn't understand the attraction. Francie was an unsophisticated, unspectacular little brunette who seemed to have pushed her way into Paul's affections despite being out of her depth. In fact she was to be Paul's secret weapon for avoiding a one-on-one showdown with Jane over Linda Eastman with whom he was falling head over heels in love. Inevitably, Jane, returning from an out-of-town theatre date, was devastated to find Francie in residence. Far too well-bred to force a major confrontation, Jane hurried off to her parents' home, leaving her mother to collect her things later. By September, having served her purpose, Francie was packed off home to New Jersey or wherever and in next to no time Linda filled the vacated place that the in-between girl had kept warm for her.

When the feisty and formidable Linda Louise Eastman arrived on the scene I was not alone in showing surprise at Paul's latest choice, although we were careful to do so behind his back. Linda was a 25-year-old American divorcée with a six-year-old daughter. Personally, I expected him to marry some fresh-faced young English rose or maybe a former Miss Great Britain. Instead, Paul was completely captivated by this hard-nosed, intelligent and very worldly rock and roll photographer from New York. Clearly we got it wrong and Paul got it exactly right because his lengthy and very happy marriage with Linda was an absolute success.

Like Paul's Jane Asher, George's lover at the peak of Beatlemania was an ambitious career woman, a successful model named Pattie Boyd who caught George's eye when she had a bit-part in *A Hard Day's Night* and he made a beeline for her. She played a schoolgirl with only one word to say: "Prisoners?" Amazingly beautiful, Pattie completely captivated George who determinedly dismissed those of his friends who suggested that she had put herself up for the movie role with the sole intention of seducing "a Beatle" and found him to be the only one currently available. As a chat-up line Pattie asked George to autograph a photograph and dedicate it not only to her but also to her sisters, Paula and Jennie. She was delighted that he put more kisses beside her name than those of the other two. Also like Jane, Pattie kept a low profile about her relationship and carefully restricted her media interviews to topics concerning her career, not her new love. Because the two women shared a great mutual interest in fashion and the latest catwalk trends, the New York publisher Gloria Stavers was able to persuade Pattie to write a regular column for 16 but this was about the London "in crowd", the capital's "beautiful people" in general, rather than her private life with George. The couple were inseparable and eventually married in 1966 after living together for a year or so and setting up home in a smart and spacious bungalow at Esher. It was Pattie who indirectly pointed George towards the music and culture of India by persuading him to escort her to a London lecture on spiritual regeneration given by Transcendental Meditation salesman, the Maharishi Mahesh Yogi. Later, she claimed with some validity that her husband's obsessive interest in Indian music actually outgrew his allegiance to The Beatles. George, who once told me that his idea of paradise would be unlimited sex at all hours of the day or night, continued to see other girls before and after his marriage to Pattie and I got the impression that she was aware of his reputation and ready to cope with it. But George never went in for long-term affairs. He took his pleasure from largely unplanned one-night stands. Hearing that George and Pattie had set a wedding date, John said: "He's put her in the club, he must have." But he hadn't and didn't, which may have contributed towards the unstable nature of their married life later on.

One August night during the 1965 US concert tour, five months before George's wedding with Pattie, I returned to my Minneapolis hotel room to find a trio of nubile young girls curled up on my floor, one of them a crude attempt at a Pattie Boyd lookalike. I came across quite a few of those. The security guys would have called them jail-bait. Each girl had instructions to await a phone call from George to say it was her turn to join him. I asked the Boyd-alike: "Why my room?" She replied: "George said you'd like us." Even after the touring ended twelve months later, The Beatles had more freedom than the average married man to meet other women and enjoy brief virtually anonymous affairs simply because they spent such a lot of time on business that could keep them away from home overnight or longer. In the case of George and Pattie, her policy appeared to be one of joining 'em if you couldn't beat 'em. In its initial stages at least, many of the couple's showbusiness colleagues looked upon her liaison with guitarist Eric Clapton as a straightforward tit-for-tat affair, although the biggest surprise was that Messrs Harrison and Clapton remained such good chums. According to the way he talked to me, George recognised that Pattie was going to give as good as she got in terms of extramarital flings and that for the rest of his first marriage his best option was to accept an open relationship that they could both put up with. Why on earth any man with a partner as gorgeous as Pattie should want to stray is beyond my comprehension but I suppose George had his reasons. In the early and middle Sixties I always took George for a fairly jealous sort of guy, particularly where an attractive girl was concerned, but he must have changed radically in later years.

Of the four Beatles as I knew them through the Sixties, the most committed to love and marriage was Ringo. I had the impression that there was a greater degree of true romance between Ringo and the Liverpool hairdresser Maureen Cox than any of the group's other couples. Six years younger than Ringo, Mo, or Mitch as she was known to most of her closest hometown mates, was an avid follower of the top Mersey Beat bands, a frequent visitor to the Cavern where she lined up with early arrivals several hours before they opened the doors, and a casual girlfriend of several leading local musicians. Like the rest of his family, Mo knew Ringo as Rich or Richie – typical Liverpudlian shortenings of his real name, Richard. Long before Ringo joined The Beatles, Mo saw him drumming for Rory Storm's Hurricanes, another top Mersey Beat combo. She told me: "I fancied him then but couldn't possibly have made the first move. It was up to Richie. Our eyes met a few times at Rory's gigs but nothing happened. I began to make up my mind that I wasn't his type." They started dating in earnest only after Ringo plucked up the courage to ask her for a dance one night at the Cavern. But when The Beatles took him away from Liverpool and she stayed at home, it looked as though their relationship would die. At the end of 1964 Ringo checked into London's University College Hospital to have his tonsils taken out and a concerned Maureen raced to his bedside to comfort him. She told me: "I wasn't trying to take advantage of the situation and I had no idea whether me visiting him would lead to anything more. To tell you the truth, the idea of having to move to London permanently was putting me off." Two months later the couple married in a civic ceremony at Westminster's Caxton Hall and the first of their three children was born on September 13, 1965. In contrast to the Lennons, the marriage of the Starkeys seemed to be a reliable and much more substantial affair founded on a long-established, slow-burn love affair rather than a resented pregnancy. Mo made a point of keeping their home life as normal, tranquil and ordinary as possible even in the extraordinary environment of the Beatlemania years. And when the boys began to spend whole nights in the recording studio, Mo would still have a hot meal ready for her husband when he returned from work at breakfast time. In the early years of their marriage at least, Ringo respected the sanctity of his marriage more than the average rock'n'roller of the era and I was both shocked and sorry to hear that he and Mo were to be divorced in 1975.

The first wives of John, George and Ringo got together at one another's houses on a regular basis, almost every day when the group was away. Being married to members of the world's most famous pop group meant that there was a unique bond between the women. It was impossible for the rest of us to imagine what it was like to be envied by millions of near-hysterical love rivals including many who were fanatical enough to wish you serious harm, a painful death even. Cynthia and Maureen were the closest, partly because they were Liverpudlians in exile and had this additional bond, but also because Pattie often bowed in and out of the circle to undertake modelling commitments. Jane Asher was a very occasional fourth participant but this was a country-based girlie group and townies like Paul and Jane didn't fit into the pattern. All three women were unashamedly fans of The Beatles and would often ring my office to find out about forthcoming tour or recording dates rather than pressing their partners for the details. When Cynthia, Maureen and Pattie got together it was usually in the kitchen, for many cups of tea or coffee if it was middle of the day or several bottles of wine if it was the afternoon. There were two main types of topic for discussion among this close-knit clique: family gossip that circulated solely within The Beatles' own tight inner circle and the wider issues that arose from sometimes scandalous rumours that were rife among the group's fans. I saw this group as the glue that helped to hold The Beatles' marriages together at least for the time being. To share happiness and sorrow, success and disappointment, was a good way of patching up the cracks as soon as they appeared. As part of such a warm and secure little group they felt more at ease than if they had been dealing with the traumas and crises of their extraordinary lives on their own. But for the sharing of information on the perks, pitfalls, problems and sheer insanity of successfully partnering a Beatle, the womenfolk might have teetered on the brink of despair or simply broken free even sooner than they did. It is to their credit that these faithful first partners kept their lives so private over the years. The media would have agreed to almost any conditions to get their individual stories, but I was never allowed to fix any interviews or photo shoots for the women other than at general photo calls for showbusiness functions or exclusive pictures to mark weddings and births.

I never saw the disbanding of The Beatles as a disaster. I regarded it as a positive move that freed up a quartet of tethered artistic spirits to go their separate ways. The Beatles actually finished being the Fab Four at the end of their touring era in 1966. From then on, they were more like a limited company trading as The Beatles. It was no coincidence that George had such an enormous hit with 'My Sweet Lord' soon after emerging from the shadows of Lennon and McCartney. The collapse of The Beatles was not only inevitable, it was the right thing to happen for all concerned in the prevailing circumstances. Nor did I cast John's new love, Yoko Ono, or Paul's latest partner, Linda Eastman, in the roles of Wicked Witches of St John's Wood. In 1966 The Beatles were ready to defy those who had controlled the business side of their lives and master-minded their development as top-selling musicians. By 1968 they were defying one another. A series of childish actions and reactions by John and Paul created a bad atmosphere in their recording sessions. Both men openly broke the Fab Four's rule that womenfolk should be barred from the studio along with all other non-essential visitors. It was a sensible policy with which Cynthia, Jane, Pattie and Maureen had been content to comply. On occasions where some or all of them were going to socialise after work, the women would congregate in a West End club or restaurant and wait there to meet up with their men. This was not a problem and did not cause contention. Then John began to show up at sessions with Yoko. Paul counter-attacked first by fetching Francie Schwartz to work with him and then bringing in Linda Eastman. Lennon and McCartney used to sit there like generals in two opposing camps – John and Yoko huddled in secretive conversation on one side of the studio, Paul with

Linda on the other. Paul's guest had the good sense to keep her voice down and simply watch what went on. Yoko Ono on the other hand couldn't keep her mouth shut and insisted upon giving herself more of a speaking part in the proceedings, a cardinal sin according to The Beatles' book of unwritten rules. Yoko was a catalyst for change but, far from seeing her as the evil opportunist as the fans portrayed her, I saw her as the vital stimulating influence which John, Paul, George and Ringo needed to bring on the break-up at just the right time. The first time Yoko spoke out at full volume during a recording session it was to convey some relatively trivial word of advice to John about whatever he was singing at the moment. The other Beatles looked around, straight-faced, startled, stunned. There was a moment's dead silence that was broken by Paul: "Fuck me! Did somebody speak? Who the fuck was that?" Of course he knew full well who had spoken. The others joined in: "Did you say something, George? Your lips didn't move!" "Have we got a new producer in?"

From such small beginnings grew not merely some additional unpleasantness among the group but also the wider-circulating gossip that Yoko and Linda were breaking up The Beatles, a theme that the media was pleased to pick up and run with. By the end of 1968, sink or swim, it was not Yoko or Linda but The Beatles who took executive responsibility for the group's destiny and that included the decision to call it a day sooner rather than later. What they didn't need at that stage was heavyweight intervention from contentious outsiders. In February 1969, John's hero Allen Klein came in with a mission to rescue and re-cultivate the rotting Apple. His job was to cut out the dead wood before putrefaction set in. One of his first victims was the long-serving and long-suffering Alistair Taylor, who had never even met Klein. Taylor came round to my new offices to cry on my shoulder, telling me: "I've called Paul and each of the others in turn and nobody will speak to me. Being sacked by the American is bad enough but being ostracised by old friends without explanation has made me feel physically sick."

Almost immediately after Klein's appointment, Paul brought in his own advocate, Linda's brother, the New York lawyer John Eastman who was handed the somewhat cryptic job title of free-lance "general counsel to Apple Corps". The two opposing camps within The Beatles consolidated their personal positions – within just over a week of one another in March 1969 Paul married Linda and John married Yoko Ono. The two titles on The Beatles' new single, 'Get Back' and 'Don't Let Me Down', were bizarrely appropriate. In August the group worked together for the last time at Abbey Road, putting the finishing touches to the album of that name and posing for album cover photographs on the zebra crossing outside EMI's studios. George Martin's assessment of *Abbey Road* was that "one side was very much what John wanted and the second side was what Paul and I wanted".

From this point on, the formal disbanding of the no-longer-even-slightly-Fab Four took on all the griminess, hostility and verbal violence of a seriously acrimonious divorce, with Paul accepting professional advice that he must sue the others to survive or drown in the financial and emotional quagmire of what he called "personal differences, business differences and musical differences". Paul said that, although he had never been divorced, he thought the process of disbanding The Beatles was very similar, "a loving relationship turned sour". Meanwhile, John was well on the way to becoming a full-blown drug addict. By 1970, he confessed he must have had a thousand LSD trips since 1964: "I used to just eat it all the time." He was also into heroin but he was keeping quiet about that.

As with the end of touring, no formal media announcement was made by the group's management, now Apple Corps, about the winding up of The Beatles, but in April 1970 a release to publicise Paul's solo album, called *McCartney*, prompted the world's press to declare that the band no longer existed. John had started the band back in 1957 and the balance of power had shifted in Paul's direction over the years. Eventually, more or less ignoring the eccentric albums John and Yoko were putting together, Paul contrived to finish the band's active lifespan by noisily beginning his solo career. He chose to by-pass the Apple press office and release news of the *McCartney* album via his brother-in-law, John Eastman, in New York. In August 1970 Apple's press department shut up shop and in January 1971 McCartney began High Court action to dissolve The Beatles' partnership. John retaliated by calling the *McCartney* album rubbish and claiming that the other three Beatles were "fed up of being sidemen for Paul", a complaint that harked back to McCartney's predominant role in the making of *Magical Mystery Tour* four years earlier.

One late phase of the public war between Lennon and McCartney was waged in the pages of *Melody Maker* in November 1971. In an interview with the paper Paul said: "There was a little bit of hype on the back of the *Let It Be* sleeve for the first time ever on a Beatles album. It was said to be a new-phase Beatles album and there was nothing further from the truth. That was the last Beatles album and everybody knew it – Klein had it re-produced because he said it didn't sound commercial enough." It was a somewhat confused quote and I for one wasn't sure what Paul was complaining about, but John took up the challenge and dragged my name into his reply: "*Let It Be* was not the 'first bit of hype' on a Beatles album. Remember Tony Barrow? And his wonderful writing on 'Please Please Me' etc." John went on to claim that the *Let It Be* notes were "written in the style of the great Barrow himself" and added: "We were intending to parody Barrow originally, so it was hype." Finally, John referred to Paul's much publicised *Life* magazine article inferring that Paul's interview for that piece was itself packed with hype: "Tony Barrow couldn't have done it better."

When the stormy legal battle that raged on behind the scenes over intellectual properties, divided responsibilities and hard cash, had blown itself out, Paul finally wrote an open letter to the group's fans, addressing them as "Beatle People", the simple but sexy name I had given them back in 1963: "The time has come for me to withdraw from The Beatles' Fan Club. As you may know, the band split up over a year ago and has not played together since. Each of us is getting together his own career and for this reason I don't want to be involved with anything that continues the illusion that there is such a thing as The Beatles. Those days are over. Thanks for everything."

At the time we were unable to see the full picture. We were like people with our noses pressed up against an enormous CinemaScope screen so that we could take in only a fraction of what was happening. It was afterwards when, as Paul said, those days were over, that we had an opportunity to go back and sit in the stalls and re-run the whole Beatlemania movie for ourselves. Only then did we appreciate the full musical and social significance of The Beatles and understand the magnitude of the revolution of which the Fab Four were unarguably the pioneers. The Beatles had massively influenced the music business, getting rid of record company red tape that had regulated the length of studio sessions, reducing the dictatorship of the record company A&R departments to so much rubble and placing power more appropriately in the hands of the musicians and their independent producers. Their adventurous songwriting and ingenious musical productions started trends and set benchmarks for the rest of the business, and for decades to come their work was emulated by other ambitious bands and solo singer-songwriters. Because they refused to spend time touring regional and international television stations, The Beatles invented and successfully launched the independently produced promotional film clip as a generally accepted means of promoting new releases. The pre-recorded clip was to become the paramount marketing tool of the modern pop and rock music industry. Through the unprecedented strength of their music and by the example of what they said and wore, The Beatles also influenced the thinking of an entire generation of adolescents and young adults, who now saw the world in a new light and treated their children with a greater degree of tolerance, respect and understanding.

The Beatles hadn't happened before and would never happen again. Over the years there would be claims from different quarters of the recording business that yet another new musical Messiah was on the way but nobody, not even The Beatles' producer George Martin, found it possible to clone the individual or combined creative abilities of John, Paul, George and Ringo.

Index